Marriage and the Family
in Eighteenth-Century France

JAMES F. TRAER was a member of the faculty of Hamilton College from 1969 to 1979, when he became Vice President and Dean of Academic Affairs at Adrian College. A graduate of the College of Wooster, he received his J.D., M.A., and Ph.D. degrees from the University of Michigan.

Marriage and the Family in Eighteenth-Century France

JAMES F. TRAER

Cornell University Press, Ithaca and London

Cornell University Press gratefully acknowledges a grant from the Andrew W. Mellon Foundation that aided in bringing this book to publication.

Copyright © 1980 by Cornell University

First published 1980 by Cornell University Press.
Published in the United Kingdom by Cornell University Press Ltd., 2–4 Brook Street, London WIY 1AA.

International Standard Book Number 0-8014-1298-6
Library of Congress Catalog Card Number 80-11121
Printed in the United States of America
Librarians: Library of Congress cataloging information appears on the last page of the book.

TO MY WIFE,
MARIBETH

Contents

Preface

THIS BOOK TRACES the development of the law governing marriage and the family in France from the final decades of the ancien régime to the promulgation of the civil code in 1804. It analyzes the delicate interplay among Enlightenment ideas about man as a social being, the technical development of the law, and political events that opened the way to massive legal reform. Through the use of court records and administrative documents, it then examines the way the revolutionary laws were applied.

In addition, the book contributes some conclusions to the larger study of marriage and the family in Western Europe during the past few centuries. The nature of the evidence about marriage and family life requires several cautionary statements. Literary evidence exists and should not be ignored, but relatively few persons wrote about the most commonplace and fundamental realities of their daily lives. Those who did may be atypical in their literacy, their economic position, or their persuasion. Consequently, plays, novels, essays, diaries, and other forms of the written word must be used with care and corroboration. Statutes and court decisions regulated certain aspects of family life, but by themselves they constitute an imperfect mirror of society's actual practices. The law sets the outer limits for human behavior; it does not ordinarily identify the norm. Furthermore, in normal times the law tends to lag behind social change, while in a period of revolution it may leap ahead of prevailing practices as legislators modify it in order to instruct and change society.

I have made use of documents of the central government in Paris from the late eighteenth and early nineteenth centuries and the notarial archives and court records of the revolutionary judicial districts of Angoulême (Charente, formerly Angoumois) and Laon (Aisne, formerly Laonnois) of the 1780s and 1790s. While my conclusions apply broadly across chronology and geography, they must, when extended to other times and places, be somewhat tentative, in the nature of hypotheses. It is also important to remember that change in any fundamental social structure, such as the family, occurs very gradually. The family, John Demos has noted, "is one of those 'primary institutions' whose essential durability normally lends coherence to a wide range of more visible cultural processes."[1] Finally, a twentieth-century American Protestant of urban middle-class origin may not be ideally equipped to comprehend the deepest thoughts and feelings of the members of an eighteenth-century French Catholic agrarian society.

With these limitations carefully stated, the book attempts to present something of the reality of marriage and the family, as well as its legal and literary forms. And despite the acknowledged elements of stability in any society's marriage and family system, it asserts the existence of change in ideas, in the law, and in the practices of marriage and family life in eighteenth-century France.

The dual character of this book, as a work of legal and social history, reflects both my training as historian and lawyer and the areas of expertise of the historians and legal scholars who have assisted in its preparation. The work began at the University of Michigan, where many persons gave me aid and encouragement. I am particularly indebted to John W. Bowditch for sharing with me his broad understanding of the period and his high standards of clarity in thought and language; to Raymond P. Grew, who proposed many questions that the book might raise; and to David D. Bien, who offered valuable criticism of those portions of the work concerned with the ancien régime.

At the University of Michigan Law School, Whitmore Gray rendered useful advice on many aspects of the civil law and Eric Stein aided me in defining legal aspects of the topic. Max Rheinstein of the University of Chicago Law School contributed encouragement and his comprehensive knowledge of European family law.

1. John Demos, *A Little Commonwealth: Family Life in Plymouth Colony* (New York: Oxford University Press, 1970), p. xiii.

Elizabeth Eisenstein, Robert Forster, James Friguglietti, Ralph Giesey, and Robert R. Palmer have shared with me their reactions to my ideas and conclusions. Most recently, colleagues at Hamilton College, including Esther Barazzone, David M. Ellis, Michael Haltzel, Edwin B. Lee, Peter Marcy, and David Millar, have offered thoughtful criticisms of portions of the manuscript.

In France, former professor Antoine Prost, now dean of the Université d'Orléans, provided direction and criticism, and François Furet of the Sixième Section of the Ecole Pratique des Hautes Etudes graciously commented on my ideas and conclusions. Philippe Ariès kindly discussed his own work with me and offered some suggestions. I am indebted to a host of librarians and archivists at the major research centers in Paris, Angoulême, and Laon who have helped me to penetrate the mysteries of their bibliographic and archival collections.

I am grateful to the governments of the United States and France for their support of the Fulbright Program, which helped me to spend a year engaged in research in France. The University of Michigan and Hamilton College generously provided funds to support both research in France and preparation of the final work. Most recently, the National Endowment for the Humanities made it possible for me to spend an exceptionally fruitful summer in France.

Bernhard Kendler and Barbara H. Salazar of Cornell University Press have provided useful editorial assistance, while Merna Schaub, Joyce Poyer, Caryl Stoker, and Lydia Oprsal have typed portions of the manuscript with accuracy and enthusiasm.

While studying eighteenth-century French families, my wife and I had the good fortune to become closely acquainted with two twentieth-century French families whose friendship and assistance we have greatly valued. I express here our gratitude to Lucien and Jeanne Parizy of Vanves and to Robert and Anna Palpacuer of Ris-Orangis. My wife, Maribeth, has contributed editorial assistance and encouragement during the past ten years. This book is dedicated to her, with deep appreciation.

JAMES F. TRAER

Adrian, Michigan

Marriage and the Family
in Eighteenth-Century France

Introduction

MARRIAGE AND FAMILY ORGANIZATION under the ancien régime may best be described as traditional.[1] In the traditional marriage the husband and father exercised both legal and actual power over the person and property of his wife and children. He enjoyed management of their property and of the revenue that it produced. The law permitted him to discipline his wife and children, either by physical punishment or by confinement in a correctional institution. In short, he was the ruler of his own small realm, similar to the monarch in his kingdom.

As his children matured, he decided whether or not they might marry and, if so, how to arrange their marriages so as to help them and the family to realize economic and social goals. Marriage of a child required the transfer of property and was closely linked to distribution of family property in the form of inheritance. Family interest often dictated that most property be settled upon one child or a few children, and the law in most parts of France authorized

---

1. The terms *modern* and *traditional* are also used by Edward Shorter in *The Making of the Modern Family* (New York: Basic Books, 1975), and I am in agreement with Shorter's basic interpretation about the evolution of the modern family. Other students of the period, including Peter Laslett and Lawrence Stone, used the word *patriarchal* instead of *traditional*. I prefer not to use *patriarchal* because in the discipline of anthropology it has referred to patrilineal kinship ties (not completely a feature of French society) and because it suggests to me a society composed of extended families, clans, or tribes. See Peter Laslett and Richard Wall, eds., *Household and Family in Past Time* (New York: Cambridge University Press, 1972), and Lawrence Stone, *The Family, Sex, and Marriage in England, 1500–1800* (New York: Harper & Row, 1977), pp. 123–218. The terms *traditional* and *modern* correspond, in many ways, to the latter two of four categories of marriage and family that Stone identifies in England.

substantial inequality of inheritance. A variety of institutions and groups buttressed the traditional family, supporting its goals and helping to maintain the power of its chief. The moral and legal authority of church and monarchy provided the positive sanction of example and the negative one of potential punishment. The matrix of kin, community, and other groups (parish, confraternity, guild, corporation) afforded the traditional family stability, direction, and support.

In contrast to the "traditional" marriage and family, the "modern" marriage and family developed out of the literature and criticism of the French Enlightenment, translated into new laws and social realities during a massive political upheaval. Without the Revolution of 1789, the ideas of the *philosophes* might have remained simply the theories of an elite. But the legislators of the revolution, who sought to create a more ideal society, used them to change drastically the laws governing marriage and the family.

Freedom of choice and affection were to be the basic elements of the modern marriage. Husband and wife were to be equals, and children more nearly equal to parents and sooner freed from the disabilities of legal minority than were their counterparts under the ancien régime. The modern marriage thus became less a means of aiding the spouses' families to attain economic and social goals than an opportunity for the spouses themselves to find self-fulfillment and happiness. The creation of machinery for divorce signified not disregard for marriage but precisely this new value: that marriage should be a means to happiness.

The themes of equality and sentiment figure prominently in the new laws. Not only did they prescribe equality of spouses but, in the area of inheritance, they required scrupulously equal treatment of all children in a family. Revolutionary concern for the equality of all children sometimes ran counter to the increased emphasis on the legitimate family, as in the statutes requiring division of inheritance between illegitimate children and their legitimate half siblings. The nature of a new institution, the family court, demonstrated the widespread belief that family sentiment or affection could be useful in resolving a variety of practical problems. The court was to decide family disputes by means of arbitration by other family members. Laws sanctioning adoption as a way of creating families for orphaned children testify again to the importance of sentiment, in this case the sentiment of affection for children.

Discussion of children leads to the interpretation advanced by Philippe Ariès, which identifies the child as the key to the changing conception of the family. According to Ariès, the modern family evolved out of an increased awareness of the child as an individual, an object of amusement and affection, and a future adult. As early as the sixteenth century, moralists testified to the increased attention or "coddling" they believed children had begun to receive. Greater attachment coincided with the beginning of a decline in infant mortality among the upper classes. Mothers took an increased interest in their children's hygiene, with some going so far as to nurse their infants themselves instead of employing wetnurses. Fathers became more concerned with their children's instruction, either by tutors or in private schools or religious establishments. Schooling began to last into adolescence, which came to be viewed as a separate period between childhood and full adulthood.[2]

While the relationship between the parents and children of this new family became more intense and affectionate, at the same time the family tended to become smaller and more withdrawn from society at large. Parental concern with the development and advancement of children, together with a declining infant mortality, led to conscious efforts to limit the number of births within the family.[3] With fewer children, parents were able to devote increased attention to the education and rearing of each individual child. All of these changes spanned several centuries and occurred first among aristocratic and middle-class families, which then served as models for the families of the popular classes.

This book accepts much of Ariès's interpretation, but rejects his contention that it was exclusively a growing appreciation of the child that created the modern family. No less important was the

2. Philippe Ariès, *Centuries of Childhood: A Social History of Family Life*, trans. Robert Baldick (London: Jonathan Cape, 1960). I record here my gratitude to Mr. Ariès, who generously agreed to meet with a young graduate student in 1967 and who responded patiently and perceptively to the questions he posed in halting, rudimentary French.

3. See essays by Ariès and others in Hélène Berguès et al., *La prévention des naissances dans la famille: Ses origines dans les temps modernes* (Paris: Presses Universitaires de France, 1960).

view that proclaimed marriage rightly the product of free choice and affection and emphasized the equality of the spouses with one another and the equal treatment of children by parents.

Nor were the ideas and laws that created modern marriage products of the Industrial Revolution, which did not begin to transform France until the mid-nineteenth century. To be sure, middle-class persons of the eighteenth century were probably wealthier than their predecessors and France may then have been in a preindustrial or precapitalist period. But nothing in that increasing wealth or stage of economic development necessitated that men and women marry for affection or upon free choice or that they accept notions of greater equality between husband and wife or parents and children.

Rather, ideas and certain kinds of institutional conflicts, such as a dispute between the Catholic church and the French monarchy, yielded a new view of marriage and the family—one that appealed to many individuals particularly because of its links to such political ideas as liberty and equality and to romanticism, an important fashion in literature. The increasing wealth of professionals, *rentiers,* bureaucrats, merchants, and others afforded them or their children increased leisure, greater education, and an opportunity to accept the new view and act upon it. Their changing economic circumstances did not require them to adopt notions about a modern marriage and family. Indeed, they might as easily have followed the traditional view suggested by aristocratic ideals, which rejected the claims of sentiment and freedom of choice.

This book focuses on the relationships of husband and wife and parent with child—in short, the nuclear family. Because it makes little use of demographic data and does not attempt to study the household, it does not address the debate about the frequency with which family organization assumed an extended or stem form as opposed to a nuclear form.[4] On the one hand, it is clear that nuclear

---

4. For a discussion of the issue and a strong opinion against the likelihood of a significant number of complex families in early modern times, see the introduction by Peter Laslett in Laslett and Wall, *Household and Family,* pp. 13–23. Lutz K. Berkner presents the opposite point of view in "The Stem Family and the Developmental Cycle of the Peasant Household: An Eighteenth-Century Austrian Example," *American Historical Review* 77, no. 2 (April 1972): 398–418, and in "Inheritance, Land Tenure, and Peasant Family Structure: A German Regional Comparison," in

families acknowledged and responded to the obligations and ties of the larger kinship group and to the sense of family as lineage or a chain of humans linked by blood over time. Certainly, great and powerful families often had relatives, as well as servants, residing with them and were thus "extended." Also, despite the growth of hospitals in the eighteenth century, it was still usually the family, rich or poor, that assumed the burden of caring for the aged and infirm. On the other hand, the issues of the time were primarily those of the nuclear family: parental consent to a child's marriage, the quality of the relationship between the spouses, and the division of inheritance among children.

Most enlightened men of the eighteenth century viewed the law as an instrument capable of producing fundamental social change. Since human nature was essentially plastic, new and better laws and institutions could produce individual happiness and social justice. The coming of revolution in 1789 gave social critics and legislators the opportunity to implement a vast body of Enlightenment criticism and theory. They swept aside much of the existing structure of Catholic doctrine and royal law that had regulated marriage and family relationships for two centuries. Under the twin banners of liberty and equality they enacted legislation that they believed would create and foster a new pattern of marriage and family organization.

There followed several years during which the optimism about radical reform dimmed and revolutionary law took its practical

Family and Inheritance: Rural Society in Western Europe, 1200–1800, ed. Jack Goody, Joan Thirsk, and E. P. Thompson (New York: Cambridge University Press, 1976), pp. 71–95. For a current French point of view that finds little evidence of extended family households in seventeenth- and eighteenth-century France, see Jean-Louis Flandrin, _Familles: Parenté, maison, sexualité dans l'ancienne société_ (Paris: Librairie Hachette, 1976), pp. 54–83.

One of the significant questions that the evidence has not yet permitted Laslett, Berkner, Flandrin, and others to address is the length of time during which any individual was likely to experience an extended or stem family. It seems probable that inclusion of a nephew or niece or an aged or infirm parent in the family circle for a short time would produce a different experience from a household situation in which two generations of married couples lived together for many years. Put differently, were the instances of a resident grandparent or other relative brief departures from a fundamentally nuclear pattern or were they predictable and lengthy stages during which the family could be classified as extended or stem?

shape under the pressures and compromises of application. At the end of the decade, Napoleon Bonaparte returned to France to a centralized, authoritarian regime and achieved the old revolutionary goal of unification of the civil law into a single code.

The opening two chapters focus on the ancien régime. Chapter 1 summarizes the development of the Catholic conception of marriage, culminating in the decrees of the Council of Trent, and shows how the French monarchy increasingly arrogated to itself the regulation of marriage and family matters, especially in the two centuries before 1789. The rich burgeoning of Enlightenment thought on marriage and the family constitutes the major subject of Chapter 2. The emphasis of the *philosophes* on man as an individual, the importance of liberty and human happiness, and the possibility of a better society led them to persistent criticism of existing rules and institutions. Their thought had immediate application in efforts to achieve toleration and legal acceptance of the marriage practices of Jews and Protestants.

Chapters 3, 4, and 5 present the major works of revolutionary legislation. Chapter 3 concerns the creation of civil marriage and the records of civil status. It traces the conflict between church and revolutionary regime stemming from application of the Civil Constitution of the Clergy, the need for accurate and accessible records of vital statistics, and the further development of the theory that marriage was a civil contract subject to regulation by the state. Chapter 4 discusses divorce legislation, which came into being primarily from the conflict described in Chapter 3, together with a vigorous campaign identifying indissoluble marriage with despotism and dissolution of marriage with liberty.

Chapter 5 describes several laws that regulated relationships within the family. Primary among them were decrees establishing absolute equality of succession rights among children of a deceased parent. Others included lower ages of majority for young men and women, the creation of adoption as a means of obtaining parents for orphaned children, and a decree that permitted illegitimate children to claim inheritance from their parents. Finally, Chapter 5 explains the creation and functioning of a family court that sought to mobilize family sentiment for the resolution of conflict through the use of relatives in a form of private arbitration. Since the court dispensed with professional judges and men of law, its founders calculated it would render speedy, economical, and equitable justice.

Chapter 6 recounts the creation of the civil code and analyzes its provisions in the light of the conservative attitudes of the First Consul, Bonaparte, and the political theorist de Bonald. The code was neither a blind reaction to revolutionary legislation nor a wholesale return to the law of the ancien régime, although it included elements of both viewpoints. Rather, as the concluding Chapter 7 indicates, it reconciled many of the revolution's achievements with the needs of an authoritarian state.

Neither the thought of the Enlightenment nor the speed with which it was proclaimed law during the revolution yielded the immediate replacement of traditional forms of marriage and family by modern ones. The pace of change was slow. For many individuals, the revolutionary experience culminated in a sense of disillusionment about the possibility of perfecting human relationships and institutions. A petitioner who wrote to the councils of the Directory in 1796, stating plaintively that although she had married for love her marriage had produced unhappiness, voiced a common complaint.[5] Freedom of marital choice, marriage based on affection, equality of spouses, availability of divorce, and equal treatment of children did not automatically or necessarily create human accord and happiness. Yet despite the slowness of social change, the more conservative attitudes of the framers of the civil code, and some retrograde legislation such as the elimination of divorce from the civil code between 1816 and 1884, the direction of change was clear. In ideas, in the law, and in their everyday lives, men and women began gradually to reject earlier, traditional relationships in favor of a modern marriage and family.

5. Petition of Suzanne Rauly to the Council of Five Hundred and the Council of Ancients, 30 floréal Yr. 4 (May 19, 1796), Archives Nationales, D xxxix 4.

Sacrament and Contract: Catholic Doctrine and Royal Authority over Marriage and the Family

THE WORDS *sacrament* and *contract* summarize the legal definition of marriage in eighteenth-century France.[1] For many men, marriage referred primarily to a religious act, a sacrament in which the church blessed the union of a man and a woman, declaring it indissoluble and pleasing in the sight of God. For others, jurists and

1. The term *contract* here refers exclusively to the juridical theory whereby the monarchy asserted its right to regulate marriage. Excluded is any consideration of the marriage contract with which the spouses and their families regulated property matters during the marriage and beyond. The marriage contract was governed by customary or Roman law, which remained essentially unchanged during the revolution until they were unified by the provisions of the civil code. See Jacqueline Brisset, *L'adoption de la communauté comme régime légal dans le code civil* (Paris: Presses Universitaires de France, 1967). There was no controversy or reform effort, and even the practice of the drafting of marriage contracts by notaries did not evolve during the revolution (Jacques Lelievre, *La pratique des contrats de mariage chez les notaires au Châtelet de Paris de 1769 à 1804* [Paris: Cujas, 1959]).

For an introduction to the marriage contract as a means of studying social groups and social mobility, see Adeline Daumard and François Furet, *Structures et relations sociales à Paris au milieu du dix-huitième siècle* (Paris: Armand Colin, 1961); Adeline Daumard, "Structures sociales et classement socio-professionnel: L'apport des archives notariales aux XVIIIᵉ et XIXᵉ siècles," *Revue historique* 227 (1962):140–54. For an example of the method together with a useful discussion of the way data can be organized and prepared for recording and manipulation on a computer, see Marcel Couturier, *Recherches sur les structures sociales de Châteaudun (1525–1789) (Paris: S.E.V.P.E.N., 1969).

those who had been involved in the processes of the law, marriage meant a contract subject to the rules of royal law and the jurisdiction of royal courts. Beyond the law, marriage meant many things: an alliance of fortune and social rank, a property settlement regulating the duties and rights of the spouses and their families, a personal relationship between two individuals founded upon sentiment and free choice, cohabitation with the intent to remain together. Yet if in the popular mind marriage often meant simply living together, it was still important to obtain the church's blessing. An old legal proverb expresses both the private, consensual nature of the institution and the involvement of the church:

> To drink, to eat, to sleep together,
> It appears to me is all of marriage,
> But it is necessary that the church give its approval.[2]

The Catholic dogmas of the sacramental and indissoluble nature of marriage developed over centuries of doctrinal controversy and reached their most complete expression in the decrees of the Council of Trent. Beginning with the background of Roman law and scripture, this chapter summarizes the development of Catholic doctrine of marriage to the end of the sixteenth century.[3] After discussing the decisions reached at Trent, the chapter's focus shifts

2. "Boire, manger, coucher ensemble, / Est mariage ce me semble, / Mais il faut que l'église y passe" (Antoine Loisel, *Institutes coutumières*, bk. 1, tit. 2, rule 6, as quoted in Ernest Glasson, *Le mariage civil et le divorce dans l'antiquité et dans les principales législations modernes de l'Europe*, 2d ed. [Paris: A. Durand et Pedone, 1880], p. 231).

3. Several multivolume histories of the Catholic church trace the evolution of Catholic doctrine and the institutional development of the church. The series Histoire de l'église depuis les origines jusqu'à nos jours, ed. Augustin Fliche and Victor Martin (Paris: Bloud et Gay, 1935-), is particularly useful for the sixteenth, seventeenth, and eighteenth centuries. A shorter work by a distinguished British Catholic historian which covers the period up to the Reformation is Philip Hughes, *A History of the Church*, 3 vols. (London: Burns & Oates, 1947-49). Henry Daniel-Rops has published an eight-volume study, *L'histoire de l'église de Christ* (Paris: A. Fayard, 1952-65), most of which has been translated into English; it is popular, colorful, and sometimes lacking in objectivity. A recent series entitled Nouvelle histoire de l'église, ed. L.-J. Rogier, R. Aubret, and M. D. Knowles, 5 vols. (Paris: Seuil, 1963-68), provides extensive current bibliographical references and heavy emphasis on church history in France and the Low Countries.

For an analysis of marriage in canon law, the best work remains Adhémar Esmein, *Le mariage en droit canonique*, brought up to date by R. Genestal, 2 vols. (Paris: Sirey, 1928). Another highly useful source is Gabriel Le Bras, "La doctrine du

to the growth and expansion of royal authority over marriage and family law. In the two centuries before the French Revolution the monarchy asserted its power in legislation, in the jurisdiction of royal courts, in attempts to supervise the records of marriage, birth, and death, and in the formulation of a new theory that marriage was a secular contract as well as a sacrament.

Roman law provided the earliest influence on the Christian tradition, and in vulgarized form it became the basis of private law in the southern portion of France.[4] In its primitive stages, the Roman law of marriage involved the concept of *manus,* by which the husband exercised power over his wife. With the celebration of a marriage, a young woman thus passed from the authority of her father to that of her husband, who might in turn still be subject to the authority (*patria potestas*) of his father or eldest male relative.[5] In the later or classical period of Roman law, however, marriage involved a much greater degree of equality between the spouses, and was formed by their free consent alone. Even when a son remained under his father's authority, absence of parental consent did not invalidate a marriage, although it might lead to disinheritance or other penalties.[6]

mariage chez les théologiens et les canonistes depuis l'an mille," *Dictionnaire de théologie catholique* (Paris: Letouzey et Ane, 1927), vol. 9, pt. 2. Le Bras also initiated a series entitled Histoire du droit et des institutions de l'église en Occident (Paris: Sirey, 1955-), which will run to twenty volumes.

The number of works on Christian marriage is legion. Two of the most frequently cited are George Herbert Joyce, *Christian Marriage: An Historical and Doctrinal Study,* 2d ed. (London: Sheed & Ward, 1948), and George E. Howard, *A History of Matrimonial Institutions,* 3 vols. (Chicago: University of Chicago Press, 1904). The anthropological data in the latter work are outmoded, but both volumes provide a good discussion of the historical development of Christian marriage in doctrine and practice.

4. The best brief introduction to Roman law is Barry Nichols, *An Introduction to Roman Law* (Oxford: Clarendon Press, 1962). Herbert Felix Jolowicz, *An Historical Introduction to the Study of Roman Law,* 2d ed. (Oxford: Oxford University Press, 1952), is a classic study. Other books dealing with Roman family and marriage law include Percy E. Corbett, *The Roman Law of Marriage* (Oxford: Clarendon Press, 1930); Fritz Schulz, *Principles of Roman Law* (Oxford: Clarendon Press, 1936); Fritz Schulz, *Classical Roman Law* (Oxford: Clarendon Press, 1951).

5. Nichols, *Introduction to Roman Law,* pp. 65-68, 80-90.

6. Paul Ourliac and J. de Malafosse, *Le droit familial,* vol. 3 of *Histoire du droit privé* (Paris: Presses Universitaires de France, 1968), pp. 165-66.

While no special form or ceremony was required to manifest the consent of the

Since the basis of marriage in classical Roman law was the free consent of the parties, divorce might be obtained where such consent no longer existed. Thus the spouses could divorce by mutual agreement, or one might repudiate the other without having to justify the action. Divorce was available to husband and wife on largely equal terms, and the parties did not have to resort to judicial intervention to dissolve their marriage. They merely followed certain forms designed to assure their serious intentions and furnish proof that the marriage had indeed been terminated.[7] One scholar has described classical Roman law of marriage and divorce as essentially humanistic in nature, because it emphasized the liberty and equality of the parties to a marriage that was based solely on their consent, rather than on the coercive powers of family or society as represented by the state.[8]

Roman law governing paternal control over children did not experience the liberalization that characterized the law of marriage and divorce. Even during the classical period, the father's authority over his unemancipated children remained virtually undiminished. He retained full control and enjoyment of their property, and he might discipline them largely as he wished. The law permitted adoption where a childless person wished to bestow his name and property on another individual, and it included a highly developed system of guardianship for orphans and incompetents. Major family decisions, such as those involving marriage or divorce, were usually made with the advice of a family council.[9]

The structure of marriage, divorce, and the family in Roman law is reasonably clear, but little evidence exists as to how these institutions functioned in reality and particularly the extent to which divorce was actually practiced. It would be useful to have more information because the men of eighteenth-century France spoke

---

parties and to create a marriage, the existence of a dowry (*dos*) and the prenuptial gifts (*donatio ante nuptias*) generally distinguished marriage from more casual relationships. During the period of the Late Empire, the law required evidence of prenuptial gifts for valid marriages of persons of social rank (John J. Carberry, *The Juridical Form of Marriage* [Washington, D.C.: Catholic University of America Press, 1963], p. 9).

7. Esmein, *Mariage en droit canonique*, 1:49.
8. Schulz, *Classical Roman Law*, pp. 103–8.
9. Nichols, *Introduction to Roman Law*, p. 85.

constantly of the Roman experience with divorce, either attributing the purity and simplicity of marriage and morals under the Republic to the institution, or damning it and claiming that its widespread abuse had contributed to the decline and fall of the Empire. The practice of divorce appears to have been more widespread during the later centuries of the Empire; whether it was a substantial factor in the social disintegration of the period remains in dispute. In any event, early Christian emperors attempted to restrict divorce by requiring that repudiation be based on certain specified grounds and by prohibiting the spouse who sought repudiation from marrying again immediately.[10]

Any discussion of Christian thought on marriage begins with reference to the Holy Scriptures. Thus God created woman as a companion for man (Gen. 2:23–24), and the Gospels repeat the injunction of the Old Testament that man and wife are become as one flesh and that no man may break apart that which God has joined together (Matt. 14:3–6; Mark 10:2–9).[11] Mark and Luke taught that marriage was indissoluble, without any exceptions or qualifications (Mark 10:11–12; Luke 16:18), but Matthew permitted a man to divorce a wife who had been guilty of adultery (Matt. 19:9; 5:31–32).

Paul preferred celibacy to marriage, but he spoke frequently of marriage in his letters to the early churches. In one case, he seemed to sanction a physical separation but not divorce, forbidding a wife to depart from her husband, but adding that "if she depart, let her remain unmarried or be reconciled to her husband" (1 Cor. 7:10–11). In the same passage, Paul called upon Christian husbands and wives to retain their unbelieving spouses, but if the unbeliever leave, to let him go, "for a brother or sister is not under bondage in such cases." Paul warned that a married woman was bound by the law to her husband so long as he was alive, but she might marry again after his death (Rom. 7:1–3). Finally, in his letter to the church at Ephesus, Paul called marriage a mystery and explained that the

---

10. Esmein, *Mariage en droit canonique*, 1:49.
11. The passages relating to marriage in the King James Version and in the authorized translation of the Rheims-Douay Version of the Bible contain virtually the same wording.

union of a man and wife mirrored the union of Christ with the church (Eph. 5:22–23).

Most thinkers in the early centuries of the Christian era stressed the moral perfection of celibacy, but for those persons who could not hope to maintain themselves in such a state, they developed the conception of marriage found in the statements of Jesus and Paul. In describing marriage, the church fathers used the Latin word *sacramentum* for the Greek term meaning mystery, and they taught that the sacraments were visible signs or ceremonies by which man might seek and obtain divine grace. In the Pauline tradition, many theologians constructed elaborate comparisons between human marriage and Christ's relationship to the church.[12] Emphasis on the sacramental nature of marriage supported the view that it was also indissoluble and that ideally it ought not to be followed by a second marriage after the death of a husband or wife.

In the case of divorce, theologians sought to reconcile the strict teachings of Jesus and Paul with the more permissive law and custom of the Roman Empire. Many church fathers insisted on the absolute indissolubility of marriage. Augustine classified indissolubility as one of the three blessings of marriage, along with the mutual faith of the spouses and the generation of children, and after centuries of debate the Catholic church in Western Europe ultimately adopted his viewpoint.[13] Some authors argued from the text in the book of Matthew that divorce might be permitted on the ground of adultery of a wife, or occasionally that of a husband, and they often defined adultery in a spiritual sense to include idolatry, apostasy, and other sins. The Eastern or Orthodox church accepted their reasoning and permitted divorce.[14]

The practice of marriage during the early Middle Ages in Western Europe rested on a compromise between the doctrines that the church was slowly formulating and the popular practices drawn

---

12. A. Michel, "Sacrement," *Dictionnaire de la théologie catholique*, 14:486–89.

13. Dennis J. Burns, *Matrimonial Indissolubility* (Washington, D.C.: Catholic University of America Press, 1936), pp. 2–4. For an excellent discussion of the development of Catholic doctrine and practice during the closing era of the Roman Empire, see Jean Gaudement, *L'église dans l'empire roman (IV–VIe siècles)*, vol. 3 of *Histoire du droit et des institutions de l'église en Occident* (Paris: Sirey, 1955).

14. Howard, *History of Matrimonial Institutions*, 2:23–28.

from remembered Roman law and tradition and from Germanic custom. In theory, the basis of marriage remained the free consent of husband and wife; in practice, parents or feudal lords usually arranged marriages for their children or vassals. The marriage ceremony frequently included the transfer of the father's authority over his daughter to the bridegroom.

Various church councils insisted on the necessity of public celebration of marriage and blessing by a priest, but since these injunctions did not include the sanction of nullity, marriages were often celebrated privately, without the assistance of a cleric. When marriages were celebrated publicly, the ceremony was conducted outside of the church, and afterward the celebrants entered the church to hear mass and receive communion.[15] Indissolubility of marriage remained a difficult principle to enforce, for Germanic custom had permitted repudiation and sometimes multiple wives. Except for a brief revival of temporal authority under the Carolingian monarchs, however, the church steadily advanced its claim to be the sole institution charged with authority over marriage.[16]

More sophisticated theoretical formulations accompanied increased church control over marriage and substantial agreement on the principle of indissolubility. During the tenth through the twelfth centuries, two conceptions of marriage competed for dominance, one emphasizing the consent of the parties as the constituting factor and the other insisting that a valid marriage was concluded only after the physical consummation of the union. Papal decrees ultimately resolved the dispute in the thirteenth century by formulating the "classical doctrine" of marriage. According to the classical doctrine, marriage existed as a sacrament when formed by simple consent alone, but it might be dissolved by the pope so long as it had not been consummated.[17] The requirement of consummation (*copula carnalis*) provided one means of evading the rule of abso-

---

15. Carberry, *Juridical Form of Marriage,* pp. 11–13.
16. Howard, *History of Matrimonial Institutions,* 2:49.
17. John Gilissen, *Introduction historique au droit civil* (Brussels: Presses Universitaires de Bruxelles, 1960), pp. 227–28; Charles Donahue, Jr., "The Case of the Man Who Fell into the Tiber: The Roman Law of Marriage at the Time of the Glossators," *American Journal of Legal History* 22, no. 1 (January 1978):1–53.

lute indissolubility. Those who wished to escape from an unsatisfactory marriage might allege that it had never been consummated,
accusing their marital partners of impotence.[18] Actions for nullity
based on impotence were very important in canon law and were far
more frequent than the probable physical incapacities of the persons involved.[19]

Another way to end a marriage was to allege that it had never
been validly constituted. The church used the term *impediments* for
all of those conditions or requirements necessary for a valid marriage. Some of the impediments were absolute in the sense that
failure to satisfy them rendered a marriage wholly null and void,
whereas violation of others merely entailed spiritual penalties that
fell short of depriving the relationship of the status of marriage.
Defects in consent, prohibited degrees of family or spiritual relationship, prior marriage, previous holy vows taken by one of the
parties, all offered grounds by means of which a marriage might be
declared null.[20]

Finally, a physical separation of the parties, if it did not leave
them free to conclude new marriages, at least relieved them of the
duty of living with one another and determined their rights with
respect to property. In canon law, the term *divortium*, or divorce,
was used to designate both actions to annul a marriage and those
for physical separation (also called *separatio quod torum et men-
sam*). Separation might be based on an agreement between the
parties that one of them might carry out a wish to enter a religious
institution or take a vow of continence, or one spouse might obtain
a decree against the other for adultery, heresy, and, later, hatred
that made continued life in common dangerous to the complaining
spouse.[21]

The Council of Trent, meeting intermittently from 1545 to 1563,
completed the work of formulating Catholic doctrine regarding
marriage and divorce. "If anyone says that matrimony is not truly

18. Esmein, *Mariage en droit canonique*, 1:259–96.
19. Antoine Hotman, *Traité de la dissolution du mariage par l'impuissance et
froideur de l'homme ou de la femme* (Paris: M. Patisoon, 1581), pp. 3–6.
20. Ourliac and de Malafosse, *Droit familial*, pp. 193–96.
21. Gilissen, *Introduction historique au droit civil*, pp. 229–30.

and properly one of the seven sacraments of the evangelical law instituted by Christ the Lord, let him be anathema," announced the first canon of the twenty-fourth session of the council.[22] Thus in the face of criticism begun by Luther and other Protestant reformers, the church reaffirmed the doctrine of marriage as a sacrament, with the accompanying corollary that it was by nature indissoluble. The council denied that marriage might be dissolved, whether on account of adultery of husband or wife or because of heresy, absence, or physical defects (*molestam cohabitationem*) of one of the parties—all grounds for which some Protestants would permit divorce.[23]

Probably the most difficult problem before the council involved the form and manner of celebration of Catholic marriage. Until this time, the minimum requirement for a valid marriage had remained simply the consent of the parties to it. Canon law recommended public celebration and a priestly benediction, but absence of either or both of these elements did not invalidate a marriage. The very simplicity of the required act gave rise to a variety of problems: multiple marriages, inability to ascertain a child's legitimacy or the proper devolution of a succession, frequent cases of young persons marrying without their parent's consent. Clandestine marriages in violation of parental authority were particularly repugnant to the French monarchy, and the cardinal of Lorraine, chief French repre-

---

22. Heinrich Joseph Dominik Denzinger, *The Sources of Catholic Dogma*, trans. Roy J. Deferrari (St. Louis: B. Herder, 1957), p. 296. No useful one-volume history of the Council of Trent exists in English. A brief introduction to the proceedings of the council may be found in Philip Hughes, *The Church in Crisis: A History of the Twenty Great Councils* (London: Burns & Oates, 1961). A German scholar has begun a multivolume work on the council, of which two volumes have appeared to date: Hubert Jedin, *A History of the Council of Trent*, trans. Dom Ernest Graf (London: Thomas Nelson, 1957, 1961). Jedin's work includes both the clash and settlement of doctrinal disputes and the full range of European diplomacy and politics that accompanied the meetings of the council, but the volumes published so far cover only its first few sessions. For the last sessions of the council, which include the doctrinal conclusions regarding marriage and the manner of its celebration, the same author has published a brief work: *Crisis and Closure of the Council of Trent*, trans. N. D. Smith (London: Sheed & Ward, 1967).

23. Denzinger, *Sources of Catholic Dogma*, p. 297. Other canons affirmed the moral excellence of virginity or celibacy over the state of marriage, the church's authority to establish qualifications for marriage, and its right to decree physical separation of husband and wife.

sentative at the council, urged that marriages of minors against their parents' wishes should be denied any validity in canon law.[24]

The council rejected the cardinal's demand, maintaining the church's traditional viewpoint that the sacraments should be readily available to all those who wish to partake of them. It did establish formal requirements for publicity in connection with marriages, however. According to the Decree Tametsi, marriage could be celebrated only after a parish priest had on three successive occasions publicly announced the intent of the contracting parties to marry. The marriage had to be performed in the presence of two or three witnesses, among them the parish priest who had published the banns. The decree warned priests not to celebrate marriages of persons not belonging to their parish, and instructed that only a bishop could dispense with the requirements of publication of the banns. Finally, the council admonished temporal lords and magistrates to resist such worldly inclinations and desires as might tempt them to interfere with the freedom of marriage as governed by the law and doctrine of the church.[25]

Thus the Council of Trent completed the work of centuries of doctrinal and theoretical development of the Catholic conception of marriage. In response to Protestant criticism, it reaffirmed the sacramental and indissoluble nature of the institution. In so doing, the council rejected those aspects of the Roman legal tradition and those sources of Christian belief that would have provided exceptions to the principle of indissolubility. The careful provisions governing the valid celebration of marriage by parish priests were designed to ensure that the church's conception and control of marriage would be realized in the secular world.

At the same time as the Catholic church was completing its doctrinal formulation and extending its claims to regulate the marital relationship, the French monarchy began to stipulate its requirements for valid celebration of marriage. Ever since the development of feudalism under the Carolingians, the monarch had exercised control over the succession to fiefs and marriage choices of his

24. Carberry, *Juridical Form of Marriage*, pp. 21–23; Esmein, *Mariage en droit canonique*, 2:172–89.
25. Denzinger, *Sources of Catholic Dogma*, pp. 300–301.

vassals.[26] In addition, although property questions involving marriage contracts and inheritance had sometimes been heard by the church tribunals, these disputes were more frequently settled in various civil courts.[27] The creation of venal offices from the late fifteenth century gave the servants of the crown a motive to expand the jurisdiction of royal courts: litigation yielded revenue to royal judges and officials, thereby enhancing the value of their offices to the state. In addition, the crown was eager to support the authority of the heads of families, analogous to that of the monarch himself, against rebellious subjects. Finally, the intense impulse of the absolute monarchy to regulate all manner of human affairs provides another explanation for royal efforts to secure control over the marital relationship.

French Catholics who supported the authority of the monarchy claimed that the right to legislate and adjudicate concerning marriage was one of the "ancient liberties" of the Gallican church.[28] Initially, the issue was whether the Tridentine decrees would be directly applicable as canon law in France.[29] Later, royal lawyers and Gallican churchmen began to modify the exclusively sacramental view of marriage in order to justify increased legislation in the entire area of family law. The growth of royal legislation intensified disputes over whether cases involving marriage and family law should be heard in religious or secular courts. The monarchy also claimed the right to supervise the church's function of keeping records of marriages, births, and deaths. By the end of the eighteenth century, the French monarchy had assumed substantial control over legislation and litigation involving marriage and had fostered the development of doctrinal change to justify that control. Church and monarchy sometimes worked out face-saving compromises, but royal authority was in fact predominate.

---

26. Ourliac and de Malafosse, *Droit familial*, p. 203.

27. Paul Viollet, *Histoire du droit civil français* (Paris: Sirey, 1905), pp. 435–38.

28. For a discussion of Gallicanism in the sixteenth and seventeenth centuries, including abundant bibliographical references, see Léopold Willaert, *La restauration catholique (1563–1648)*, vol. 18 of L'histoire de l'église depuis les origines jusqu'à nos jours (Paris: Bloud et Gay, 1960).

29. Victor Martin, *Le gallicanisme et la réforme catholique: Essai historique sur l'introduction en France des décrets du Concile de Trente (1563–1615)* (Paris: A. Picard, 1919), pp. 1–165.

The Edict of 1556 against "clandestine marriages" constituted the state's first effort to regulate the valid celebration of marriage. King Henry II issued it in order to further the marriage of his illegitimate daughter with a young man of the Montmorency family. The Montmorency youth had previously been secretly married, and when the pope hesitated to annul the earlier marriage, the king responded with a statute.[30]

The edict forbade young men under the age of thirty and young women under twenty-five to marry without obtaining the consent of their parents or relatives. It could not attack the validity of such secret marriages directly, since marriage was regulated by church law, but it invoked the formidable penalty of disinheritance. In addition to disinheriting the offending child, a parent might revoke any gifts he had made to the child, and the latter might not claim any benefits that would normally accrue to the marriage by means of a marriage contract or the law. The edict gave no precedent for royal legislation regarding marriage. Instead, it emphasized the Christian duty of obedience to parents and relied on the authority of the king as the "executor of the will and commandments of God."[31]

Following the conclusion of the Council of Trent, assemblies of the French clergy urged acceptance and application of the Tridentine reforms regarding marriage. Proponents of royal power hesitated to recognize the council's authority within France, however, and King Henry III finally resolved the problem by issuing his own legislation. The Edict of Blois of 1580 proclaimed the rules decreed by the council, but with some modifications and additions. Instead of two witnesses to a marriage, the edict required the presence of four. The Tridentine reformers had stipulated that a priest should be present at a marriage as a witness, while the edict required his presence indirectly by forbidding notaries to hear promises of marriage.

Like the decrees of the council, the Edict of Blois emphasized the importance of the element of publicity for marriage. Article 40

---

30. Ourliac and de Malafosse, *Droit familial*, pp. 204–5.

31. François André Isambert, *Recueil général des anciennes lois françaises, depuis l'an 420 jusqu'à la révolution de 1789* (Paris: Berlin-le-Prieur, 1822–1833), 13:469–71.

forbade dispensing with the three publications of intent to marry (the banns) save for urgent and legitimate reasons and upon the request of the parties and their nearest relatives. Curés and vicars were warned to inquire carefully into the status of persons who wished to marry, and if they were minors, to refuse to celebrate their marriage without the consent of father and mother, tutor, or curator.[32] Instead of employing a civil penalty of disinheritance, the edict provided that anyone who married a minor against family wishes was guilty of the crime of rape. The statute defined rape in this case as seduction of a minor below twenty-five years of age, notwithstanding the consent of the minor, and it decreed the penalty of death for the crime.[33]

According to subsequent royal lawyers, the Edict of Blois did not constitute a "reception" of the Council of Trent's decrees. It was distinctly royal legislation, not ratification of church law. In the articles of the edict concerning marriage, Henry III may have been consciously trying to create royal secular law, or he may have viewed himself as acting in his capacity as head of the Gallican church, or, more probably, he may not have been conscious of any clear distinction between the two areas of authority. In any event, since the legislation dealt with the validity of marriage, not only French jurists but Pope Gregory XIII viewed it as an attempt by a secular power to regulate marriage, and so did assemblies of the French clergy after 1580.[34] The particular significance of the Edict of 1556 and the Edict of Blois is that they formed the basis of two centuries of effort by lawyers, magistrates, jurists, and some churchmen to extend the power of the king over marriage.

Royal edicts of 1606, 1629, 1639, and 1697 repeated and ex-

---

32. Tutors and curators were guardians. In both Roman and customary law, a tutor served as a legal guardian for a minor if the minor's parents were dead or incapable of exercising parental authority. Curators were appointed for insane persons, spendthrifts, and other legally incapable persons (Ourliac and de Malafosse, *Droit familial*, pp. 86–122).

33. Isambert, *Recueil général*, 14:391–92.

34. René Louis marquis d'Argenson and P. de Motte, *Histoire du droit canonique et du gouvernement de l'église* (London: 1750), p. 45; Jules Basdevant, *Des rapports de l'église et de l'état dans la législation du mariage du Concile de Trente au code civil* (Paris: Sirey, 1900), pp. 66–67. Although old, Basdevant's work remains important and useful.

panded the provisions of the earlier legislation.[35] In support of the legislation, seventeenth-century jurists advanced a contractual theory that stated that the monarch might create absolute impediments or barriers to marriage. A professor of theology at the University of Paris named Hennequin taught the doctrine, and his disciple Launoy published in 1674 a major treatise on the subject, *Regia in matrimonium potestas.* A doctrinal battle ensued in which the Parlement of Paris sustained Launoy's arguments and forced his critics to modify theirs.[36] Subsequently another doctor of the Sorbonne, Gerbais, extended the argument by contending that marriage had originally been a natural contract left by God to the control of princes and had existed long before Jesus Christ had raised it to the dignity of a sacrament.[37] One example of royal creation of an absolute impediment to marriage was the rule that members of the royal family might not marry without the express consent of the king. Gaston of Orléans challenged the rule when his brother, Louis XIII, failed to grant consent to a projected marriage with Margaret of Lorraine. The king won the support of both a national assembly of the clergy and the Parlement of Paris, which in 1634 declared the couple's union invalid.[38]

The doctrinal work of Hennequin, Launoy, and Gerbais, the intervention of the Parlement of Paris, and the royal edicts establishing rules for valid celebration of marriage and prohibiting clandestine marriages clearly indicate growing theoretical royal control in the area, but the practical application of this authority encountered repeated difficulties. The Edict of Blois and the Edict of 1639 had specified that a person contracting a secret marriage with a minor against parental consent would be convicted of rape and punished by death. The crime that the decrees described was clearly

35. Isambert, *Recueil général,* 15:307; 16:234–36, 520–24; 20:287–95.
36. Maurice Covillard, *Le mariage considéré comme contrat civil dans l'histoire du droit français* (Paris: Arthur Rousseau, 1899), pp. 38–44.
37. Gerbais, *Traité du pouvoir de l'église et des princes sur les empêchements du mariage avec la pratique des empêchements qui subsistent aujourd'hui* (Paris: Antoine Dezallier, 1690), pp. 292–334.
38. Basdevant, *Des rapports de l'église et de l'état,* pp. 107–11. For a more complete discussion of the attempted marriage of Gaston d'Orléans, see Monique Valtat, *Les contrats de mariage dans la famille royale en France au XVIIe siècle* (Paris: Picard, 1953), pp. 40–49.

against the authority of the parents over a minor child, and the minor's consent to the relationship was irrelevant. Nevertheless, treatises on French jurisprudence before 1730 tended to confuse this crime with rape involving sexual relations with an adult woman without her consent.[39]

A curious development occurred in Brittany, where Article 42 of the Edict of Blois was incorporated into a revised version of the *Coutume de Bretagne,* which applied rape by seduction, as the crime was now termed, to any case of intercourse between unmarried men and women, regardless of the age of the parties involved. On complaint and proof of a woman who claimed to have been seduced, the seducer was convicted and sentenced to death, but he was reprieved if he would agree to marry the woman he had wronged. Thus many a man came to the church with his feet in irons, and engagements begun in casual sexual relations led to marriages whose effects were unlikely to be happy for the parties involved or for society.[40] This misinterpretation of Article 42 of the Edict of Blois had begun to spread to other provinces when, in 1739, Louis XV issued a declaration further defining the crime of rape by seduction and attempting to eliminate its misapplication. The preamble explained that the law was directed against unions that were unworthy because of corruption of morals or inequality of condition of the two spouses. The edict prescribed the death penalty for the seducer and stipulated that he might not be able to avoid it by marrying the person he had ravished.[41]

Jurists and courts could hardly misunderstand the nature of the crime of rape by seduction after the ordinance of 1739, but they shrank from applying the extreme penalty of death.[42] Courts ruled that the crime had to include intent to conclude an unlawful marriage, which they then failed to find, thus reducing the offense to simple illicit commerce. Sometimes they convicted persons of rape

39. Jean François Fournel, *Traité de la séduction* (Paris: Demonville, 1781), pp. 304–6.
    40. Isambert, *Recueil général,* 21:338–40.
    41. Ibid., 338–41.
    42. Paul Viollet, *Précis de l'histoire du droit français* (Paris: L. Larose et Forcel, 1886), pp. 344–45. For an excellent discussion of the development of the crime of rape by seduction Léon Duguit, "Etude historique sur le rapt de séduction," *Nouvelle revue historique de droit français et étranger* 10 (1886):587–625.

by seduction but refused to apply any penalty beyond disinheritance.[43] The repeated legislation on the subject of parental control over marriage and the increasing severity of the penalties directed against secret marriages suggests grave difficulties in enforcement of the law. While the monarchy may have wrested control of legislation in the area from the church, it was less successful in requiring observance of its own laws.

The growth of royal secular legislation in an area formerly the exclusive domain of the church led inevitably to conflicts over which system of courts should adjudicate disputes involving marital legislation. Although the church claimed broad competence in the area, the seventeenth and eighteenth centuries witnessed a steady movement of litigation from ecclesiastical courts into royal secular ones, with the transfer of cases being effected by means of an action known as the *appel comme d'abus*. The theory of the action was simply that the court hearing the case was acting beyond the bounds of its jurisdiction, or that its decision infringed upon the rights of the secular power.[44] For example, although cases involving an alleged rape by seduction were sometimes begun before church courts, one party or the other often used the *appel comme d'abus* to move these cases before royal judges. Appeal ran from royal courts to the *parlements,* and it was the *parlements* that developed the body of interpretation governing the crime of rape by seduction.[45]

In addition to the whole issue of marriage by minor children, the French monarchy used the *appel comme d'abus* to assert control over questions of bigamy, impediments to marriage, formal oppositions filed by relatives of one of the parties, demands for damages

---

43. Fournel, *Traité de la séduction,* pp. 323–27.

44. Marcel Marion, *Dictionnaire des institutions de la France aux XVIIe et XVIIIe siècles* (Paris: Picard, 1963), pp. 21–24. The *appel comme d'abus* is comparable to the writ of prohibition in the common law which the English crown used to establish royal jurisdiction over litigation in church courts. The writ of prohibition is very old, however, dating from the reign of Henry II (1154–89), whereas the *appel comme d'abus* appears only after sixteenth-century royal legislation concerning marriage. For a discussion of the early use of the writ of prohibition, see G. B. Flahiff, "The Writ of Prohibition in the Thirteenth Century," *Medieval Studies* (Toronto) 6 (1944):261–313; 7 (1945):229–90.

45. G. Pacilly, "Contribution à l'histoire de la théorie du rapt de séduction: Étude de jurisprudence," *Tijdschrift voor rechtsgeschiedenis* (Haarlem) 13 (1934):306–318.

or return of gifts after a broken engagement, and all questions involving property relations of spouses, children, and parents. The crown did not always deprive the *officialités,* or church courts, of jurisdiction in these cases, but if they failed to enforce royal law, it would use the *appel comme d'abus* to void a judgment and have the whole matter taken out of the church's hands. Thus where the *appel* did not deprive the *officialités* of their actual jurisdiction, it effectively abolished their freedom of independent action.[46]

New theoretical formulations of marriage accompanied royal legislation and the growing involvement of royal courts. In 1753 the jurist Pierre Le Ridant published a work in which he contended that marriage was in essence a secular contract, subsequently blessed by a sacrament. Thus it followed that the state was the sole authority with the right to regulate the validity of marriage. Le Ridant's argument tended to replace the older view advanced by Launoy and Gerbais, that marriage was somehow both contract and sacrament on a more or less equal basis. It was useful in justifying what courts were in fact doing and it strongly influenced later commentators.[47] Le Ridant also published a practical manual for magistrates and men of law; it included a thorough treatment of Catholic doctrine and canon law, but focused primarily on royal law and practice.[48] Other eighteenth-century writers echoed Le Ridant's emphasis on marriage as a civil contract. Pothier called it the oldest and most excellent of contracts and insisted that it was subject to the authority of the secular powers that God had placed on earth to govern men.[49] Claude de Ferrière made similar asser-

---

46. Charles Fevret, *Traité de l'abus et du vrai sujet des appelations qualifiées du nom d'abus,* new ed. (Lyons: Chez Duplan, 1736), pp. 400–543.

47. Pierre Le Ridant, *Examen de deux questions importantes sur le mariage* (Paris, 1753), pp. i–xvi; Covillard, *Mariage comme contrat civil,* pp. 59–61.

48. Pierre Le Ridant, *Code matrimonial ou recueil complet de toutes les loix canoniques et civiles de France,* new ed. (Paris: Herissant le Fils, 1770).

49. Robert-Joseph Pothier, *Contrat de mariage* in *Oeuvres,* ed. Bugnet (Paris: Cosse et N. Delamotte, 1846), 6:1. Pothier was probably the best-known French legal scholar of the period. His commentaries touched all areas of the law and his efforts to synthesize Roman and customary law, royal ordinances, the interpretation of *parlements,* and canon law into one rational, coherent body of national law helped to prepare the way for the codification of French law at the end of the century.

tions in his dictionary of law and legal practice.[50] Pierre-Toussaint Durand de Maillane's dictionary of canon law virtually avoided the notion of marriage as a sacrament altogether, except when defending Catholic doctrine against Protestant criticism.[51]

The primary goal of these jurists was to champion the monarchy's unquestioned control over the legislation and practice of marriage. Often they were less concerned with the content of that legislation and how it might be changed or improved. None of them seriously questioned the Catholic principle of indissolubility, for example, although the rule had been subjected to a barrage of criticism from enlightened thinkers and divorce was a popular topic of conversation in educated society.[52] Only an article by the lawyer and publisher Desessarts in a legal encyclopedia dealt with the subject, in a long discussion of divorce in Jewish, Roman, and Christian tradition, with numerous references to current debate in France. Desessarts suggested that the principle of toleration required that the French state permit divorce of Jews and Protestants according to their religious principles, even though it might deny divorce to the great majority of Frenchmen who were Catholics.[53]

If most legal theorists found no reason to question the dogma of indissolubility, they were greatly interested in the action of physical separation, which was the only acceptable Catholic remedy when the parties to a marriage no longer wished to associate with one another. A separation relieved the spouses of the obligation to live together, but it could never destroy the spiritual ties that bound them in marriage. The basic scriptural justification for separation was the passages in Matthew that spoke of a man putting away his wife for adultery. Church courts applied the ground of adultery

---

50. Claude de Ferrière, *Dictionnaire de droit et de pratique*, 3d ed. (Paris: Bauche, 1771), pp. 203–7.

51. Pierre-Toussaint Durand de Maillane, *Dictionnaire de droit canonique et de pratique*, 2d ed. (Paris: Benoit Duplain, 1770), 3:275–76. The dictionary is a long, disorganized work. It would be of little significance except for the author's importance as a proponent of the liberties of the Gallican church before 1789 and his later role in drafting civil legislation concerning marriage during the revolution.

52. See Chapter 2.

53. Nicholas Lemoyne Desessarts, "Divorce," in Joseph Nicolas Guyot, *Répertoire universel et raisonné de jurisprudence*, 2d ed. (Paris: Visse, 1784), 5:734–50.

equally to either partner and also permitted separation for serious injury, lengthy absence, corruption of morals, or adoption of false or heretical religious beliefs.[54]

At least as early as the sixteenth century, royal courts began to hear suits involving the property aspects of separations. Furthermore, since adultery, bad morals, and injury to a marital partner were all crimes, they fell under the jurisdiction of the secular state. As in the case of rape by seduction, the action of *appel comme d'abus* proved particularly useful in transferring separation cases out of the church's courts.[55] Royal judges enjoyed substantial latitude regarding the grounds for separation, and the monarchy made no effort to legislate on the subject, as it had in the case of the validity of clandestine marriages. In contrast to the church's emphasis on equal standards of conduct for both husband and wife, royal courts developed their own policy, which tended to discriminate against women and give legal sanction to a double standard of sexual conduct. A husband's adultery ceased to be a ground for separation except under the most extreme circumstances.[56] A wife's adultery, on the other hand, provided the ground for separation and also for detention in a convent for an indeterminate time.[57]

The wife who managed to obtain a separation from her husband remained severely handicapped in the management of her own property. Separation gave her only limited rights to receive income and revenues and administer leases; the law still required the consent of her husband for major decisions affecting property. Since separations usually involved discord between husband and wife, that consent was usually refused, whereupon the wife had to resort to legal action to obtain the right to administer her own property.[58]

As in the case of separations, the law governing relations between children and parents, primarily fathers, developed outside the pur-

54. Esmein, *Mariage en droit canonique,* 2:110–13.

55. Gérard Thibault-Laurent, *La première introduction du divorce en France sous la Révolution et l'Empire* (Clermont-Ferrand: Imprimerie Moderne, 1938), pp. 21–22.

56. Georges Dumas, *Histoire de l'indissolubilité du mariage en droit français* (Paris: Arthur Rousseau, 1902), p. 46.

57. Pothier, *Contrat du mariage,* pp. 242–43.

58. Marcel Planiol, *Treatise on the Civil Law,* with the collaboration of Georges Ripert, 12th ed., trans. Louisiana State Law Institute, 1 (St. Paul, Minn.: West Publishing Co., 1959), p. 729.

view of the church. Paternal power (*puissance paternelle*) consisted of Roman law in the south and customary law in the north, both modified and interpreted by royal statutes and court decisions (*jurisprudence*). Paternal authority admitted broadly defined rights of correction and of management and enjoyment of a child's property. In both a legal and practical sense, emancipation from this *puissance paternelle* usually came when a son or daughter married and/or established a separate residence for over a year. The issue of marriage provided the most frequent challenge to paternal power in the seventeenth and eighteenth centuries, and, as has been shown, the French monarchy consistently sought to reinforce, supplement, and extend paternal control over the marriage of children. It was as though the *père de famille* were, within his own small realm, a kind of absolute monarch against whom the law would not tolerate disobedience.[59]

A second aspect of the relationship between parents and children involved succession or inheritance rights, which were remarkably varied and complex.[60] They required classification of the legal status of the persons involved, the nature of the property being transmitted, and the province or region in which the persons and/or the property were located. A variety of legal instruments—wills, gifts, renunciations, marriage contracts, and other agreements— might in some instances alter the transmission of a succession otherwise governed by the rules applying to a particular category of person, property, and locality. The entire area of the law afforded ample employment for notaries, attorneys, and barristers, often to the considerable expense of their clients.

The rules of the ancien régime admitted two main categories of persons: nobles and commoners (*roturiers*). The law governing noble successions usually applied only when both the person and

59. For the history of paternal authority, see Marie-Paul Bernard, *Histoire de l'autorité paternelle en France* (Paris: Montdidier, 1863); Emile Masson, *La puissance paternelle et la famille sous la Révolution* (Paris: A. Pedone, 1910); and the works cited in Chapter 5, notes 5 and 6.

60. For an introduction see Charles Lefebvre, *L'ancien droit des successions*, 2 vols. (Paris: Sirey, 1912); Emile Chenon, *Histoire générale du droit français public et privé des origines à 1815*, 2 vols. (Paris: Sirey, 1929); and Gabriel Lepointe, *Droit romain et ancien droit français: Régimes matrimoniaux, libéralités et successions* (Paris: Montchrestien, 1958).

the property involved were "noble," although in some areas it might apply to noble property held by a commoner, for example, a fief owned by a merchant who continued to engage in trade. The most prominent feature of noble succession was the rule of primogeniture (*droit d'aînesse*), awarding the eldest male child the castle or principal manor and between one-half and four-fifths of his parents' immovable family property (*propres*). In some areas an eldest daughter could succeed by right of primogeniture when a noble family had no sons. The rule of primogeniture applied throughout France, wherever land was held by feudal tenure. In medieval times it had been important to keep the fief undivided in order not to reduce the fighting capacity of the vassal who held it, but in the seventeenth and eighteenth centuries the only justification for primogeniture was that it maintained intact the property, and hence the status, of illustrious families.[61]

The law classified property as to whether it was land or attached to land and therefore immovable (*immeuble*) or movable (*meuble*). But in addition to this division, the law distinguished between immovable property received from one's parents or relatives (*propres*) and movable and immovable property acquired in one's lifetime by labor or good fortune (*acquêts*). The immovable *acquêts* of one generation became *propres* when they passed to the next by gift or inheritance. The classification of *propres* was originally intended to facilitate the return of family property to paternal and maternal relatives when a marriage produced no descendants who survived to inherit from their parents. Thus defined, *propres* looked backward to ancestral lines. In practice, however, restrictions on alienation of *propres* made them "family property," a kind of trust for future generations. To add a further refinement, various categories of movable property came to be classified legally as *propres*. These categories included *rentes foncières* (perpetual annuities in exchange for alienation of land), *rentes constituées* (perpetual annuities in exchange for capital sums), and venal offices, which became heritable after 1604. While the law of each locality controlled the succession to *propres* and *acquêts*, the general rule was that

61. Marion, *Dictionnaire des institutions*, pp. 12–13.

propres remained within the family while *acquêts* and *meubles* could be freely alienated at the expense of potential heirs.[62]

In the south under Roman law, it was customary for both rich and poor commoners, men and women alike, to enjoy considerable freedom in disposing of their property by executing wills, by gift, or by means of provisions in their children's marriage contracts. That freedom was limited by a guaranteed share (*légitime* or *réserve*) for children, and for ascendants when there were no children. The *légitime* varied between one-fourth and one-half of the deceased person's *propres,* or his *acquêts* when there were no *propres,* or even movable property, depending on the numbers of heirs and whether they were children or ascendants.[63] In the southwest, Roman law combined with numerous local customs to yield varying results in various localities.[64] In both regions, children, usually daughters or younger sons, might renounce or assign their succession rights at the time they received a dowry or share establishing them in marriage, an office or employment, or a religious order.

In the northern regions of customary law, *roturier* individuals enjoyed less freedom in disposing of their property than did those in the south, and property more frequently passed by intestate succession. Wills were less common and were usually made only by persons with substantial fortunes.[65] Four distinct categories of customs governed the succession of children to their parents' property. In a small western part of Picardy and Normandy along the Atlantic coast, the customs accorded the eldest non-noble son a right of

62. Philippe de Renusson, *Traité des propres* (Paris, 1681); Charles Lefebvre, *Les fortunes anciennes au point de vue juridique* (Paris: Sirey, 1912). An excellent discussion of these categories appears in Ralph Giesey, "Rules of Inheritance and Strategies of Mobility in Prerevolutionary France," *American Historical Review* 82, no. 2 (April 1977):271–89.

63. Lepointe, *Droit romain*, pp. 464–70; Roger Aubenas, *Testaments et successions*, vol. 3 of *Cours d'histoire du droit privé* (Aix-en-Provence: Librairie de l'Université, 1954), 17–29.

64. See Jacques Poumarède, *Les successions dans le sud-ouest de la France au moyen âge* (Paris: Presses Universitaires de France, 1972). Robert Wheaton describes the practical application of succession law in "Custom and Will in Seventeenth-Century Bordeaux," a paper delivered at the Twenty-second Annual Conference of the Society for French Historical Studies, Rochester, New York, April 9–10, 1976.

65. Ourliac and de Malafosse, *Droit familial,* pp. 393–402.

primogeniture (*droit d'aînesse en roture*) amounting to between two-thirds and four-fifths of the parent's *propres,* in much the same fashion as if the succession were noble. A second category of regions, including Auvergne, Bourbonnais, Berry, Nivernais, Burgundy, Lorraine, Artois, and parts of Picardy and Flanders, permitted a parent to grant an advantage (*préciput*) to one child by means of a gift or provision in a marriage contract. The favored child subsequently obtained an equal share of the parent's *propres* that remained at death.

A third group of customs governing the Ile-de-France, Orléannais, and much of Champagne, sometimes referred to as the Orléano-Parisian group, created a system of "simple equality" whereby any child who wished to share in a succession had to return for purposes of division of the estate (*rapporter*) any family lands received by him from the deceased parent. This system of "simple equality" did not prevent the child from renouncing the succession, however, and retaining property previously received if it happened to be a more substantial share than he would receive by equal distribution. Finally, there existed a custom of "strict equality" requiring all children to return for purposes of division of the estate all advantages that were *propres* received from a deceased parent, whether or not they wished to participate in the succession. This system of strict equality prevailed in the provinces of the west, ranging from most of Normandy and Brittany in the northwest through Anjoy, Maine, and Touraine to Poitou, Aunis, Saintonge, and Angoumois in the southwest.[66] As in the south, daughters and younger sons sometimes renounced their succession rights upon establishment in marriage, in an office or employment, or in the church. Although much of the customary law of northern France permitted some kind of inequality of succession rights among non-noble children, it is unclear whether significant numbers of parents sought to use the option to favor one child above

66. Jean Yver, *Egalité entre héritiers et exclusion des enfants dotés: Essai de géographie coutumier* (Paris: Sirey, 1966). Yver's book treats an unusually complex subject and is sometimes difficult to follow. Emmanuel Le Roy Ladurie has summarized Yver's conclusions in "Système de la coutume: Structures familiales et coutume d'héritage en France au XVIe siècle," *Annales E.S.C.* 27 (1972):825–46. A translation of the article appears in Goody, Thirsk, and Thompson, *Family and Inheritance,* pp. 37–70.

others.[67] In any event, disputes involving both successions and paternal power were litigated almost exclusively in royal courts.

If the insistent pressure of magistrates and jurists had impelled the French monarchy to acquire effective control over the legislation and practice of marriage and family law, the state continued to yield primary responsibility to the church in the area of record keeping. Priests had traditionally kept records of the persons they baptized, married, and buried, and the decrees of the Council of Trent enjoined them to continue to do so.[68] The earliest royal legislation on the subject appeared in the Ordinance of Villers-Cotteret, issued by Francis I in 1539. The relevant provisions of the ordinance were essentially feudal in nature, in that they were designed to verify the deaths and births of persons who held or might hold benefices that, when vacant, would revert to the control of the king. The statute provided that at the end of each year, curés and religious establishments were to deposit records of baptisms and interments with the nearest royal bailiff or seneschal.[69]

The Ordinance of Villers-Cotterets was later supplanted by the provisions of the Edict of Blois, which introduced the first royal legislation concerning vital statistics applicable to all men and women and which included marriage as well as birth and death. Article 181 of the edict of 1579 enjoined royal registrars (*greffiers*) to obtain from all curés or vicars within their area of jurisdiction yearly copies of the registers of baptisms, marriages, and burials.[70]

67. Professor Giesey, in "Rules of Inheritance," pp. 272–278, contends that well-to-do commoners found means to avoid the requirements of equality in order to maintain and build family fortunes. On the other hand, a recent work by Xavier Martin, *Le principe d'égalité dans les successions roturiers en Anjou et dans le Maine* (Paris: Presses Universitaires de France, 1972), insists that advantaging one child was practically impossible in that area of western France. Lenard Berlanstein's *The Barristers of Toulouse* (Baltimore: Johns Hopkins University Press, 1975), pp. 62–67, concludes that Toulousan barristers, unlike their noble colleagues of the *parlement,* usually divided their fortunes in substantially equal fashion among their children. My study of succession practices in Angoulême (an area of "strict equality") before and during the French Revolution, "Equality in the Year Two" (a paper delivered at the annual meeting of the American Society for Legal History, Philadelphia, October 21–24, 1976), indicates that significant departures from rules of equal division were uncommon among *roturiers* of the Angoumois. The problem needs greater study in depth.

68. Denzinger, *Sources of Catholic Dogma,* pp. 300–301.

69. Isambert, *Recueil général,* 12:160.

70. Ibid., 14:423.

A later statute of 1668 instructed curés and other priests to keep two original registers and to submit one of them to the registry (*greffe*) of the nearest royal court at the end of each year. Records of baptism required mention of the child's date of birth and the names of two close relatives or friends as witnesses. For marriage, the parties were supposed to include their names, ages, social rank, place of residence, whether they were under the power of parents or another person, the names of four witnesses, and their relationship to the witnesses, if any.[71]

Before the statute of 1667, royal officials had in fact only rarely obtained the yearly copies of the registers. After 1667, compliance with the law gradually became more general.[72] At no time before the Revolution of 1789 did the state make a serious effort to assume the function of recording these statistics. The parish priest, or curé, retained the job of registering the significant events in the lives of the members of his flock.

The most important feature of the development of the law of marriage in France during the two centuries after the Council of Trent was the growth of the monarchy's authority. Instead of accepting the council's decrees, kings began to legislate on the subject of marriage. Royal courts eroded the jurisdiction of church courts over the marriage bond, while developing a massive body of doctrine and decisions in areas of unquestioned civil authority, such as property rights, paternal power, and successions. Jurists formulated a contractual theory of marriage to justify royal authority. At the end of the ancien régime, the church had not ceased to claim jurisdiction over marriage but substantial power had passed into the hands of the monarchy.

The substance of marriage and family law evolved with the change in the authority sanctioning and administering it. Catholic doctrine had sought to make the sacraments, including matrimony, readily available to all men. It favored early marriage as a means of avoiding sin. Canon law governing separation had emphasized

71. Ibid., 18:137–38.
72. Michel Fleury and Louis Henry, *Nouveau manuel de dépouillement et d'exploitation de l'état civil ancien* (Paris: Institut National d'Etudes Démographiques, 1965), pp. 22–24.

equal treatment of husband and wife for the same marital offenses. Royal law, on the other hand, attempted to extend parental control over the marriage of children to age twenty-five or thirty, despite great resistance against the enforcement of its edicts. The terrors of disinheritance and the effort to redefine the crime of rape to fit clandestine marriages proved relatively ineffective, given the actions of courts that deliberately misinterpreted the law or refused to apply its more extreme penalties. Royal law controlling separation increasingly condoned marital offenses by the husband while applying stiffer penalties to the same actions by the wife. Only on the subject of indissolubility did royal lawyers and clerics easily agree; whether a contract or a sacrament, the institution of marriage remained indissoluble.

2

The Rise of Criticism: The Thought of the French Enlightenment

DESPITE DISPUTES concerning their respective areas of authority, the Catholic church and the French monarchy had created an orthodox view of marriage in the seventeenth and eighteenth centuries. Marriage was both contract and sacrament, with the relative importance of the two elements depending on the primary allegiance of the speaker. It was indissoluble. While royal courts had acquired much of the judicial business involving marital and family disputes, some of it remained in the hands of the church courts, acting under the supervision of the *parlements*. Courts of both systems applied royal legislation and canon law. The state showed increasing interest in maintaining an improved system of records of vital statistics, but it used clerical personnel and worked within the existing framework of church organization.

Outside the areas of theology and law, political and social theorists of the French Enlightenment contributed a variety of new ideas about marriage and the family to the established conceptions of Catholic doctrine and royal law and jurisprudence. Their contributions may be classified under the concepts of diversity, utility, and sentiment. First, eighteenth-century thinkers studied foreign societies and political systems, both in Europe and in the exotic lands that lay beyond. Real and imaginary travelers brought home tales of marriage practices, family relationships, and child-rearing customs that differed from those of France. Other investigators compared the institutions of the classical or early Christian eras with those of their century. Increasingly, men became aware of the diversity of customs, laws, and attitudes governing marriage and the family in other cultures and at other times.

Second, many *philosophes* urged changes in the law or in the popular conception of marriage in the interest of utility. They would secularize marriage, permit divorce, and limit paternal power in the interest of good public morals, population increase, and a better society. The advocates of toleration of the marriage practices of religious minorities voiced the same argument. Protestants and Jews were useful, productive members of French society; therefore the state should respect and protect their marriage customs. The contention won wide acceptance, first in judicial decisions and finally in royal legislation that recognized the legality of the marriages of French Calvinists.

Third, as the century passed, literary men and social critics increasingly advanced the claims of sentiment in marriage and family relationships. They argued that marital partners ought to choose one another freely, out of mutual affection and esteem. They praised marriage as a means to personal happiness rather than as a convenient social and economic relationship. They insisted that the bonds joining husband and wife and parents with children ought to be those of affection, not authority. In their emphasis on diversity, utility, and sentiment, the eighteenth-century philosophers fostered a spirit of critical and comparative inquiry directed especially at ideas and institutions closely connected with the church and the monarchy. Their thoughts on marriage, divorce, and the family became the property of most educated men and helped to produce the "modern" conception of marriage and the family that was subsequently expressed in the legislation of the revolution.[1]

In addition to the background of Catholic doctrine and secular legal thought, eighteenth-century writers drew upon two groups of ideas from the preceding century. They frequently cited the works

1. Numerous pamphlets on the issue of divorce, for example, marshaled an unvarying succession of secular, "enlightened" authorities, just as clerical tracts mobilized the standard, predictable citations to the views of church fathers and councils.

of jurists who discussed marriage and the organization of the family in connection with larger problems of natural law and the principles of political organization. To these theoretical formulations they added the realism found in the reflections of Montaigne.

Natural-law theorists emphasized the essential similarity between the family and the state and contended that the husband and father should be the sovereign within the domestic commonwealth. In keeping with his authority in marriage, Bodin believed he should be permitted to divorce his wife at will.[2] Hugo Grotius found no sanction in natural law for either parental control over the marriage of children or monogamy. He further argued that while God probably favored indissoluble marriage, divorce had been permitted freely among the Hebrews, Persians, Indians, Egyptians, Greeks, and Romans.[3] Pufendorf emphasized the contractual nature of marriage and reasoned that such actions as desertion, refusal to cohabit, and adultery of the wife constituted breach of the contract sufficient to justify divorce.[4]

John Locke approached the question of marriage and family organization in terms of paternal power, for he was writing partly to refute Sir Thomas Filmer's *Patriarcha*, which justified divine-right monarchy as being essentially patriarchal. Locke argued that paternal power over children meant providing them with nurture and

2. Jean Bodin, *The Six Books of a Commonweale*, trans. Richard Knolles, corrected and revised by Kenneth D. McRae (Cambridge: Harvard University Press, 1962), pp. 10–19.

3. Hugo Grotius, *The Law of War and Peace*, trans. Francis W. Kelsey et al. (Oxford: Clarendon Press, 1925), pp. 234–38. The work appears to have been widely circulated in France. The catalog of the Bibliothèque Nationale lists sixteen Latin editions, four French editions, and numerous extracts and summaries in French published between 1625 and 1773.

4. Samuel Pufendorf, *The Law of Nature and of Nations*, trans. C. H. Oldfather and W. A. Oldfather (Oxford: Clarendon Press, 1934), 2:389–877. Of the seven editions of the work appearing in French in the eighteenth century, that of Jean Barbeyrac particularly helped to popularize Pufendorf's ideas. The son of an émigré Calvinist minister, Barbeyrac taught at Berlin, Lausanne, and Groningen. In a note appended to his translation, he suggested that since the sole end of marriage is the procreation and rearing of children, its duration need not exceed the time required to fulfill these goals. Furthermore, since marriage is a contract, Barbeyrac urged that the contracting parties should be able to stipulate that it should last for a lifetime or for some shorter period (Jean Sourdois, "Le mariage et le divorce sous la législation intermédiaire," *Revue générale du droit, de la législation et de jurisprudence* 33 [1909]:422).

guidance until they reached the age of reason and sound judgment. He emphasized the equality of the sexes and contended that, while marriage had to last long enough to achieve procreation and rearing of young, it did not need to be perpetual:

> But though there are ties upon mankind which make the conjugal bond more firm and lasting than [among] the other species of animals, yet it would give one reason to inquire why this compact, where procreation and education are secured and inheritance taken care for, may not be made determinable, either by consent, or at a certain time, or upon certain conditions, as well as any other voluntary compact, there being no necessity in the nature of the thing that it should always be for life.[5]

In addition to the ideas of natural-law theorists and political philosophers, most eighteenth-century men were familiar with the more informal reflections on marriage found in the essays of Montaigne. Montaigne compared marriage to a cage of birds: those outside are anxious to enter, while those within want only to escape. When asked whether or not a man should marry, he repeated a response that he attributed to Socrates: whichever a man does, he will repent it.[6] Montaigne reasoned that since marriage is beset by a thousand cares that trouble the course of affection, the marital tie is far inferior to simple friendship.[7]

In his essay entitled "On Some Verses of Virgil," Montaigne wrote at length about love. He praised passionate love, human sexual desires, and their fulfillment, but he warned that love was no proper basis for marriage:

> Love hates people to be attached to each other except by himself, and takes a laggard part in relations that are set up and maintained under another title, as marriage is. . . . We do not marry for ourselves, whatever we say; we marry just as much or more for our posterity, for our family. The practice and benefit of marriage concerns our

5. John Locke, *Two Treatises of Government*, ed. Peter Laslett (Cambridge: University Press, 1960), p. 339.

6. Michel Eyquem de Montaigne, "On Some Verses of Virgil," in *The Complete Works of Montaigne*, trans. and ed. Donald M. Frame (Stanford: Stanford University Press, 1948), p. 647. Frame's *Montaigne: A Biography* (New York: Harcourt Brace & World, 1965) provides a particularly useful introduction to the essayist and his writings.

7. Montaigne, "Of Friendship," in *Complete Works*, pp. 137–38.

race very far beyond us. Therefore, I like this fashion of arranging it rather by a third hand than by our own. How opposite is all of this to the conventions of love. . . . I see no marriages that sooner are troubled and fail than those that progress by means of beauty and amorous desires.[8]

The essayist adopted a casual attitude toward adultery. He noted that many honorable men have been cuckolds and have not really suffered for it, despite gossip.[9] With regard to divorce, he argued that human nature resisted external efforts to force it to be constant:

We have thought to tie the knot of our marriages more firmly by taking away all means of dissolving them; but the knot of will and affection has become loosened as the knot of constraint has been tightened. And on the contrary, what kept marriages in Rome so long in honor and security was everyone's freedom to break them off at will. They loved their wives the better because they might lose them; and, with full liberty of divorce, five hundred years passed before anyone took advantage of it.[10]

Montaigne and the natural-law theorists cited human inconstancy, the law of nature, and contractual theory to challenge the Catholic dogma of marital indissolubility. On the other hand, with the exception of John Locke, they supported the absolute authority of the husband and father within the family. And they identified marriage with the broader concerns of the social and economic status of the family and the political stability and welfare of the state.

The first common theme in eighteenth-century writing on marriage and the family is fascination with the diversity of customs and

8. "On Some Verses of Virgil," in ibid., pp. 645–46.
9. Ibid., p. 642.
10. Montaigne, "That Our Desire Is Increased by Difficulty," in *Complete Works*, p. 466. Many readers absorbed Montaigne's thought through the writing of his disciple, Pierre Charron. Charron reorganized Montaigne's reflections under such general topics as man's weakness, vanity, inconstancy, and the need for knowledge; his *Traité de la sagesse* proved popular even though it greatly diminished the wit and richness of the original essays. Charron restated Montaigne's comments on divorce with such emphasis and clarity that the church censured editions of the work published in 1601 and 1604. Even in later, revised editions, Charron stressed that all nations except France rendered marriage "more easy, free and fertile" by polygamy, repudiation, or both (Pierre Charron, *Traité de la sagesse* [Paris: Lefebvre, 1836], pp. 220–23).

forms of social organization found in other societies. Writers most often reported and interpreted the practices of other cultures to justify divorce, but the evidence they presented also indicated different sexual mores and relationships within the family. Many authors surveyed the history of the practice of marriage. In the seventeenth century, Pufendorf had presented a lengthy discussion of comparative marriage and sexual customs in ancient and modern times, while Charron had argued that divorce had been practiced in the classical world by pagans and Christians alike.[11] In *The Spirit of the Laws,* Montesquieu ended a chapter on divorce and repudiation with a discussion of marriage during the Roman Empire.[12] Jean-Charles de Lavie, a former president of the Parlement of Bordeaux and a student of Bodin, argued in his *Des corps politiques* that neither public morals nor the rearing of children had suffered from the practice of divorce in Rome.[13]

In Diderot's *Encyclopedia,* Boucher d'Argis organized his entry entitled "Divorce" as a historical essay. With the opening sentence he acknowledged the orthodox Catholic view, noting that "divorce is certainly contrary to the first institution of marriage, which by its nature is indissoluble."[14] Then he traced the development of divorce in the law of Moses and Jesus and its use during the Roman Empire and the early period of the French monarchy. Under the heading "*Mariage à terme,*" d'Argis related the story of a manuscript, dated 1297, which had been found in the royal library and which purported to be a contract of marriage between two nobles for a term of seven years, with the possibility of renewal. In it, the parties had agreed that if they chose to separate, they would divide their children equally between them, drawing lots for the final child in case of an uneven number.[15] Voltaire's discussion of divorce in the *Philosophic Dictionary* borrowed the historical background

11. Pufendorf, *Law of Nature,* pp. 839–59; Charron, *Traité de la sagesse,* pp. 222–23.

12. Charles de Secondat de Montesquieu, *The Spirit of the Laws,* trans. Thomas Nugent (New York: Colonial Press, 1900), 1:261–63.

13. Jean-Charles de Lavie, *Des corps politiques et de leurs gouvernements* (Lyons: P. Duplain, 1764), 1:71–72.

14. *Encyclopédie ou dictionnaire raisonné des sciences, des arts et des métiers* (Paris: Briasson, 1754), 4:1083. Boucher d'Argis was a lawyer who practiced before the Parlement of Paris.

15. Ibid., 10:113.

from the *Encyclopedia* and criticized the church for having been unwilling to accept divorce legislation decreed by the eminent Christian and lawgiver, Justinian.[16]

In reference to the practice of other contemporary societies, Montesquieu reminded Frenchmen that indissolubility was far from a universal rule by examining it through the eyes of foreign visitors. In the *Persian Letters*, Usbec writes to Rhédi about the curious customs of French Christians. He notes that they have succeeded in abolishing divorce, which was permissible under the Roman Empire, and consequently most marriages are rent by quarrels and disgust. They have forgotten that nothing contributes to mutual attachment so much as the facility of divorce; a husband and wife will sustain domestic difficulties willingly if they know it is within their power to put an end to them. Discord in a Christian marriage may be resolved only by permitting the parties to separate, and usually the husband then seeks pleasure with *filles de joie*—a commerce harmful to himself and also to society, since it fails to produce legitimate children.[17]

In *The Spirit of the Laws,* Montesquieu reported that the extent of parental authority varied from country to country. He noted that in England the principle of respect for parents was frequently abused by daughters who married according to their own fancy, without consulting their parents. Such a practice was perhaps tolerable, since the laws of that country did not recognize monastic celibacy, and hence daughters had no state to choose but that of marriage. In France, on the contrary, young women always had the alternative of celibacy, and therefore the law that required them to obtain the consent of their fathers to marry was more acceptable.[18]

---

16. François Marie Arouet de Voltaire, "Philosophic Dictionary," in *The Works of Voltaire,* trans. William F. Fleming (New York: Dingwall-Rock, 1927), 4:147–48. Similar discussions of Roman and Christian practice recur constantly in less well-known pamphlets and treatises. See, for example, Simon-Nicolas-Henri Linguet, *Théorie des lois civiles ou principes fondamentaux de la société* (London: 1769), 1:12–13. In 1774, the notes to an edition of Plutarch's treatise on marriage argued that the practice of divorce in Greek and Roman marital law had not led to abuses or damaged public morality (*Manuel des époux ou maximes de conduite dans le mariage: Traité de Plutarque traduit par M. * * * * [London, 1774]).

17. Charles de Secondat de Montesquieu, *Lettres persanes* (Paris: Nelson, 1951), pp. 240–42.

18. Montesquieu, *Spirit of the Laws,* 2:5–6.

Montesquieu explained the existence of polygamy in some societies by reference to climate, geography, and other physical factors. He concluded that in southern countries a man's body matures so much more rapidly than his character or reason that his sexual passions tend to be violent and undisciplined. In northern countries, where growth is slower, physical and moral maturity more nearly coincide and passions are less strong. Hence polygamy is common in the south, but monogamy is the general rule in the north.[19]

Montesquieu's fictional Persian visitors had been shocked to find France a nation where a man might have only one wife rather than several. David Hume's essay on polygamy and divorce, which he published in *Mercure* in 1757, disapproved of both practices but nevertheless cited numerous instances of polygamy. Hume explained that the citizens of Athens had once taken additional wives to remedy a population deficit and that even primitive Britons were said to have practiced a form of group marriage in which the children belonged to the group rather than to individual parents.[20] Similarly, Prémontval's tract against polygamy demonstrated that it had been found at various times in many societies.[21] Jean Nicolas Démeunier reported similar findings in a study based on the reports of explorers, travelers, and historians. In the chapter on marriage, he further noted that while most civilized nations have rejected the practice of polygamy, they have thought it unwise to chain together two unhappy spouses for life, and hence they have permitted divorce.[22]

Numerous authors contrasted the effects of the Catholic rule of indissolubility in France with those of the usage of divorce in the Protestant states of Europe. Lavie argued that the practice of re-

19. Ibid., 67–68.
20. David Hume, *Essays Moral, Political, and Literary*, ed. T. H. Green and T. H. Grose (London: Longmans, Green, 1875), 1:237–239.
21. André-Pierre Le Guay de Prémontval, *La monogamie, ou l'unité dans le mariage; ouvrage dans lequel on entreprend d'établir, contre le préjugé comun, l'exacte et parfaite conformité des trois loix de la nature, de Moïse et de Jésus-Christ, sur ce sujet*, 3 vols. (The Hague: P. Van Cleef, 1751).
22. Jean Nicolas Démeunier, *L'esprit des usages et des coutumes des differens peuples, ou observations tirées des voyageurs et des historiens* (Paris: Pissot, 1776), 1:177–230. The author's name is also sometimes given as Desmeuniers.

pudiation had had a favorable effect on the population of the Protestant states of Germany.[23] Cerfvol contended that the Protestant nations of northern Europe were enjoying both population growth and prosperity while the Catholic states of southern Europe were suffering from declining population and poverty. He stated further that divorce even existed in Catholic Poland, where bishops dissolved marriages without the necessity of referring the cases to Rome.[24] The *Encyclopedia* discussed the practice of divorce in the states adhering to the Confession of Augsburg, while Voltaire noted in the *Philosophic Dictionary* that the Eastern or Greek Orthodox church permitted dissolution of marriage, in conformity with the teachings of the Scriptures, the views of most of the church fathers, and the practice of early Christians.[25]

While European Protestants enjoyed greater marital liberty than Catholics through the facility of divorce, eighteenth-century writers often saw non-Western societies as completely free from artificial and constraining rules regarding marriage. David Hume had first explained that the sailors of Tonkin married only for a season, and the *Encyclopedia* also discussed the practice.[26] Similarly, Helvétius praised the customs of those African countries where a lover and his mistress lived together for a period of time and tested the compatibility of their characters before they married. He urged that such a custom might be applied in France, on condition that the law provide for the care and rearing of the children of such unions.[27]

In 1772, a year after Bougainville had described his travels in the South Pacific, Diderot composed a tale in which he depicted an idyllic Tahitian society, untroubled by the repression and restrictions of Western civilization. In this paradise all young women were held in common by the men; the Tahitians knew nothing of

23. Lavie, *Des corps politiques,* p. 74.

24. Cerfvol, *Législation du divorce* (London, 1769), pp. 48–49, 13. The practice of the Polish Catholic church actually involved actions to nullify marriage, which were adjudicated by the Polish bishops rather than being sent to Rome. The practical result was that the parties were free to marry again, on the ground that a valid marriage had never existed.

25. *Encyclopédie,* 4:1083; Voltaire, *Works,* 4:147.

26. Hume, *Essays Moral,* 1:231–35.

27. Claude Adrien Helvétius, *A Treatise on Man: His Intellectual Faculties and His Education,* trans. W. Hooper (London: Albion Press, 1810), 2:274.

adultery or incest. Sexual relations were open and natural and young women felt honored to conceive and bear children, which were then reared by all members of the tribe. Given man's inconstant nature, the laws made no effort to chain a man and a woman together for the duration of their lives.[28]

Thus while the writings of all of these authors emphasized the diversity of marriage and family customs in classical and contemporary times, almost all praised the custom of divorce. Divorce had been an acceptable practice in Roman and early Christian society. Citizens of Protestant states employed it according to the rules of their religion, and members of non-European cultures enjoyed great freedom in determining the duration of their marriages. All of these accounts encouraged Frenchmen to question the Catholic doctrine of indissolubility and to borrow elements of marital or family organization from the customs and laws of other societies.

Other ideas about marriage and family law in the eighteenth century may be grouped under the concept of utility, which in turn implied a particular understanding of human nature. Most writers of the French Enlightenment adhered to the doctrine of environmentalism as it had been developed by John Locke.[29] They believed that man at birth was neither good nor evil and had no fixed or innate qualities. Rather, the human personality began as a *tabula rasa*, ready to receive the sense impressions of environment and society. Human nature was malleable and was formed by parental training, education, social custom, law, and the entire experience of living. Individuals who held this conception of human nature placed great faith in the utility of law to reform marriage and family relationships. They also believed that changes in the law of marriage could further larger social goals.

Numerous writers argued that the introduction of divorce would be useful as a means of furthering population growth.[30] The Mar-

28. Denis Diderot, *Supplément au voyage de Bougainville* (Geneva: Droz, 1955), pp. 224–35. Diderot did not publish the work during his lifetime; it first appeared in 1796.

29. Peter Gay, *The Science of Freedom*, vol. 2 of *The Enlightenment: An Interpretation* (New York: Alfred A. Knopf, 1969), pp. 177–80.

30. Joseph J. Spengler has surveyed the eighteenth-century literature on population in *France Faces Depopulation* (Durham, N.C.: Duke University Press, 1938)

shal de Saxe believed with many men of his day that the population
of Europe had been diminishing since Roman times and that the
decline had been particularly marked in France. Since a state's
prosperity and military capacity depended on its size, the marshal
argued that marriage should be contracted for a term of years, to be
renewed at the end of the period only if the spouses had had children. He believed that making marriage dissoluble in this manner
would also discourage debauchery, which destroyed man's ability
to procreate. Spouses who had renewed their marriage pact three
times would become inseparably wedded to one another and they,
along with mothers who had borne ten, fifteen, and twenty children, would receive awards from the state. The marshal argued that
his program could scarcely be objectionable to theologians, for it
implemented God's first commandment to man: that he should
increase and multiply.[31]

The Parisian lawyer and journalist Linguet praised the social
utility of divorce, for it allowed the parties to an unproductive
marriage to dissolve their relationship, permitting at least one of
them to produce children in a second marriage. He further contended that the existence of divorce encouraged bachelors to undertake lawful marriage, knowing the relationship need not necessarily
endure a lifetime.[32] Cerfvol's *Mémoire sur la population* noted that

---

and *French Predecessors of Malthus: A Study in Eighteenth-Century Wage and
Population Theory* (Durham, N.C.: Duke University Press, 1942). Both mercantilist
and physiocratic writers believed that the state should foster population growth.
During the eighteenth century, royal officials began to assemble statistical data that,
although admittedly incomplete, suggested that the nation's population had in fact
been increasing during the century. Despite such evidence, many authors continued
to believe that the nation's size was decreasing. One possible explanation for this
inconsistency may lie in recent suggestions that some Frenchmen had begun to adopt
contraceptive techniques within marriage during the period. The writers who com-
plain of supposed population decline attribute it in part to couples who wrong
nature (*trompe la nature*) in order to keep their families small and satisfy their love
of luxury. For research on attitudes toward contraceptive practices in the family in
the eighteenth century, see Hélène Berguès, *La prévention des naissances dans la
famille: Ses origines dans les temps modernes* (Paris: Presses Universitaires de
France, 1960); Jacques Dupaquier, "Sur la population française au XVIIIᵉ siècle,"
Revue historique 239 (March–April 1968):43–79.

31. Maurice comte de Saxe, "Réflections sur la propagation de l'espèce
humaine," in *Mes rêveries,* published posthumously by the abbé Perau (Amsterdam,
1757), 2:155–60.

32. Linguet, *Théories des lois civiles,* 1:340–465. Although brilliant, Linguet
apparently had a talent for making enemies. The biographies refer to his arrogance,

spouses who abhor each other are more likely to produce children out of wedlock than within it. With the aid of divorce, they might achieve happy, fruitful marriages with other persons. Cerfvol argued that if priests and single persons of both sexes were strongly encouraged to marry, the decline of French population might be reversed.[33]

Morelly's *Code de la nature*, which appeared in 1755, is one eighteenth-century writer's proposal for the creation of a new society by means of improved laws. After a bitter critique of existing customs and institutions, Morelly presented model legislation for a state that he declared would be organized according to the intentions of nature. The *Code* depicted an authoritarian society in which marriage and divorce were carefully regulated in the interests of the state. All young men and women were to be married after reaching the age of puberty; youths might select partners during the course of an annual public festival. First marriages were to be indissoluble for ten years, after which time the parties might divorce, having first participated in reconciliation efforts supervised by a group of older heads of families. Divorced persons might remarry only on the condition that they choose a partner their own age or older. In the event of divorce, children of both sexes were to remain with their father.[34]

Claude Helvétius also urged changes in the law of marriage in

---

disloyalty to his profession, and unbalanced conduct. His career as a lawyer was ended by expulsion from the Paris bar about 1774, after which time he worked as a journalist in Switzerland, the Netherlands, and England. He returned to France at the beginning of the revolution and was guillotined in 1794. See Jean Cruppi, *Un avocat journaliste au XVIIIe siècle: Linguet* (Paris: Hachette, 1895); Henry Vyverberg, "Limits of Nonconformity in the Enlightenment: The Case of Simon-Nicolas-Henri Linguet," *French Historical Studies* 4, no. 4 (Fall 1970):474–91.

33. Cerfvol, *Mémoire sur la population* (London, 1768), pp. 4–83. The name Cerfvol also sometimes appears as de Cerfvol or Chevalier de Cerfvol. It was probably a pseudonym, for none of the biographical reference works for the period are able to provide any information about him other than noting his vocation as a pamphleteer who wrote about marriage, women's rights, and the family. Cerfvol reiterated his arguments in *Législation du divorce* (London, 1769). In this work he included a draft code that would have permitted divorce for adultery, absence, insanity, severe mistreatment, unreasonably dissolute living, and infamous criminal punishments. The code included sensible provisions governing the division of property, the custody of children, and the maintenance of the former wife.

34. Morelly, *Code de la nature; ou le véritable esprit de ses lois,* ed. Gilbert Chinard (Paris: Raymond Clavreuil, 1950), pp. 310–18.

order to further broad social ends. He reasoned that indissoluble
marriage was suitable for peasants, because their lifelong occupation was to cultivate and improve the soil. Other classes in society
should be governed by different marriage rules. Soldiers, for example, should not marry at all, for marriage reduced their warlike
spirit. Rather, they should be free to contract liaisons as they
wished, and when the relationships were terminated, the children of
these unions should be reared by the prince to provide the state with
soldiers. The civil laws permitting divorce must make careful provision for the education and marriage of children, who would remain
with the mother or depart with the father according to their sex. If
the parents lacked sufficient funds, the state ought to use some of
the income of the clergy to maintain these children. Society could
profit from human desire for change or variety in marriage, since

> if it be true that the desire of change be so conformable as is said to
> human nature, the privilege of change may be proposed as the re-
> ward of merit, and by this soldiers may be made more brave, magis-
> trates more just, artisans more industrious, and men of genius more
> studious.[35]

Arguments for toleration of Jewish and Protestant marriage customs repeated the theme of utility. Jews and Protestants were useful
members of French society; discrimination against their marriage
practices would encourage them to emigrate, thus depriving the
state of their talents and wealth. In theory, all Frenchmen had been
Catholics since the Revocation of the Edict of Nantes in 1685. In
fact, the country's population included perhaps as many as a million Calvinists, who were located mainly in the south. The wars of
Louis XIV had extended France's eastern frontiers to include parts
of Alsace inhabited by German-speaking Lutherans and Jews.
Other Jews lived in the towns near the papal city of Avignon and in
Bordeaux. The legal status of these minority groups varied. The
Jews of Bordeaux had fled religious persecution in Portugal, and
were considered resident aliens. The Peace of Westphalia had
guaranteed the Lutherans of Alsace the right to practice their own
religion, while the statutes of that province extended limited religious toleration to Jews. The state refused, however, to recognize

35. Helvétius, A Treatise on Man, 2:273–75.

French Calvinists as a separate religious group or to authorize special practices connected with their faith, such as the celebration of marriage before their own pastors.[36]

The existence of communities of Jews and Protestants within the predominantly Catholic French state and their desire to observe their own marriage laws constituted a potential exception to the institutional and doctrinal pattern of marriage that had been established by the church and the monarchy. The rule of marital indissolubility was especially vulnerable, since both Protestant and Jewish religious law sanctioned divorce under some circumstances and because both groups practiced it outside of France. The Jewish practice of divorce gave rise to two lengthy and well-publicized disputes in which lawyers and pamphleteers questioned the rule of absolute indissolubility of marriage.

Borach Lévi, later called Joseph-Jean-François Elie Lévi, was an Alsatian Jew from the city of Haguenau, who converted to Christianity while in Paris in 1752. Lévi had previously married according to Jewish law and had fathered two daughters, but after his conversion he sought to marry again within the Catholic religion. Lévi's wife urged him to return to her and to the religion of his ancestors, and when he refused, she demanded a divorce according to Jewish law. Meanwhile a Catholic curé refused to marry Lévi and his intended bride on the ground of Lévi's previous marriage, and the *officialité* of Soissons affirmed the curé's decision. Lévi obtained an *appel comme d'abus* attacking the jurisdiction of the church court and having the matter transferred to the Parlement of Paris.[37]

36. Arthur Hertzberg, *The French Enlightenment and the Jews* (New York: Columbia University Press, 1968), contains an excellent introduction to the life of Jewish communities in France before 1789. For articles and bibliography, see the special issue of *Annales historiques de la Révolution française* 233 (January–March 1976). The opening chapters of Burdette C. Poland's *French Protestantism and the French Revolution* (Princeton: Princeton University Press, 1957) describe the situation of French Protestants under the ancien régime.

37. One collection of pleadings and memoirs on the Lévi case is located in the Bibliothèque Nationale under the call numbers Ld[184] 10–15. Another collection, including most of the documents and pleadings from the case, appeared in Amsterdam in 1761 as *Consultation sur le mariage: Recueil sur la question si un juif marié dans sa religion peut se remarier après son baptême, lorsque sa femme juive refuse de le suivre et d'habiter avec lui.* Many of the participants in the suit published their opinions separately.

Lévi's lawyers argued that since the rule of indissolubility did not exist according to Jewish custom, Lévi might divorce his wife under the same law by which he had married her. Even assuming that the state would not allow the Jewish practice of divorce, they contended that Christian doctrine permitted a convert to remarry within the Christian faith when his unconverted spouse refused to reside with him. As a precedent for such a solution, one advocate analogized Lévi's situation to that of a Muslim who converted to Christianity while traveling in France in 1720. Assuming the name of Sieur Albert, he remarried in Paris with the consent of the cardinal de Noailles, despite the existence of four wives in Constantinople. The same lawyer cited a recent decision of the Sovereign Council of Colmar in 1749, upholding the right of a newly converted Christian to remarry, and produced letters from the bishops of Verdun, Toul, Metz, and Strasbourg attesting that Jews converting to Christianity in their bishoprics had always been allowed to remarry Christians.[38]

Loyseau de Mauléon, a celebrated counselor and frequent advocate of "enlightened" causes, urged that the law must accommodate legal institutions to the imperfections of human beings. While it might be most admirable for Lévi to live in continence for the rest of his life, the legitimate demands of human nature urged him to take a lawful companion. Therefore, Loyseau de Mauléon concluded, if the law wished to encourage conversion to Christianity, it must offer the newly converted Christian the opportunity of marriage, not simply the choice between continence and illicit pleasures.[39] On the other hand, a consultation written by the prominent legal scholar Le Ridant argued that the decision of the Council of Trent making marriage absolutely indissoluble must be controlling, despite the conflicting opinions of church fathers and earlier councils on the question of remarriage by a new convert.[40]

The Parlement of Paris rendered judgment on January 2, 1758,

38. Le Gras, *Mémoire pour Joseph-Jean-François Elie Lévi* (Paris: Du Mesnil, 1757), pp. 60–70.

39. Alexandre-Jérôme Loyseau de Mauléon, "Plaidoyer pour Joseph-Jean-François Elie Lévi," *Plaidoyers et mémoires* (Paris: Le Breton, 1762), pp. 1–48.

40. Pierre Le Ridant, *Consultation sur le mariage du juif Borach Lévi* (Paris: Du Mesnil, 1758), pp. 1–28. Le Ridant also recounts the story of the Lévi affaire in *Code matrimonial* and in *Examen de deux questions importantes sur le mariage*.

declaring that Lévi's appeals from the judgment of the *officialité* could not be sustained. Attorney General Seguier justified the rule of indissolubility of marriage by reference to natural law, divine law, and civil law.[41] Although the decision of the Parlement of Paris in the Lévi case did not expressly prohibit the practice of divorce according to Jewish law, its sweeping reaffirmation of the rule of indissolubility suggested that no exceptions would be allowed for minority religious practices in France. Yet the same court reversed its position in the 1770s when confronted with efforts to dissolve a marriage linking two prominent Jewish families of Bordeaux.

Samuel Péixotto was born in Bordeaux in 1741 to a merchant family, and as a young man was sent to Holland and England to work in the banking houses of Mendes Dacosta. In 1762 Péixotto contracted a marriage with the banker's sister, Sara Mendes Dacosta, and the couple celebrated their union in the Portuguese Jewish synagogue in London. They returned to Bordeaux, where they lived together for five years before separating in 1776. Sometime in the 1770s, Péixotto brought an action before the Châtelet, a law court in Paris, requesting that his marriage be declared null or be dissolved by divorce. Péixotto gave his wife's domicile as Paris instead of Bordeaux, and when she failed to respond to the suit, he obtained a judgment of nullity by default.[42]

Sara Dacosta attacked the judgment before the Parlement of Bordeaux, and the Parlement of Paris resolved the conflict between the two jurisdictions by returning the case to the Châtelet with instructions that it be judged on its merits. The Châtelet rejected Péixotto's contention that his marriage should be nullified because of defects in the manner in which it had been celebrated. Péixotto's second argument rested squarely on the Jewish law of divorce. Royal edicts had given the Portuguese Jewish community permission to live in France "according to their customs and usages," and hence, Péixotto urged, he should be entitled to a divorce, the French law of marital indissolubility notwithstanding. Sara Dacosta's lawyers replied that divorce among the Jews was not an automatic right and

41. Jean-Baptiste Denisart, ed., *Collection de décisions nouvelles et de notions relatives à la jurisprudence,* placed in new order, corrected, and augmented by Camus and Bayard (Paris: Desaint, 1783), 6:570–85.
42. Ibid., p. 586.

that a tribunal of rabbis would reject Péixotto's claim as without foundation.[43]

The Parlement of Paris responded by referring the case to the Sephardic Jewish community of Bordeaux to determine whether or not Péixotto was entitled to a divorce according to Jewish law. The elders of the community delayed, probably because both parties to the dispute belonged to powerful families, and the issue ultimately became academic when Péixotto went to Spain, where he converted to Catholicism in 1781.[44] The importance of the case lies in the willingness of the Parlement of Paris to admit the possibility of divorce in France, at least for members of a minority religion.

Instead of divorce, French Protestants were primarily concerned with the validity of their marriages. These "new converts," as Calvinists had been called after 1685, had been forced to marry before Catholic priests, but by the eighteenth century they had adopted the practice of marrying "*au désert.*" This meant simply that they celebrated their marriages before their own pastors in private homes or in the countryside. French law refused to recognize the validity of these Protestant marriages, however, with resulting frequent difficulties over the legitimacy of children and the devolution of property. A French Protestant constantly feared that at his death the law would declare his children bastards and his wife a concubine, depriving them of their name and their inheritance.[45]

An increasing number of Frenchmen believed that the law's refusal to recognize the validity of Protestant marriages was inhumane and harmful to society. As early as 1755, the canonist and legal scholar Le Ridant contended that a means must be found to legalize marriages and births among French Calvinists without offending the Catholic clergy.[46] The first publication of Jean Portalis, who went on to enjoy a lengthy career as an advocate and civil servant, was a consultation on the validity of Protestant marriage.[47]

---

43. Ibid., pp. 586–88.
44. Hertzberg, *French Enlightenment and the Jews,* pp. 207–8.
45. On the problem of Protestant marriage, see Roger Chastanier, *L'état civil des protestants, 1550–1792* (Nîmes, 1922); Pierre Taillandier, *Le mariage des protestants français sous l'ancien régime* (Clermont-Ferrand: Dumont, 1919).
46. Pierre Le Ridant, *Mémoire théologique et politique au sujet des mariages clandestins des protestants de France* (n.p., 1755).
47. Jean-Etienne-Marie Portalis, *Consultation sur la validité du mariage des protestants* (n.p., 1770).

Sometime in the 1760s, Louis XIV had instructed Gilbert de Voisins to study the problem and to suggest how it might be resolved. De Voisins proposed that the state should permit Protestant worship in homes and allow a limited number of pastors to travel in the country and conduct private services. Marriages might be celebrated before these pastors, and the spouses could then register their marriage with a royal magistrate or a curé acting in his capacity as a royal official. De Voisins' plan was not adopted, but it provided the model for the Edict of Toleration, which the monarchy enacted on the eve of the revolution, after two decades of increasing propaganda on behalf of Protestant marriage.[48]

The arguments of some individuals for toleration of minority religious practices were part of a larger offensive directed against the Catholic church. Voltaire had begun his campaign against superstition and fanaticism in the 1760s with the battle cry "*Ecrasez l'infâme*."[49] In the *Philosophic Dictionary* he explained that marriage was primarily a civil contract and that the church had seized control of it in an age when civil governments were weak. Thus the church was able to maintain the prohibition against divorce, except for persons of wealth or political influence. "This custom, established in ignorant times, is perpetuated in enlightened ones only because it exists. All abuse eternizes itself; it is an Augean stable, and requires a Hercules to cleanse it."[50]

Voltaire criticized royal prohibitions against the marriage of non-Catholics with Catholics and urged legislation to protect the million French Protestants whose marriages were of questionable validity because they had not been celebrated before a priest.[51] In "The Memoir of a Magistrate," which he published as part of the discussion of adultery in the *Philosophic Dictionary*, Voltaire denounced the sterility and inhumanity of the Catholic rule of indissolubility when a man's wife had wronged him by adultery:

> If I look around among the nations of the earth, I see no religion except the Roman Catholic which does not recognize divorce and

48. Armand Lods, "Les partisans et les adversaires de l'édit de tolérance: Étude bibliographique et juridique," *Bulletin de la Société de l'Histoire du Protestantisme Français* 36 (1887):551–65.
49. Peter Gay, *Voltaire's Politics: The Poet as Realist* (Princeton: Princeton University Press, 1959), pp. 239–58.
50. Voltaire, *Works*, 4:147–48.
51. Ibid., 6:197–204.

second marriage as a natural right. What inversion of order, then, has made it a virtue in Catholics to suffer adultery and a duty to live without wives when their wives have thus shamefully injured them? . . . A separation of person and property is granted me, but not a divorce. The law takes from me my wife, and leaves me the word *sacrament*! I no longer enjoy matrimony, but I am still married! What contradiction! What slavery!

Nor is it less strange that this law of the church is directly contrary to the words which it believes to have been pronounced by Jesus Christ: "Whosoever shall put away his wife, *except it be for fornication*, and shall marry another, committeth adultery."[52]

"Let the priests and monks abstain from women if they wish," declared Voltaire's magistrate. "They are victims of the pope and deserve the misfortune they have contrived for themselves. . . . But I, a magistrate who serves the state the whole day long, have occasion for a woman at night."[53]

In the two decades before the revolution, the efforts of the *philosophes* to obtain toleration and a legal status for the marriages of French Calvinists won increasing acceptance. Even Catholic

---

52. Ibid., 3:81.

53. Ibid., p. 82. In earlier versions of the incident that Voltaire recounted in "Memoir of a Magistrate," the principal figure was a carpenter from the Alsatian city of Landau whose wife had deserted him and run off with a soldier. A number of authors of pamphlets urging divorce and condemning the church control of marriage law presented the story, but none told it so effectively as Voltaire. See Philibert, *Cri d'un honnête homme, qui se croit fondé en droit naturel et divin à répudier sa femme* (n.p., 1769); Desnoyers, *Réfutation du système porté en la consultation faite à Lucienne le 16 août 1771, qui établi que le mari que sa femme a quitté, et s'est allé marier en pays étranger, peut obtenir le divorce et la liberté de se remarier en France* (Paris: Houry, 1771); Simon-Nicolas-Henri Linguet, *Mémoire à consulter et consultation pour un mari dont la femme s'est remariée en pays protestant, et qui demand s'il peut se remarier de même en France* (Paris: Cellot, 1771); *Réponse au mémoire et à la consultation de M. Linguet touchant l'indissolubilité du mariage* (Paris: Lambert, 1772).

The facts of the story of the carpenter of Landau were remarkably similar to those of a divorce suit brought by a Lutheran baker of the same city in 1722. The baker demanded a divorce from his unfaithful wife on the basis of the guarantees of religious rights contained in the treaties of the Peace of Augsburg. Previously, church consistories had routinely granted divorce on those grounds permitted by the Lutheran religion. This time, however, the Sovereign Council of Alsace, acting under orders from the king, refused to permit any exception to the rule of marital indissolubility. The decision of 1722 ended the practice of divorce by Lutherans in France (*Recueil des édits, déclarations, lettres patentes, arrêts du Conseil d'Etat et du Conseil Souverain d'Alsace* [Colmar: Jean-Henri Decker, 1775], 1:570–76.

judges sought ways to maintain the de facto validity of such unions or at least to mitigate the law's harsh penalties against them. Although these men were mostly conservatives, they adopted the view that the French state should tolerate and value useful, productive citizens, whatever religion they might profess.

The Parlement of Toulouse had acquired the reputation of continuing hostility toward Protestants with its condemnation of Jean Calas in 1762, and shortly thereafter it permitted a Protestant to marry a second time in the Catholic faith on the explicit ground that the alleged first marriage had no existence in the law. Yet by the 1770s, the court was devising means of protecting the successions of Protestant children against the claims of Catholic collateral relatives. This effort involved shifting the burden of proof, relying on statutes governing Protestant marriage just before 1685 which had not been specifically repealed by the Revocation of the Edict of Nantes, and a variety of other technical maneuvers. The results were the same: to thwart challenges to the validity of Protestant marriages after the death of one of the spouses.[54]

Outside the courts, such men as Turgot, Condorcet, Voltaire, Lafayette, Rulhière, the baron de Breteuil, and Malesherbes argued for the modification or elimination of Protestant disabilities in the area of marriage.[55] Malesherbes's two memoirs are usually given substantial credit in persuading Louis XVI and his advisers to legislate on the subject.[56] All of these men contended that Protestants were useful citizens to the French state, which in turn should grant them the same benefits and legal protection it afforded the rest of society. In addition to the argument of utility, the critics advanced the principle of tolerance; the need for better population statistics, which would include Protestant births, marriages, and deaths; and

---

54. David D. Bien, "Catholic Magistrates and Protestant Marriage in the French Enlightenment," *French Historical Studies* 2 (1962):409–29. On the Calas case and the growth of toleration in late-eighteenth-century France, see David D. Bien, *The Calas Affair: Persecution, Toleration, and Heresy in Eighteenth-Century Toulouse* (Princeton: Princeton University Press, 1960).

55. Léonce Anquez, *De l'état civil des réformés de France* (Paris: Grassart, 1868), pp. 106–210.

56. Chrétien-Guillaume Lamoignon de Malesherbes, *Mémoire sur le mariage des protestants* (n.p., 1785) and *Second mémoire sur le mariage des protestants* (London, 1787).

the harmful effect of the present system on public morals. Early in 1787 the Parlement of Paris passed a resolution urging the king to establish more certain means of guaranteeing the civil status of Protestants, and the issue received support in the Assembly of Notables, which was meeting at the same time.[57] Finally, in November 1787, Louis XVI affixed his signature to an edict drafted by Malesherbes with the aid of Breteuil, Lafayette, and Rabaut Saint-Etienne, a pastor and Protestant leader from Nîmes.[58]

Although the Edict of 1787 did not guarantee freedom of Protestant worship, it recognized that conversion efforts after the Revocation of the Edict of Nantes had failed, leaving the nation's Protestants with the alternatives of profaning the sacraments by simulated conversions or compromising their civil status and that of their children by marriages that were not recognized by law. The edict created two means by which Protestants could conclude valid marriages. An engaged couple might have their banns published by the curé resident at the domicile of one of them and, after a private religious ceremony, they could present a declaration of their marriage together with the testimony of four witnesses to the same curé. Curés were not required by the edict to receive declarations of non-Catholic marriage. If they did so, they acted in the capacity of civil officials of the monarchy. Reception of the declaration involved record-keeping duties and implied no sacramental blessing or other religious act. The second means made available by the law followed the same pattern, except that the banns were published and the declaration received by the first official of justice of the locality, who was either royal or seigneurial, depending on the part of France.[59]

The Edict of 1787 specifically excluded Alsatian Lutherans from its application, indicating that their status and marriages would continue to be governed by treaties, but the use of the term *non-Catholic* in the law gave no indication of whether or not it would apply to the marriages of Jews living in France. Many of the same men who had championed the cause of Protestant marriage—

57. Jules Basdevant, *Des rapports de l'église et de l'état dans la législation du mariage du Concile de Trente au code civil* (Paris: Sirey, 1900), p. 167.

58. Poland, *French Protestantism*, pp. 78–79.

59. Isambert, *Recueil général*, 28:472–82.

Linguet and Malesherbes, for example—were also proponents of increased toleration and liberalized legislation for Jews. In Nîmes and in Metz, Jewish communities sought to record their marriages after the manner provided by the statute, but word from Paris established that the king had not intended and did not wish the edict to apply to his Jewish subjects.[60]

Protestant reception of the Edict of 1787 was favorable, and in many areas two and even three generations flocked to royal officials or curés to record their marriages and thus legitimate their children.[61] Individual Catholic clerics were often prepared to cooperate with the provisions of the edict, but the General Assembly of the Clergy protested against the innovation. In its Remonstrance of August 3, 1788, the clergy formally informed the king that no power on earth was able to authorize its pastors to declare that heretics, who married without any religious rite, solely by dispensation from a secular authority, contracted a legitimate marriage.[62] On the other hand, by early 1789 the pastor Rabaut Saint-Etienne urged that the Catholic clergy should be instructed that they must receive proofs of Protestant marriage without obstruction or delays.[63] On the question of religiously mixed marriages, the guard of the seals, de Barentin, responded to several inquiries early the same year that the edict did not supersede or abolish earlier ordinances forbidding marriage between Catholics and Protestants.[64]

Within the area of marriage and the family, only the issue of Jewish divorce and Protestant marriage produced a response from conservative and clerical critics of enlightened ideas. Thus the Lévi and Péixotto cases called forth numerous brochures upholding the role of indissolubility of marriage, while the movement for toleration of the marriages of Calvinists met objection from the church. To be sure, the Enlightenment did not lack critics, such as Bergier, Gauchat, Pluquet, Pluche, Barruel, and the authors of the Jesuit

60. Zosa Szajkowski, "Protestants and Jews of France in the Fight for Emancipation, 1789–1791," *Proceedings of the American Academy for Jewish Research* 25 (1956):119–35.

61. Poland, *French Protestantism*, pp. 83–84.

62. Archives Nationales, BB³⁰ 88. Hereafter cited as AN.

63. Rabaut Saint-Etienne to M. Le Garde des Sceaux, February 1788, AN, BB³⁰ 88.

64. Ibid.

Journal de Trévoux, but these men responded to the broader issues of the validity of the Christian message and the authority of the church and to such major publications as the *Encyclopedia.*[65] Several scholars have noted how eighteenth-century Christians tried to meet the thought of the Enlightenment on its own ground, asserting the "reasonableness" of Christianity and providing only a muted and sometimes eccentric defense of the faith.[66] In any event, the century simply did not see the development of a literary and polemical tradition supporting indissoluble marriage, paternal and marital authority, and inequality between children in opposition to those writings that urged the "modern" view of marriage and the family.

Despite its limitations, the Edict of 1787, permitting Protestant marriage, was a worthy product of the Enlightenment's ideals of tolerance and utility. It also represented one major exception to the French monarchy's general inability to reform itself at the end of the eighteenth century. Its significance for the later development of marriage and family law is substantial, for it is the first instance of a purely secular law governing the marriages of a large number of French citizens and, as such, it foreshadowed the introduction of civil marriage for all Frenchmen during the revolution.

A third major theme in eighteenth-century thought proposed sentiment as the key to marriage and family relationships. Dramatists and novelists contrasted the marriage of inclination, initiated by the free choice of two individuals and founded on their mutual affection, with the marriage of convenience, contracted by two families for their children and intended to further the families' social and economic goals. The idea that marriage might properly be based on

65. Robert R. Palmer, *Catholics and Unbelievers in Eighteenth-Century France* (Princeton: Princeton University Press, 1947), pp. 23–102.

66. See ibid., pp. 3–22; Gay, *The Enlightenment,* 1:322–57; and Bernard Groethuysen, *The Bourgeois: Catholicism vs. Capitalism in Eighteenth-Century France* (New York: Holt, Rinehart & Winston, 1968), pp. 37–128. The introduction to the last volume states confusingly that it is both a translation from a French edition and a condensation of the author's two-volume work, *Die Entstehung der bürgerlichen Welt- und Lebensanschauung in Frankreich* (Halls: M. Niemeyer, 1927–30).

sentiment or love was new. Literary tradition, from the courtly poetry of the troubadours and the myth of Tristan and Iseult through the drama of Corneille and Racine and the essays of Montaigne, had declared passionate love and marriage to be incompatible. As Denis de Rougemont has noted, the essence of passionate love was its quality of unsatisfied longing, whereas marriage included the obligations and gratifications of the nuptial bed. Since passionate love could exist only in a state of unfulfilled desire, the troubadours addressed their poetry to married women whom they could never hope to possess. And the theme of the impossibility of permanent physical and spiritual union recurs in the tales of Tristan and Iseult, Heloise and Abelard, and the *Romance of the Rose*.[67]

For the eighteenth century, Robert Mauzi has emphasized the extent to which the *philosophes* proposed worldly human happiness as the legitimate end of man. While they differed as to the nature of that happiness and the means by which it might be attained, many writers praised human love (*l'amour*) and sought to retain an idealized image of it without renouncing the pleasures of possession. In contrast to de Rougemont's formulation, their view of love was one of longing leading to satisfaction. Love might be realized in opposition to unchosen marriage ties or in the context of middle-class domesticity. In any case, Mauzi declares that by the end of the century, love had become, in the words of Rousseau's Julie to Saint-Preux, "the great matter of life" (*la grande affaire de la vie*).[68]

Many eighteenth-century authors still saw or felt some contradiction between love and marriage, however, and hence they chose other, related words, describing the relationship between husband

---

67. Denis de Rougemont, *Love in the Western World*, rev. and augm. ed., trans. Montgomery Belgion (New York: Pantheon Books, 1956), pp. 32–37, 50–55. For a similar view, see C. S. Lewis, *The Allegory of Love: A Study in the Medieval Tradition* (London: Oxford University Press, 1936). Edward Shorter, in *The Making of the Modern Family* (New York: Basic Books, 1975), also contends that eighteenth-century men and women began to seek marriages based on sentiment or romance, rejecting the older forces of family, community, and custom that had formerly controlled their courtship and marital choices.

68. Robert Mauzi, *L'idée du bonheur dans la pensée française au XVIIIᵉ siècle* (Paris: Armand Colin, 1960), p. 458.

and wife as founded on sentiment, mutual affection, esteem, friend-ship, or "rational" love.[69] This "modern" conception of marriage emphasized the marital happiness and domesticity of the spouses at the expense of ties and obligations to their families. While the modern conception of marriage began as a literary and dramatic creation, moralists and social critics soon sought to translate it into a legal and social reality.

The conflict of love with family and social obligations was a favorite theme of eighteenth-century French dramatists.[70] In Marivaux's *Le jeu de l'amour et du hasard,* first performed in 1730, two wellborn persons destined by their parents for marriage disguise themselves as servants, meet, and fall in love. The young man, Dorante, discloses his true identity and, after considerable internal conflict, agrees to marry Silvia despite the supposed difference in their social stations. Content with having been chosen for herself alone, Silvia then abandons her disguise and the play ends with the couple happily contemplating their coming marriage.[71] In Nivelle de la Chaussée's *La préjugé à la mode,* which was produced five years later, a foolish husband neglects his wife because it is socially unfashionable to show love for one's spouse. He is ulti-

69. Gay, *The Enlightenment,* 2:31–34. For a general discussion of French litera-ture in the eighteenth century, see Robert Niklaus, *A Literary History of France: The Eighteenth Century, 1715–1789* (New York: Barnes & Noble, 1970). For the de-velopment of love as a literary theme, see Paul Kluckhohn, *Die Auffassung der Liebe in der Literatur des 18. Jahrhunderts und in der deutschen Romantik* (1922; reprint ed. Tubingen: Max Niemeyer, 1966). Pierre Fauchery in *La destinée féminine dans le roman européen du dix-huitième siècle, 1713–1807: Essai de gynécomythie romanesque* (Paris: Armand Colin, 1972), pp. 364–99, contends that love seldom led to a happy marriage in the eighteenth-century European novel, but concedes that for reasons of plot, novelists preferred unhappy marriages to happy ones or to successful divorces. A useful article is Xavier Lannes, "Le XVIIIᵉ siècle: L'évolution des idées," in *Renouveau des idées sur la famille,* ed. Robert Prigent (Paris: Presses Universitaires de France, 1954), pp. 33–49.

70. Eleanor F. Jourdain, *Dramatic Theory and Practice in France, 1690–1808* (London: Longmans, Green, 1921); Hildegard Leib, *Les cas de mésalliances dans le roman et le théâtre français aux XVIIIᵉ et XIXᵉ siècles* (Berlin: E. Ebering, 1936); Elaine Mauzey, "Des évidences de la critique sociale dans le théâtre du dix-huitième siècle," *Northwest Missouri College Studies* 23:4 (1959), 1–34.

71. Pierre Carlet de Chamblain de Marivaux, *Le jeu de l'amour et du hasard,* in *Eighteenth-Century French Plays,* ed. Clarence D. Brenner and Nolan A. Goodyear (New York: Century, 1927), pp. 233–58. For an analysis of Marivaux's works, see E. J. H. Greene, *Marivaux* (Toronto: University of Toronto Press, 1965).

mately convinced of his error and reconciled to his wife amid tears of joy.[72]

In 1749, Voltaire's *Nanine* again raised the issue of marriage across class lines, with Voltaire refusing to blunt his criticism of the prejudice against the *mésalliance* by use of disguises, such as Marivaux had employed. Despite the objections of his family, the count d'Olban persists in his determination to marry his beloved Nanine, the daughter of a peasant.[73] Finally, Diderot's *Père de famille* further develops the theme of marriage for love. The *fils de famille* here, Saint-Albin, falls in love with Sophie, a virtuous young woman of humble origin who believes him to be a workingman. His father finds the young lady attractive, but not of sufficient fortune for marriage. The couple's love survives numerous obstacles, including Sophie's confinement under a *lettre de cachet* obtained by Saint-Albin's uncle. At last, Saint-Albin's father is reconciled to his son's marital choice and grants his blessing to the happy couple.[74]

In the realm of the novel, Jean-Jacques Rosseau treated the theme of sentiment and family relationships most fully in *La nouvelle Héloïse* and *Emile*. The former work presents the story of Saint-Preux's love for Julie d'Etanges, a love that Julie sacrifices by her obedience to her father's insistence that she marry Monsieur de Wolmar. Ultimately, Julie develops esteem and a measure of affection for her husband, and from their life together, far from the convention and artifice of cities and society, she finds a sense of inner peace. When Saint-Preux returns to visit the couple, still cherishing his love for Julie and having abandoned all other human ties, Julie refuses to resume their passionate relationship, and her refusal elevates their love to a higher, "spiritual" level. Thus most readers of *La nouvelle Héloïse* could find in Rousseau the celebration of a romantic love that they had known or hoped to know, while deriving consolation and a sense of moral superiority from

72. Pierre-Claude Nivelle de la Chaussée, *Le préjugé à la mode*, in *Eighteenth-Century French Plays*, ed. Brenner and Goodyear, pp. 261–97. The play is an example of the genre *comédie larmoyante* (sentimental domestic comedy).

73. François Marie Arouet de Voltaire, *Nanine*, in ibid., pp. 349–70.

74. Denis Diderot, *Le père de famille*, in ibid., pp. 373–413. For an analysis of the relationship of the play to Diderot's personal life, see Arthur M. Wilson, *Diderot: The Testing Years, 1713–1759* (New York: Oxford University Press, 1957).

endurance in marriages dictated by their parents and by social conventions.[75]

Although primarily a treatise on education, *Emile* presents the ideal of a happy, affectionate marriage. Emile's tutor tries to prevent his premature acquaintance with the opposite sex, on the ground that early passion hinders a youth's final development to maturity. When Emile and Sophie meet and discover their love, the tutor insists that they test their affection by separating so that Emile may spend two years studying abroad. After his return, Emile and Sophie marry, and the book closes with Emile happily awaiting the birth of the couple's first child.[76]

Another similar representation of marriage appeared in the baron d'Holbach's *La morale universelle*. Holbach praised marriage as the basis of all private society and criticized those who chose a life of celibacy. He contended, however, that a successful marriage required two human beings who loved one another. When the basis of the relationship was "sordid interest, vanity of birth, false ideas of convenience," the marriage would almost certainly prove a failure.[77] Honest pleasures, consolation, and mutual happiness of the

75. Ronald Grimsley presents a particularly useful discussion of the novel in *Jean-Jacques Rousseau: A Study in Self-Awareness* (Cardiff: University of Wales Press, 1961), pp. 116–51. Rousseau repeated his disapproval of parental control of marriage in later editions of the *Discourse on the Origins of Inequality*. In a footnote to the edition that was published in 1782, after his death, he condemned fathers who force their children to marry against their will or prevent a marriage desired by a child. Rousseau argued that such action led to broken and discordant marriages and the spectacle of innumerable unhappy spouses who give themselves over to vice or self-pity (*The Political Writings of Jean-Jacques Rousseau*, with introduction and notes by C. E. Vaughn [Cambridge: University Press, 1915], 1:205).

76. In addition to promoting an idealized view of marriage, Rousseau also criticized the church's control of the institution in French society. He argued that theological intolerance inevitably affected civil affairs, after which the sovereign ceased to be sovereign even over temporal matters. Priests became the real rulers:

> Marriage, for instance, is a civil contract, with civil effects essential to society's survival. Now: let us assume a situation in which the clergy has arrogated to itself exclusive power to approve such a contract—this being a power that the clergy of any intolerant religion must of course get into its hands. Is it not clear that the clergy, in winning this power for the church, will have reduced that of the prince to naught? Is it not clear that the prince will in the future have just as many subjects as it suits the clergy's book to make available? [*Social Contract*, in *Political Writings*, 2:221]

77. Paul Henri Thiry baron d'Holbach, *La morale universelle, ou les devoirs de l'homme fondés sur la nature* (Amsterdam: Marc-Michel Rey, 1776), 3:2–32.

spouses were among the primary aims of marriage, in Holbach's view, and where these ends remained unfulfilled, the law should permit the parties to terminate their relationship.

Marriage must be the intimate connection of the hearts and minds of two persons and of all of their physical and moral faculties, the abbé Pichon explained in his *Mémoire sur les abus dans les mariages*. He waxed indignant at marriages that were only unions of riches or titles, and criticized the institution of the dowry, which discouraged choices based on the sentiments of the two spouses. He concluded that laws that required fathers to dower their daughters should be repealed and replaced by a prohibition against daughters' inheriting any property from their parents, thus ensuring that young men would seek to marry them for their personal qualities alone.[78] Another work, *Pensées sur les femmes,* celebrated the marriage united by conjugal love. The author maintained that all too often parents selected a husband for their daughter with no consideration in mind except his fortune—as if wealth alone were sufficient to make a wife happy.[79]

The same theme of marriage for love as against marriage for worldly considerations appeared in Roucher's poem *Les mois.* In the twelfth canto the author sang of the unhappiness of spouses united against their wishes by the ambition and avarice of relatives and urged that they should be able to dissolve their union and marry the persons they truly loved:

> ... if the wisely paternal law
> Did not oppress marriage into an eternal bondage,
> There would be no more hatred, no more bitterness; its pure and
>   serene face
> No longer would be darkened with the shadow of regret.
> One would dare to punish furtive adultery.
> O you then who must create happiness on the earth,
> Kings and legislators! Open at last your eyes:
> Too long man has groaned under an odious yoke.
> Let this yoke be broken; let there be a more fruitful law,
> Permitting mortals to redeem the world.

78. Thomas-Jean Pichon, *Mémoire sur les abus dans les mariages* (Amsterdam, 1776), pp. 40–54.
79. *Pensées sur les femmes et le mariage* (Kiel, 1783), 1:60–70.

And as liberty is the bond of hearts,
Even love will bring his sweetness to marriage.[80]

Not only did the poet urge divorce as a guarantee of human liberty and love in marriage, but in the 1779 edition of the poem a commentator named Garat added a lengthy footnote reviewing all of the arguments that had been advanced in favor of divorce.

About 1770, the plight of the unhappily married woman became a favorite theme for authors who wrote in favor of divorce. The pamphleteer Cerfvol criticized the system by which a young woman who married simply moved from the authority of her father to that of her husband. He contended that divorce would give her equality with her husband and would also serve as protection against marriage dictated exclusively by parental wishes.[81] In another work, the same author presented all of the arguments for divorce in the form of a conversation between the countess of R and the marquise of L, both of whom are unhappily married.[82] The *Cri d'une honnête femme* was a similar tract consisting of a series of letters from a

---

80.   ... si la Loi, sagement paternelle,
                    N'opprimoit pas l'Hymen d'une chaîne eternelle,
                    Plus de fiel, plus d'aigreur; son front pur et serein
                    Ne se noirciroit plus des ombres du chagrin:
                    On oseroit punir le furtif adultère.
                    O vous donc, qui devez le bonheur à la Terre,
                    Rois et Législateurs! Ouvrez enfin les yeux:
                    Assez l'Homme a gemi sous un joug odieux;
                    Que ce joug soit brise; qu'une Loi plus féconde
                    Invite les mortels à réparer le monde;
                    Et que la liberté soit le lien des coeurs:
                    L'Amour même à l'Hymen envieront ses douceurs.
                    [Jean Antoine Roucher, *Les Mois* (Paris: Quillau,
                    1771), 1:186]

81. Cerfvol, *Intérêt des femmes au rétablissement du divorce* (Amsterdam, 1770), pp. 5–52.

82. The countess and the marquise also discussed the plight of a male friend whose wife had been corrupted by an abbé. Given the widespread hostility toward the clergy in the eighteenth century, it is surprising that accusations of immoral conduct by clerics were not made more frequently. Rather than criticizing the first estate for failing to observe the standard of continence, most *philosophes* argued that the rule of celibacy had pernicious effects on society and placed unreasonable demands on human nature. See Cerfvol, *Le parloir de l'Abbaye de * * * ou entretiens sur le divorce par M. de V * * * suivi de son utilité politique* (Geneva, 1770), pp. 1–43. The Bibliothèque Nationale classifies this work as anonymous, but it was bound with *Utilité civile et politique du divorce* by Cerfvol and its style and arguments strongly suggest that it was written by him also.

noblewoman whose husband had had her confined to an isolated château in order that he might be free to dissipate her property and lead a life of debauchery.[83]

The pamphlet *Le divorce réclamé par Madame la Comtesse de * * * * vividly illustrated the dangers marriage might hold for a young girl. The narrator here was an orphan who at age seventeen fell in love with a nobleman and married him. Soon after the marriage her husband turned all of the servants against her and began a liaison with her maid. When the author was delivered of a son, her husband sent the child to the country to nurse with the mother of his mistress, with the result that the infant soon died of neglect. Then the count required his wife to sell most of her property to meet his gambling debts. In desperation, the author consulted a lawyer about obtaining a divorce, which she discovered was prohibited by the law of the church. The countess ended her account by urging France to restore the law of divorce to cleanse public morals and rescue women in situations similar to her own.[84]

The Academy of Châlons-sur-Marne's prize essay question, "What would be the best means of perfecting the upbringing of women?" prompted a vigorous response from Choderlos de Lacos, the celebrated author of the drama *Les liaisons dangereuses.* In his *De l'éducation des femmes,* Laclos argued that the best intentioned efforts to improve education for women would be of little utility, given the customs and laws of a society that made them inferior to men. He insisted that the law must restore woman's natural equality so that she was neither a slave nor an object of property. Laclos promoted divorce as a useful means of ensuring the goal of equality.[85]

Thus the praise of sentiment in human relations and particularly in marriage had begun in drama and the novel, and social reformers were soon suggesting ways in which this ideal might be translated

83. *Précis du cri d'une honnête femme qui réclame le divorce* (n.p., 1770). Although it is frequently cited in the literature of the period, I was unable to find a copy of *Cri d'une honnête femme* in the United States or in any of the major libraries in Paris. The *Précis* cited here is a summary and review of the work.

84. *Le divorce réclamé par Madame la Comtesse de * * * * (London, 1769), pp. 153–70.

85. Pierre Ambroise François Choderlos de Laclos, *De l'éducation des femmes* (Paris: Léon Vanier, 1903), pp. 13, 62.

into reality. Women should be better educated and protected in their equality with men. The law governing inheritance should be changed to encourage marriage for affection rather than for wealth. Divorce should be available to end loveless marriages and to discourage parents from attempting to dictate the marriage choices of their children. In all of these ways, legal reform might further the influence of sentiment in marriage.

The *philosophes* developed a variety of ideas and attitudes clearly contrary to the conception of marriage and the family established by Catholic doctrine and royal law. From such seventeenth-century writers as Bodin, Pufendorf, and Montaigne they adopted the suggestion that marriage need not necessarily be indissoluble. Their fascination with the diversity of ancient and contemporary cultures led them to an awareness of the practice of divorce in other societies and encouraged them to question parental authority, arranged marriages, conventional sexual morality, and even the institution of marriage itself. Writing from the viewpoint of utility, many authors stressed that changes in the law of marriage, principally the introduction of divorce, could create happier marriages, purify public morals, stimulate population growth, and achieve other socially desirable goals. Many writers who favored toleration of such minority religious practices as Jewish divorce and Protestant marriage employed the argument from social utility, while often joining with it the abstract ideal of toleration or their own personal hostility toward the church.

Increasingly during the century, imaginative literature proclaimed the importance of sentiment in human relationships. Dramatists and novelists portrayed happy marriages based on inclination or love and created by the free choice of the two spouses. They praised marriage as a source of emotional satisfaction and stressed the equality of the wife with her husband. On this basis, they argued that divorce should be available to end loveless marriages and protect a woman's liberty. In their critique of traditional religious and legal conceptions, in their emphasis on diversity, utility, and sentiment, the *philosophes* prepared the way for the legislation of the revolution and the modern form of marriage and the family it sought to create.

3

Civil Marriage and the Records of Civil Status

THIS CHAPTER and the two that follow concern the major works of revolutionary legislation governing marriage and the family: the establishment of civil marriage and the records of civil status (marriage, birth, and death), the introduction of divorce, the creation of the family court, and the modification of laws governing marital property relationships and successions. The last category, concerned with the holding and transmission of property, had long been the province of private civil law. But marital and family relationships were traditionally identified with the doctrine and law of the Catholic church.

Despite the growth of royal law and judicial authority under the ancien régime, as discussed in Chapter 1, the events of birth, marriage, and death were still celebrated by sacraments. These ceremonies had important civil effects, but in the popular mind they remained essentially religious rites, even in regions of declining piety. It was the intimate identification of religion with marriage and family organization that made the creation of civil marriage and the records of civil status seem such a departure from earlier law and practice. Thus, before we begin a discussion of the new legislation, it will be useful to comment on the religious policy of the National Assembly and the attitudes of its legislators.

Most of the members of the National Assembly were Catholics of Gallican persuasion, which is to say that under the ancien régime they had favored the increase of royal control over the French church at the expense of that of the pope.[1] To be sure, the deputies were generally familiar with the anticlerical writings of the Enlightenment and many showed themselves hostile to the privileged upper clergy and to members of religious orders that did not engage in educational, charitable, or other productive activities.[2] Similarly, members of the assembly were generally convinced of the merits of religious toleration. They early rejected a proposal to make Catholicism the religion of the state, but rather extended full legal toleration to other Christians and later to Jews.[3]

In general, however, the nation's representatives sought to reform and purify the Catholic church and to subject it to increased state control within the Gallican tradition. They did not wish to separate church and state, nor did they intend to begin a conflict with organized religion. In the words of Georges Lefebvre, the religious struggle

> was unforeseen by the deputies of the [National] Constituent Assembly. Nor did they want it: the idea of a lay state was unknown to men raised by priests and nurtured on an antiquity that knew no such concept. Far from planning to separate church and state, they dreamed of bringing the two more closely together. The *philosophes* agreed, for the state could not function without religion, and in France religion could only be Roman Catholicism.[4]

1. Antonin Debidour, *Histoire des rapports de l'église et de l'état en France de 1789 à 1870* (Paris: Félix Alcan, 1898), pp. 63–64; John McManners, *The French Revolution and the Church* (New York: Harper & Row, 1969), pp. 24–37. Ludovic Sciout has argued in *Histoire de la constitution civile du clergé* (Paris: Firmin-Didot, 1872), 1:242, that some members of the Ecclesiastical Committee were Jansenists, but most historians have seen them as committed, and in some cases ardent, Catholics of Gallican persuasion. See Albert Mathiez, *Rome et le clergé français sous la Constituante* (Paris: Armand Colin, 1910), pp. 91–94. For an excellent bibliography on the church and religion during the revolution see Bernard Plongeron, *Conscience religieuse en révolution: Regards sur l'historiographie religieuse de la Révolution française* (Paris: Picard, 1969).

2. The decree of February 13, 1790, exempted houses in charge of public education and charitable establishments from the general suppression of religious orders (Jean-Baptiste Duvergier, *Collection complète des lois, décrets, ordonnances, règlements, et avis du Conseil d'Etat* (Paris: A. Guyot, 1825), 1:100.

3. Protestants received full citizenship by the decree of December 24, 1789 (ibid., p. 89). A decree of January 28, 1790, extended the rights of full citizenship to Portuguese, Spanish, and Avignonnais Jews, but Jews of Alsace did not receive similar rights until September 27, 1791 (Arthur Hertzberg, *The French Enlightenment and the Jews* [New York: Columbia University Press, 1968], p. 1).

4. Georges Lefebvre, *The French Revolution from Its Origins to 1793*, trans. Elizabeth Moss Evanson (New York: Columbia University Press, 1962), p. 166.

The essential moderation and Catholic allegiance of the members of the National Assembly is illustrated by the background of the leading members of the Ecclesiastical Committee, which was primarily responsible for the preparation of legislation pertaining to religion and the church. The committee's chairman, Durand de Maillane, was a lawyer from Aix-en-Provence who had written extensive treatises on the history of canon law, as well as a justification of the "liberties of the Gallican church."[5] Another member, Lanjuinais, was a Breton lawyer who was thoroughly familiar with canon law and had practiced in church courts.[6] A third representative, Armand-Gaston Camus, had studied ecclesiastical law in his youth and had edited later versions of such works as Le Ridant's *Code matrimonial* and Denisart's judicial encyclopedia.[7] These men were chosen in part for their expertise in both religious and secular law, but also in part because they represented the Gallican views of the great majority of the National Assembly.

As Chapter 1 pointed out, the monarchy began to assume the power to legislate regarding marriage at the same time that the church was completing its doctrinal definition of marriage at the Council of Trent. In response to the church's reaffirmation of the sacramental character of marriage, royal lawyers and Gallican churchmen developed a contractual theory of marriage that justified royal rather than clerical control of the institution. Royal courts heard or ultimately controlled an increasing number of disputes involving marriage, and while the clergy managed to retain the function of celebrating marriage and of keeping the records of birth, marriage, and death, the royal government attempted to supervise the task with new officials and legislation. Two years before the beginning

Albert Soboul presents a similar point of view in *The French Revolution 1787–1799*, trans. Alan Forrest and Colin Jones (New York: Random House, 1975), p. 198.

5. Albert Mathiez, *Contributions à l'histoire religieuse de la Révolution française* (Paris: Félix Alcan, 1907), pp. 42–96. Durand de Maillane's *Histoire apologétique du comité ecclésiastique de l'Assemblée Nationale* (Paris, 1791) provides what little information we have about the internal organization and functioning of the Ecclesiastical Committee. Those committee records that have survived are located in series D XIX in the Archives Nationales. They contain mainly surveys of religious orders in 1789 and a few miscellaneous petitions.

6. Joseph-François Michaud, *Biographie universelle*, 2d ed. (Paris: Desplaces, 1854–65), 23:203–8.

7. Ibid., 1st ed. (1812), 6:661.

of the revolution, the monarchy had approved a form of civil marriage for the nation's Calvinists with the Edict of 1787.

In the strictly legal sense, the revolutionary law creating civil marriage and the registers of civil status completed a process of institutional development that had been initiated two centuries earlier. Unexpected and initially undesired, the law founding civil marriage and the records of civil status emerged from the widening religious conflict, the breakdown of the system of vital statistics, a heightened sense of citizenship and of the obligation of the state to treat all of its citizens equally in such an important act of life, and a growing argument favoring reformation of marriage law to promote modern marriage, founded on freedom of choice and love.

The *cahiers,* or statements of grievances, of the Estates General of 1789, the historian's traditional source for evidence of public opinion at the outbreak of the revolution, reveal relatively few demands for changes in clerical control of marriage and the records of birth, marriage, and death. Reform of marriage and family law did not command the same attention as such pressing issues as the abolition of feudal privileges, reform of the tax structure, rights of representation, and freedom of expression. Only the use of the *lettre de cachet,* both to implement political oppression and to enforce a father's paternal power over his children, attracted widespread attention.[8]

Most of the *cahiers* that did include proposals relating to marriage and family law favored more liberal rules for the celebration of marriage and complained of inadequacies in the system of keeping the records of birth, marriage, and death. Only the document of the third estate of the commune of Blanvilliers, near Paris, anticipated the law of 1792 by urging complete civil control of the registers of civil status.[9] Other statements of grievances from all three

8. See Chapter 5 for a discussion of the *lettre de cachet* in connection with paternal power and the creation of the family court.

9. Jérôme Mavidal and Emile Laurent, eds., *Archives parlementaires de 1787 à 1860: Recueil complet des débats législatifs et politiques des chambres françaises,* 1st ser. (1787–99), 2d ed. (Paris: Paul Dupont, 1879–), 5:341–42, tit. 4, art. 13. Cited hereafter as *AP.* Some additional *cahiers* were discovered after the publication of the early volumes of the *Archives parlementaires* and the work's indexing is poor, but the collection is adequate for sampling the opinion of 1789. See Beatrice Fry Hyslop, *A Guide to the General Cahiers of 1789* (New York: Columbia University Press, 1936), pp. 48–108.

estates proposed that the registers should contain more information and that they should be drafted according to a uniform pattern throughout the country.[10] Three *cahiers* favored a lowered age of majority to permit earlier marriage without parental consent, while two others urged that relatives who failed to prove their formal opposition to marriage in court should be fined or otherwise penalized.[11]

Aside from the *cahiers* there were only a few proposals to reform marriage and the records of civil status. A delegate to the third estate named Garnier, who claimed to have lost an inheritance because of missing records, charged the clergy with carelessness in keeping the registers of marriage, birth, and death.[12] A lengthy petition entitled *Doléances des femmes de Franche-Comté,* prepared by a group of women in Besançon, reached the Estates General in May 1789. The women demanded that marriage be founded on freedom of choice and inclination of the parties, rather than parental coercion:

> Marriage is a union. Persons who intend to enter this state must be suited for one another and not be constrained by the will of their parents to marry someone whom they find repugnant. This happens very often. A young person is made to marry an old person, a young man an old woman or an ugly heiress, without other consideration than their property or their names—as if that sufficed to make a complete union.[13]

10. *AP,* 5:359, art. 13; 532, art. 44; 383 84, art. 66; 446, art. 15. At least two documents complained that the requirements for marriage were too costly, particularly when dispensations had to be obtained (*AP,* 4:424, art. 25; 568, art. 17).

Two assemblies of the clergy sought to limit Protestant marriage rights under the Edict of 1787, while one group of representatives of the third estate argued that the law should permit intermarriage between persons of different religions (*AP,* 3:293; 5:270, art. 2; 238, art. 17).

11. *AP,* 2:84 (nobility of Artois: age twenty-five for both sexes); 4:72 (third estate of Morlaix: age twenty for both sexes); 5:101, art. 14 (third estate of Saint-Prix: age twenty-one for both sexes); 3:89, arts. 10, 11; 293. Under royal law, the opposition was a vaguely defined legal action that might be brought by a relative or another interested party to prevent the celebration of a marriage. Oppositions could be based on the existence of ecclesiastical vows or a prior marriage or on the insanity, notorious immorality, or loathsome disease of one of the parties. Even oppositions that had no substance in fact could be highly damaging to an intended marriage.

12. Jean-Baptiste-Etienne Garnier, *Moyens d'établir un ordre propre à consigner . . . les noms de famille* (n.p., 1789), pp. 1–20.

13. *Doléances des femmes de Franche-Comté* (Besançon, April 27, 1789), p. 25.

The petitioners further contended that the law should permit easier judicial separations and provide greater protection of a wife's dowry against her husband and his creditors. The same theme of freedom of choice in marriage appeared in the writings of the count of Antraigues, who urged that the age of majority be lowered in order to limit a father's power over his sons and daughters and thus reduce the likelihood of forced unions.[14]

The first problem involving the relationship of the National Assembly with the church concerned dispensations for marriage. Canon law included a wide range of prohibitions or impediments to marriage that might be waived by means of an appeal to Rome. Obtaining a dispensation was time-consuming and costly, however, and such appeals to Rome were among the "feudal practices" abolished by the National Assembly on the night of August 4. The implementing decree of August 11, 1789, instructed bishops to grant marital dispensations without delay and without charge.[15] Nevertheless, the National Assembly continued to receive frequent complaints of financial exactions and episcopal unwillingness to grant dispensations.[16]

Another issue reflected unfavorably on clerical control of the marriage ceremony. The church had traditionally denied the sacraments of marriage and extreme unction to actors because of their allegedly immoral profession. Consequently, early in 1790 the curé of Saint-Sulpice refused to publish banns for a marriage planned by the celebrated François-Joseph Talma, an actor of the Théâtre Français. Talma had been an early member of the Cordeliers Club, and his acquaintance with Danton, Mirabeau, Marie-Joseph Chenier, and other political figures encouraged him to petition the National Assembly to overrule the curé's decision.[17] The assembly

14. Emmanuel-Louis-Henri de Launay, comte d'Antraigues, *Observations sur le divorce* (Paris: Imprimerie Nationale, 1789), pp. 15–17.

15. Duvergier, *Collection complète des lois*, 1:40.

16. Jules Basdevant, *Des rapports de l'église et de l'état dans la législation du mariage du Concile de Trente au code civil* (Paris: Sirey, 1900), p. 174.

17. Chenier was the author of the controversial play *Charles IX*, which had opened in November 1789 and which royal officials had attempted to close down on the ground that it contained criticism of the monarchy. Talma played the leading role, and his insistence on continuing the production's run ultimately led to his expulsion from the Théâtre Français (later the Comédie-Française) (Marvin Carlson,

referred Talma's petition to the Ecclesiastical Committee and urged it to prepare a new law reforming the rules for the celebration of marriage.[18]

During the first year of its existence, the Ecclesiastical Committee occupied itself primarily with creation of a Civil Constitution of the Clergy. On July 12, 1790, the National Assembly gave its approval to the document, which emphasized the related goals of reform of the church and increased state control over it. Church lands had already become state lands by the decree of November 2, 1789, and the law of February 13, 1790, had suppressed all monastic vows and abolished those establishments that required them. The principal provisions of the constitution provided for reorganization of the church along the lines of the country's new administrative divisions, for popular election of curés and bishops, for payment of all priests by the government, and for abolition of nonresidence, plural offices, and virtually all papal authority in France.[19] Having completed the major piece of legislation governing the organization and functioning of the church in France, the Ecclesiastical Committee turned to the problem of legislation concerning marriage.

The same familiar themes of reform and increased state control characterized the statute to govern marriage and the records of civil status proposed by the Ecclesiastical Committee near the end of 1790. In the committee's report to the National Assembly, Durand de Maillane built squarely on the tradition of royal control, arguing that marriage was above all a civil contract that must be controlled by the civil authority in society.[20] The new form of marriage in the proposed law would be applicable to all Frenchmen, whether

---

The Theater of the French Revolution [Ithaca: Cornell University Press, 1966], pp. 7–33).

18. AP, 26:186.

19. For the details of the Civil Constitution of the Clergy, see the works cited in note 1 above. Also Pierre de la Gorce, Histoire religieuse de la Révolution française, 11th ed. (Paris: Plon, 1912), vols. 1 and 2; Dom Henri Leclerq, L'église constitutionelle: Juillet 1790–avril 1791 (Paris: Letouzey et Ane, 1934); André Latreille, L'église catholique et la Révolution française, 1775–1815 (Paris: Hachette, 1946), vol. 1; Jean Leflon, La crise révolutionnaire 1789–1846 (Paris: Bloud et Gay, 1949).

20. Pierre-Toussaint Durand de Maillane, Rapport sur le projet de décret des comités ecclésiastiques et de constitution, concernant les empêchements, les dispenses et la forme des mariages (Paris: Imprimerie Nationale, 1790), p. 3.

Catholics or adherents of another faith, and while the law would not prohibit the nuptial benediction by a priest, it would require a prior civil ceremony.[21] Durand de Maillane insisted that the law should encourage freedom of marriage by young persons. To this end, the statute would lower the age at which a man might marry without parental consent from thirty to twenty-five, and that of a woman from twenty-five to twenty-one. Furthermore, it would forbid a parent to disinherit a son or daughter who married against parental wishes after attaining these respective ages.[22]

The proposition that the state should assume absolute control over the law of marriage and the registration of civil status met opposition both within and without the National Assembly. The abbé Samary, a deputy from Carcassonne, argued that Durand de Maillane's proposals would violate the established rules of the church and end by introducing divorce and the marriage of priests and nuns.[23] An anonymous pamphlet addressed to the assembly accused Durand de Maillane of attempting to subvert the Catholic religion while claiming to act as its friend.[24] The abbé Barruel, an important clerical spokesman, insisted that it would be unwise to agitate society with this kind of controversial legislation during a great revolution. He warned that the proposed law would threaten not only religion but the political and social order as well, for Catholics would necessarily consider purely civil marriages as invalid and having no legal effect.[25]

21. Neither Durand de Maillane's report nor the projected law explicitly mentioned the Edict of 1787, governing Protestant marriage, but the emphasis in both documents on religious liberty and the civil rights of all Frenchmen, whatever their belief, supports the conclusion that the draftsmen were influenced by the earlier law.

22. *Projet de loi proposé par le Comité ecclésiastique sur le mariage et sur les actes et registres qui doivent constater l'état civil des personnes* (Paris: Imprimerie Nationale, 1790), pp. 1–16.

23. Abbé Philippe Samary, *Examen du rapport sur le projet de décret concernant les mariages* (Paris: Crapart, n.d.), pp. 1–16.

24. *Ouvrez encore les yeux, sur les nouvelles erreurs du Comité ecclésiastique . . .* (Paris: Jacob-Sion, n.d.), p. 1–31.

25. Abbé Augustin Barruel, *Les vrais principes sur le mariage . . .* (Paris: Crapart, 1790), pp. 36–40. Other pamphlets mounted a violent personal attack against Durand de Maillane: *Lettre à Monsieur Durand de Maillane sur le rapport qu'il a fait à l'Assemblée Nationale* (Paris: Crapart, n.d.), pp. 2–16; Le chevalier de Sorilos (pseud.), *Lettre à M. Durand de Maillane, député à l'Assemblée Nationale de France* (Paris: Gattey, n.d.), pp. 6–17.

Not all commentators disapproved of the Ecclesiastical Committee's proposal. The Society of the Friends of the Constitution of Epinal (Vosges) urged that all citizens—Catholics, Protestants, and Jews—should be assured of uniform means for registering their births, marriages, and deaths.[26] The editor Pierre Le Noble offered an alternative proposal in which couples would be married in a municipal hall, where they would dedicate themselves and their future children to the interests of the state.[27] Durand de Maillane defended his proposal in a subsequent report, but the National Assembly postponed indefinitely any serious consideration of the projected law.[28]

With the Civil Constitution of the Clergy, the National Assembly had approved a fundamental reform of the structure of the church, yet it refused for two reasons to adopt more limited legislation to regulate marriage and the records of vital statistics. While most deputies were prepared to undertake extensive regulation of the institution and personnel of the church, the acts of marriage, birth, and death were intimately connected with its sacraments. Gallican deputies showed a reluctance to enact a law that appeared to affect a fundamental aspect of the faith. Also, the members of the National Assembly had not foreseen the widespread resistance of part of the lower clergy to the implementation of the Civil Constitution, and many members subsequently cited this resistance as a reason for postponing indefinitely any reform of marriage law.[29]

Despite the hesitation of the National Assembly, control over marriage and the records of civil status remained an issue because of the growing schism within the French church.[30] Clerical opposi-

---

26. Zosa Szajkowski, "Protestants and Jews of France in the Fight for Emancipation, 1789–1791," *Proceedings of the American Academy for Jewish Research* 25 (1956):125.

27. Pierre-Madeleine Le Noble, *Projet de loi pour les mariages presenté à l'Assemblée Nationale* (Paris: Garnery, 1790), pp. 36–48.

28. Pierre-Toussaint Durand de Maillane, *Suite et défense du rapport sur les empêchements, les dispenses et la forme des mariages* (Paris: Imprimerie Nationale, 1790), pp. 1–28.

29. *AP*, 26:156–60, 236–37.

30. In connection with the reorganization of local government, the minister of the interior issued an order requiring curés to submit the yearly registers of baptisms, marriages, and burials to the registrars (*greffiers*) of the new district courts (minister

tion to the Civil Constitution brought the National Assembly to decree on November 27, 1790, that all clerics who failed to take the prescribed oath to nation, king, and constitution would lose their offices and active citizenship and be prosecuted as rebels.[31] The pope finally broke his silence and denounced the legislation in the papal bull *Charitas,* of April 13, 1791. The pronouncement threatened those bishops who had taken the oath of allegiance with excommunication and exhorted the remainder of the clergy to stand firm against the forces of irreligion and error.[32] The best estimates available calculate that while only a few bishops swore fidelity to the nation and the constitution, nearly half of the lower clergy took the oath.[33]

The division of the French clergy into constitutional (jurant) and refractory (nonjurant) factions meant that many citizens were now celebrating their marriages, baptizing their children, and burying their dead with the help of priests who refused to recognize the authority of the state or the state-controlled church. On May 10, 1790, Bailly, the mayor of Paris, expressed concern to the National Assembly, noting that because many Catholic citizens were having their children baptized secretly before nonjurant priests, the city was unable to maintain accurate records necessary to civil society. On behalf of the municipal government, Bailly urged the National Assembly to pass legislation providing for civil registration of births, marriages, and deaths by officers of the municipal government in a form acceptable to all religious opinions.[34]

Bailly's request prompted new efforts to obtain the assembly's approval for such legislation. Durand de Maillane resubmitted the report he had presented in 1790 and in addition published the conclusions of the Ecclesiastical Committee on the complaint made by the actor Talma against the curé of Saint-Sulpice.[35] This second

of the interior to royal commissioner at tribunal of Château-Thierry, April 28, 1791, AN, BB¹⁶ 8 [Aisne]).

31. Duvergier, *Collection complète des lois,* 2:59–60.

32. Augustin Theiner, ed., *Documents inédits relatifs aux affaires religieuses de la France, 1790–1800* (Paris: Firmin Didot Frères, 1857), 1:75–88.

33. Charles Ledre, *L'église de France sous la révolution* (Paris: Robert Laffont, 1949), pp. 82–83; Plongeron, *Conscience religieuse en révolution,* pp. 17–36.

34. *AP,* 26:77–78.

35. Ibid., pp. 166–67.

report concluded that an actor had the same right to enjoy marriage and all other benefits of civil status as any other French citizen, and consequently it urged that the church should be deprived of its control over the celebration of marriage.[36] Lanjuinais, another member of the Ecclesiastical Committee, supported Durand de Maillane's conclusions and argued that the proposed legislation in no way differed from an edict promulgated by Joseph II of the Habsburg monarchy in 1784 or the law regulating the marriage practices of Catholics in the Kingdom of the Netherlands. He further contended that the Edict of 1787 applying to Protestants had already begun to establish civil marriage in France.[37]

In the same vein, the deputy Pierre Bouchotte presented a spirited defense of the right of civil government to legislate on the subject of marriage, which existed as a contract before Christ elevated it to the dignity of a sacrament.[38] The abbé Pierre Brugière, a constitutional priest, agreed, contending that the church should concern itself solely with the spiritual welfare of its parishioners and leave the control of temporal affairs to the secular powers in society.[39] Despite these arguments, the majority of the National Assembly continued to resist any change, and voted on May 19, 1791, to postpone further discussion of the projected law indefinitely.[40]

Although the National Assembly had refused to approve extensive legislation on the subject, the proponents of secularization of marriage and civil status did manage to include the principle in the new constitution that became effective on September 3, 1791. The assembly approved without debate Title 2, Section 7 of the document, which read: "The law considers marriage only as a civil contract. The legislative power shall establish for all inhabitants, without distinction, the method by which births, deaths, and mar-

36. Pierre-Toussaint Durand de Maillane, *Rapport sur l'affaire du sieur Talma, comédien français* (Paris: Imprimerie Nationale, n.d.), pp. 1–7.

37. Jean-Denis Lanjuinais, *Rapport sur la nécessité de supprimer les dispenses de mariages...* (Paris: Imprimerie Nationale, 1791), pp. 1–25.

38. Pierre-Paul-Alexandre Bouchotte, *Dernières observations sur l'accord de la raison et de la religion pour le rétablissement du divorce...* (Paris: Imprimerie Nationale, 1791), pp. 72–96.

39. Abbé Pierre Brugière, *Réflexions d'un curé constitutionel sur le décret de l'Assemblée Nationale concernant le mariage* (Paris: Du Pont, 1791), pp. 7–18.

40. AP, 26:156–60, 236–37.

riages are to be declared, and it shall designate the public officials who are to receive and preserve the records therefor."[41] Thus the National Assembly proclaimed the principle of civil marriage and secular control over the records of birth, marriage, and death even while refusing to enact specific legislation on the subject.

This inconsistency invited confusion and differing interpretations as to the present state of the law. If marriage was a civil contract according to the constitution, might it be celebrated civilly? A contemporary legal journal recounted one such marriage, performed by the court of the Fifth Arrondissement of Paris. The couple, a Swiss Protestant called Giroud and a Parisian woman named Jouffroy, had their banns published in their parish church of Notre Dame. They then appeared with witnesses and relatives before the court and declared that they wished to take one another in legitimate and indissoluble marriage, according to the provisions of the Edict of 1787 governing the marriage of Protestants. The edict did not provide for civil marriage by a magistrate, however, but only for subsequent registration by a Catholic priest or a royal judge of unions concluded in private Protestant ceremonies. Consequently, the edict was not really applicable to the situation, but the court celebrated the union anyway. According to the journal's sentimental account, the judges' faces were illumined with satisfaction and their tears attested to their emotion as the president of the court received the promises of the couple and declared them united in lawful matrimony.[42]

The records of the Ministry of Justice contain evidence of another civil marriage. On October 12, 1791, Monsieur Lasteyrie du Saillant of Paris wrote the minister, Duport, explaining that he had contracted marriage with a Mademoiselle de Grossoller "according to the constitution, which considers marriage only as a civil contract." A notary had drawn up the couple's contract, but they had not celebrated their union before a priest. The petitioner now wished to ensure the civil status and legitimacy of his child, and urged that the law provide some means of authenticating the legitimacy of children of civil marriage. Duport replied that although there was no question as to the legitimacy of a child born of a civil

41. Duvergier, *Collection complète des lois*, 3:277.
42. Drouet, *Gazette des nouveaux tribunaux* 3 (1791):84–86.

marriage, the law had not yet indicated what formalities were necessary to verify the civil status of the children of civil marriage.[43]

In addition to petitions sent to the ministries and the Legislative Assembly, an interesting pamphlet by Nicholas de Bonneville supported the cause of secular marriage and family law. It argued that marriage and rearing a family were duties all citizens owed to the state. Thus the law ought to apply penalties against bachelors unless they adopted children, and it must guarantee the freedom of marriage against religious restrictions and pressure by parents. The author presented a draft of legislation for the registration of acts of civil status, with elaborate provisions governing marriage which made it a patriotic celebration. Besides pledging their faith to one another, the spouses promised to remember the laws of the constitution and vowed allegiance to liberty and the nation.[44]

On February 15, 1792, the deputy Muraire presented the Legislative Assembly with the Legislative Committee's report on the projected law determining the requirements for marriage and the registration of acts of marriage, birth, and death. Although the language and form of the provisions differed, the legislation was essentially the same as the draft proposed by Durand de Maillane to the National Assembly in 1791. According to Muraire, a citizen of France was born and died for the *patrie*, independent of all religious belief. Therefore his first and last moments, as well as his life's most important personal engagement, should be inscribed in the records of the nation. The old laws of marriage, which maintained a father's control over his children up to age twenty-five or thirty and permitted disinheritance after that age, were intended to maintain inequality of condition and the honor of so-called illustrious families. Under the proposed law, two beings of the same nature and creation, equal in rights and before the law, might unite without fear of coercion or disgrace. Muraire concluded that happy marriages based on freedom of choice would produce numerous children, thus bringing benefits to the state and to society.[45]

43. AN, BB[30] 80. The Legislative Assembly received many similar petitions from justices of the peace and municipal officers. See *AP*, 35:165, 364, 529; AN, D III 363–65.

44. Nicholas de Bonneville, *Nouveau code conjugal établi sur les bases de la constitution* (Paris: Cercle Social, 1792), pp. 32–33.

45. Honoré Muraire, *Rapport fait à l'Assemblée Législative au nom du Comité*

Debate on the issue resumed on March 17, 1792, with François de Neufchateau delivering a long, impassioned speech in which he accused the enemies of the revolution of trying to undermine it by pressing for excessively radical measures that most of the country would not accept.[46] The assembly defeated his motion to instruct the Ecclesiastical Committee to prepare a more limited substitute decree and gave the bill its second reading.[47] The bill's opponents attacked it again in April, contending that it was intolerant of the practices of the Catholic faith and defective in its reliance on uneducated municipal officials for the maintenance of civil records. Shouting from the floor frequently interrupted the debate.[48] Speaking for the bill, Vergniaud emphasized the history of royal control over marriage during the ancien régime. He argued that the government had no wish to destroy the religious beliefs of many persons, but that the subject of the legislation must be controlled by the civil power: "The individual who serves society is for it neither Christian, nor Jew, nor Muslim. He is a citizen, and this title alone imposes on society the obligation to enable him to enjoy all of the advantages of association, and consequently of civil status, which is the most important of social rights."[49]

On June 16, 1792, the assembly received a letter from the minister of justice noting the disruption of civil records in the Vendée and other western departments and urging immediate legislative action to establish rules and procedures for the maintenance of public records.[50] In the debate on June 18, Louis-Jérome Gohier proposed that the civil marriage ceremony should be terminated with the cry "*Vivre libre ou mourir!*" to remind the spouses that they belonged not only to each other but to their country as well.[51] Emmanuel

---

de législation sur le mode par lequel les naissances, mariages et décès seront constatés (Paris: Imprimerie Nationale, 1792), pp. 1–27. The projected law is printed in *AP*, 38:690–93.

46. *AP*, 40:68–72.

47. Ibid., p. 78.

48. *AP*, 42:167–69.

49. Pierre-Victorin Vergniaud, *Opinion sur le mode de constater les naissances, mariages et décès* (Paris: Imprimerie Nationale, 1792), p. 10.

50. *AP*, 45:272–73.

51. Louis-Jérôme Gohier, *Opinion sur le mode de constater l'état civil des citoyens* (Paris: Imprimerie Nationale, 1792), p. 14.

Pastoret insisted that the new law would regenerate morals in society and end marriages dictated by opulence, while Charles-François Oudot suggested that the law might recognize unions less solemn than that of legally constituted marriage.[52] The final debates on the legislation took place amid the confusion and alarm of political struggle, popular insurrection, and foreign invasion. In June 1792 Louis XVI attempted a more independent policy, refusing to approve deportation legislation for nonjurant priests and a decree summoning provincial guardsmen to Paris. When Roland protested, the king replaced the Girondin leaders with a Feuillant ministry on June 12. The following day a Parisian crowd invaded the royal apartments at the Tuileries but failed to force the king to withdraw his vetoes or recall the Girondin ministry.

Meanwhile, on June 22, after some discussion as to which civil servants were best suited to receive declarations of civil status, the Legislative Assembly decided that these records should be kept by municipal officers rather than justices of the peace, notaries, or primary schoolteachers.[53] Title 3 of the bill regarding the registration of births presented few difficulties, except for the manner in which illegitimate births were to be recorded. Many legislators urged that a child born of an unwed mother should be recorded only under his mother's name, but the articles as passed glossed over the issue of illegitimacy, stating simply that the records should include the names, occupations, and domiciles of both parents.[54] Under Title 4, concerning registration and substantive requirements for marriage, some deputies wished to ensure indissolubility with the phrase that marriage is a "civil contract for life," but they were dissuaded on the ground that the phrase was redundant.[55] Proponents of the legislation strongly defended provisions establishing twenty-one as the age after which persons of both sexes might

---

52. Emmanuel Pastoret, *Opinion sur la manière de constater l'état civil des citoyens* (Paris: Imprimerie Nationale, 1792), pp. 12–13; Charles-François Oudot, *Opinion sur le mode de constater les naissances*... (Paris: Imprimerie Nationale, 1792), pp. 8–10. Except in special cases involving Calvinists, French law prior to 1789 had not recognized the de facto marriage or what the American system calls the common-law marriage. Oudot's suggestion did not win any support.

53. *AP*, 45:466–77.

54. Ibid., pp. 556–61, 559–96, 614–15.

55. Ibid., p. 652.

marry without parental consent as a blow against the despotism of paternal power.[56]

While the assembly debated, Paris was filling up with volunteers and national guardsmen from the provinces. News of foreign troops advancing on the frontiers and the duke of Brunswick's manifesto threatening reprisals if any harm were done the king aroused the Paris crowd. On August 10, insurrectionists replaced the city government with a revolutionary commune, attacked the Tuileries, and forced the king and royal family to flee to the Legislative Assembly. The assembly was powerless to control events, and although it continued to sit for several weeks, effective power had passed into the hands of the Paris Commune. After the Revolution of August 10, the deputies of the Legislative Assembly passed the remaining articles of the proposed decree with only perfunctory debate, promulgating the new law on the final day of the assembly's session.[57]

The law of September 20, 1792, dealt with two related subjects: the registration of birth, marriage, and death, the three major acts of civil life; and the requirements for valid marriage. It provided that the registers of civil status were to be maintained by an official appointed by the municipal government, who would also submit yearly statistical reports to the national government. The provisions governing birth and death were relatively simple, since both acts occur without reference to the laws or convenience of civil society. The decree instructed that a child's birth was to be recorded by presentation of the child at the town hall or other public place within twenty-four hours after its delivery. In addition to the time of birth, sex, and name of the child, the birth registration should include first and family names, occupations, and domiciles of the father and mother and of two witnesses. Special provisions governed the recording of births of foundlings. The event of death required that basically the same information be submitted by relatives or neighbors, or the administrators of hospitals or public houses. The law included provisions for police investigation when death occurred from violence or in suspicious circumstances.

56. Ibid., pp. 668–77; 46:214–15.
57. AP, 48:288, 563–64; 49:325–26.

The law stipulated ages fifteen for men and thirteen for women as the minimum age for marriage and provided that both sexes should reach majority at age twenty-one. Before that age, a father's consent, or that of a mother when the father was dead or unable to act, sufficed to permit marriage. In contrast to canon law, the number of impediments to marriage was held to a minimum, with no provisions for dispensations or exceptions. Persons wishing to marry had to publish their intent six days before the celebration; the statute provided for formal oppositions only by those individuals whose consent was necessary for the marriage.

The law instructed that the marriage ceremony should take place in a public room of the town hall, in the presence of four witnesses unrelated to the bride or groom. After reading aloud the relevant documents and receiving the promises of the couple, the public official was to draw up a certificate detailing the first and family names, ages, places of birth, occupations, and domiciles of husband and wife, parents, and witnesses, as well as mention of publication of the banns, oppositions, and consent of the parents or families. Persons who had been married civilly before passage of the law were required to submit all of this information to the public official in charge of the records of civil status. Finally, the law provided for registration of acts of divorce, which had also been instituted in the closing days of the Legislative Assembly.[58]

While the law of September 20, 1792, contained little that was wholly new, civil control of marriage and the records of marriage, birth, and death did deprive the church of record-keeping functions. Given the strength of popular custom and the significance to Catholics of the sacraments connected with birth, death, and marriage, it was highly important to obtain clerical cooperation to establish the new law. Most clerics of the constitutional church accepted the provisions without difficulty. Bishops admonished their curés to instruct parishioners to have births, marriages, and deaths recorded civilly.[59] In January 1793, the provisional executive council of the constitutional church urged all clerics to transfer

---

58. Duvergier, *Collection complète des lois*, 4:562–69.
59. C. B. Roux, bishop of Bouches-du-Rhône, to his curés, Aix, November 8, 1792, AN, AA 62 (1350).

their records to civil officials and to enjoin their flocks to observe the law—a position that the subsequent council of 1797 reaffirmed.[60] Jurant clerics reasoned that civil society had the right to regulate man's civil life, but that such legislation did not abrogate the validity of canon law for Catholics.[61]

Nonjurant clergy, on the other hand, usually refused to give up their records and cautioned their communicants against observance of the new law. Five years after its passage, reports and complaints of the obstructions of the refractory clergy continued to reach the minister of the interior.[62] "We battle against fanaticism every day," reported a commissioner from the department of the Ardèche.[63] The administration of the department of Lot-et-Garonne attempted to implement the civil recording system by printing large posters warning citizens that failure to record marriage would cause their children to be illegitimate.[64] François de Neufchateau, who had argued in 1792 that the legislation was too radical, reported as commissioner of the Executive Directory from the department of the Vosges in 1797 that the countryside was still full of superstition:

> In the departments, the republican era, public instruction, and national holidays are eclipsed everywhere by the Roman calendar, the Catholic catechism, and the solemnities of the church.

60. *Proclamation du Conseil Exécutif Provisoire*, January 22, 1793, signed by Garat, Clavier, Lebrun, and Monge, AN, AD II 35; Basdevant, *Des rapports de l'église et de l'état*, pp. 192–93.

61. François de Torcy, *Vrais principes sur le mariage*... (Paris: Le Clere, 1793), p. 5; Pierre-Claude Lejeune, *Discours sur l'exécution de la loi qui détermine le mode de constater l'état des citoyens* (Troyes: Sainton, 1792), pp. 4–9.

62. Commissioner of the Executive Directory at the court of Laon to minister of the interior, 9 *brumaire* Yr. 5 (October 31, 1796), AN, F² I 381; report adopted by the central administration of the department of Drôme, 28 *vendémiaire* Yr. 5 (October 19, 1796), AN, F² I 387; departmental administration of Ille-et-Vilaine to minister of the interior, June 27, 1793, AN, F² I 390; commissioner of the Executive Directory, central administration of the department of Meurthe, to minister of the interior, 19 *vendémiaire* Yr. 7 (October 10, 1798), AN, F²I 396; letter from the administration of Fontainebleau, 14 *frimaire* Yr. 6 (December 4, 1797), AN, F² I 404; minister of police to minister of the interior, forwarding a complaint from the department of Deux-Sevres, 4 *pluviôse* Yr. 5 (January 23, 1797), AN, F² I 405; letter to the Executive Directory from a postmaster in the department of Tarn, 28 *nivôse* Yr. 7 (January 17, 1799), AN, D XXXIX 7—to cite just a few.

63. Letter from the commissioner of the Executive Directory in Ardèche, *germinal* Yr. 5 (March–April, 1797), AN, F² I 382.

64. Central administration of Lot-et-Garonne to minister of the interior, 14 *nivôse* Yr. 5 (January 3, 1797), AN, F² I 394.

One of the new laws that is not enforced because of priests is that of civil registration of marriage, birth, and death. They do everything that they can to lead the citizens astray and to arm them against this law. They are only too well served by the lack of intelligence of the greater part of the officers supervising the civil acts.[65]

Enforcement of the law met not only sabotage by hostile clergy but the pitfalls of ignorance and incompetence of public officials as well. The minister of the interior forbade communes to elect their curés as the public officers charged with keeping the civil registers; numerous departmental administrators responded that in many communes there was no one else capable of writing and drafting documents.[66] Five years later the system still functioned poorly. On 21 *messidor* Yr. 5 (July 9, 1797) the minister of the interior reported to the Executive Directory's Committee for the Classification of Laws that he had instructed all public officers as to the proper method of maintaining the registers of civil status, but that "all of these measures have been wrecked by the carelessness of most of these functionaries. This ignorance is carried to the point where some registers state that 'the husband has given birth,' or forget to explain whether the children are born in or out of wedlock, or [omit] the names of their fathers and mothers."[67] Some correspondents suggested that better compensation for the public officers would help to remedy the situation. "Thus far, we have been compensated primarily by the satisfaction of knowing that the public registers are well kept," complained two public officers in the city of Strasbourg.[68]

The most novel suggestion for improving the records of civil

65. Letter from the commissioner of the Executive Directory, central administration of the Vosges, Epinal, 5 *vendémiaire* Yr. 5 (September 26, 1796), AN, F² I 408.

66. General administrative council of department of Corrèze to minister of the interior, January 19, 1793, AN, F² I 385; administrators of the department of the Meuse to minister of the interior, November 15, 1792, AN, F² I 396.

67. Minister of the interior to Committee for the Classification of Laws, 21 *messidor* Yr. 5 (July 9, 1797), AN, D XXXIX 5. In 1796 the members of the Executive Directory had urged the Council of Five Hundred to pass legislation requiring strict observance of the law of civil status, but the council failed to act (Antonin Debidour, ed., *Recueil des actes du Directoire exécutif* [Paris: Imprimerie Nationale, 1913], 1:743).

68. Report made to the general council of the commune of Strasbourg concerning the office for the recording of acts of civil status, 16 *pluviôse* Yr. 3 (February 4, 1795), AN, D XXXIX 3.

status came from the national agent of the commune of Blois during the height of the Terror. In a letter of June 1794 to the Committee of Surveillance of the Convention, he proposed that every citizen be marked at birth with a number representing the commune and department where he was born. He explained that the number might be made by an injection of powder under the skin, after the manner of certain savage peoples who put indelible markings on their bodies. The marking could be made without pain or danger to health, and such a system would greatly facilitate the job of keeping track of Frenchmen. He added ominously that with it, one could easily ascertain the commune of origin and hence the identity of a man dead in Paris.[69]

With the exception of minor supplementary decrees, the legislatures after 1792 avoided any major changes in the law governing civil marriage and civil registration of birth, marriage, and death.[70] Interpretations of the law of marriage given by the minister of the interior consistently sought to extend freedom of marriage for adults and limit it for minors. Thus the minister reproved a public official of Angers who refused to permit a widow of five months to remarry—the ancien régime law having required a delay of ten months—and instructed him to enforce the law as written rather than his own personal moral standards.[71] Similarly, soldiers and foreign prisoners of war were permitted to marry freely, despite the opposition of military officials.[72] The minister refused, however, to

69. National agent of the commune of Blois to Committee of Surveillance of the National Convention, 3 messidor Yr. 2 (June 21, 1794), AN, F² I 392.

70. An additional law of December 19, 1792, clarified the original act, requiring payments for copies of official records, establishing special provisions governing the law's application to large cities, and creating some exceptions to harsh penalties for failure to report births or deaths promptly (AP, 55:151–54). A decree of 1793 provided that a notarized act composed of the sworn statements of three relatives, friends, or neighbors might serve as evidence of date and place of birth for purposes of the marriage ceremony (AP, 74:98). The legislators resolved the problem of obtaining consent for the marriage of minors who were orphans or whose parents were under some kind of disability by referring the matter to the jurisdiction of the family court (Duvergier, Collection complète des lois, 5:125).

71. Minister of the interior to public officer of municipality of Angers, 12 messidor Yr. 4 (June 30, 1796), AN, F² I 394.

72. Minister of the interior to central administration of department of Jura, 21 ventôse Yr. 7 (March 11, 1799), AN, F² I 391; minister of the interior to commissioner of Executive Directory at canton of Ecoui, 21 nivôse Yr. 5 (January 10, 1796), AN, F² I 388.

allow private, unpublicized marriages of minors, deeming such marriages likely to encourage clandestine unions against parental authority.[73] He insisted that minor children, even when widowed, divorced, or living outside the parental home, required parental consent to make a legitimate marriage, and he upheld a divorced father's right to withhold consent to a marriage of his minor child.[74] Finally, the minister of justice indignantly denied a young woman the right to take any legal action against her father in an attempt to secure a dowry in order to establish herself in marriage.[75]

Given the hostile attitude of nonjurant clergy and the reluctance of many Frenchmen to substitute new procedures for traditional forms and observances, legislators sought ways to make the practice of civil marriage attractive, popular, and patriotic. The statute of 1792 prescribed only a very simple ceremony. The parties were to appear at the town hall with witnesses, birth certificates, and statements of parental consent when necessary. After the public officer had read the documents aloud, the parties recited their vows to one another and the officer declared them married. The ceremony lacked any references to religion, the *patrie,* love, or the moral and social responsibilities of marriage, and many persons complained of its unimpressive nature. A description by La Révellière-Lépeaux gives a vivid impression of civil marriage as practiced in Paris:

> I have only once attended a marriage in the commune of Paris; I
> have never in my life seen anything that shocked me so much. The
> aisle of the hall where the public officer was located was blocked by a

73. Minister of the interior to commissioner of Executive Directory at municipal administration of Saint-Thiery, Marne, 25 *fructidor* Yr. 4 (September 11, 1796), AN, F² I 395.

74. Minister of the interior to public officer of Avignon, 28 *ventôse* Yr. 5 (March 18, 1797), AN, F² I 407; minister of justice to Citizen Machemin, *prairial* Yr. 5 (May–June 1795), AN, BB¹⁶ 27 (Basses-Alpes). In theory, the Ministry of the Interior was responsible for the functioning of the civil administration, including the public officers who celebrated marriages and recorded births, marriages, and deaths, whereas the Ministry of Justice handled questions involving the content and meaning of laws and the functioning of the court system. In practice, both ministries responded to all kinds of problems and questions.

75. Minister of justice to Suzanne Magdaleine Armand La Baulme, 30 *messidor* Yr. 4 (July 18, 1796), AN, BB¹⁶ 87 (Bouches-du-Rhône). An action for a dowry had existed under the ancien régime in Roman-law areas.

thousand vulgar persons, whose disgusting comments and cynical gestures offended the least delicate of men. Imagine, then, a hall without cleanliness, without decoration, where everything was piled up pell-mell and without order on the tavern benches, grooms, brides, witnesses... a public officer with curled hair in a shabby frock coat, a large ugly statue of the goddess Hymen, having in her hand two old wreaths of discolored flowers of Italy... the pronouncement of four words of I-don't-know-what formula, the signature of the spouses and the witnesses at the bottom of the act, and there are twenty, thirty marriages finished! No ceremonies, no speeches, no songs, no symbols, no meeting of the two families and of friends.[76]

One critic petitioned the Legislative Assembly for an amendment to the law of 1792 which would require the public officer to place the wedding ring on the finger of the bride at the conclusion of the civil ceremony. He explained that "the people are restless with the absence of religious rites and, in the case of marriage, do not feel themselves completely married when the bride has not received the ring."[77]

Another individual writing the National Convention suggested special holidays celebrating love and conjugal love. The two celebrations would be held in the spring, ten or twenty days apart, with officials of each commune or section collecting contributions at the *fête de l'amour* to provide a dowry for the marriage of one or two virtuous girls. Following hymns to the Supreme Being and a discourse on conjugal love and love of the *patrie,* "all the youths will be allowed to embrace all the young women they know, offer them flowers and ribbons, and wish them good fortune in love."[78] The author reasoned that these democratized "*fêtes galantes*" would lead to many declarations of love and decisions to marry. Subsequently, the *fête de l'amour conjugal* would honor the young women who received the municipal dowries and would include a

76. Louis-Marie La Révellière-Lépeaux, *Réflexions sur le culte, sur les cérémonies civiles, et sur les fêtes nationales, lues à l'Institut le 12 floréal an V* (Paris: H. J. Jansen, Yr. 5), pp. 26–27.

77. AN, D III 361.

78. It is noteworthy that even this revolutionary "modern" conception of marriage, founded on notions of romantic love and emphasizing the interests of the country, recognized the importance of the dowry for a young woman's marriage prospects.

ceremony in which husbands and wives renewed vows of love and fidelity to each other, their children, and their country.[79] In 1794, deputies as diverse in political views as Robespierre and Boissy d'Anglas both urged the Convention to create a system of national holidays that would include celebration of marriage and conjugal love.[80] But it was the regime of the Executive Directory that transformed these proposals into law, with the statute of 3 *brumaire* Yr. 4 (October 25, 1795), which included a festival of marriage or *fête des époux* on 10 *floréal* (April 29 or 30, depending on the year) among the seven national holidays. The law sought to promote observance of civil marriage and to link domestic virtues to national goals by means of patriotic songs, speeches, fraternal banquets, public games, and the distribution of awards.[81] The festivals were promoted most vigorously in the years 6 and 7 (1798, 1799), with the directors Merlin de Douai, La Révellière-Lépeaux, and François de Neufchateau particularly zealous in exhorting national and local administrators to action. Frontier departments such as the Nord and the Meuse regularly celebrated the *fête des époux*, as did such cities as Nantes, Angers, and Lyon, where patriots were acutely conscious that their loyalty was not shared by the residents of the surrounding countryside. In other departments, such as Puy-de-Dôme and Charente, the holidays passed virtually unnoticed.[82]

In the rhetoric of the festival of marriage, departmental administrators urged their subordinates "to honor worthily *marriage,* that salutary and sacred institution, the principal foundation and perhaps the first cause of the social order. You will honor especially in the *fête des époux* the fathers of defenders of the *patrie* and those who, aided by their numerous children, make our countryside

79. Jacques Piron, *Invocation, hymne et autres exercises pour honorer l'Etre suprême et plan de fêtes à l'amour et à la tendresse conjugale, présentés à la Convention* (n.p., n.d.), pp. 1–6.
80. *Moniteur universel,* reprint (Paris: H. Plon, 1858–70), 19 *floréal* Yr. 2 (May 8, 1794), 20:411; François Boissy d'Anglas, *Essai sur les fêtes nationales suivi de quelques idées sur les arts et sur la nécessité de les encourager* (Paris, Yr. 2).
81. Duvergier, *Collection complète des lois,* 8:438–39.
82. James F. Traer, "Youth, Marriage, Patrie: The Family Festivals in the French Revolution," paper delivered at the annual meeting of the American Historical Association, Chicago, December 28, 1974, pp. 5–6.

fertile by their sweat and their labor."[83] A public notice in the city of Angers echoed Rousseau, proclaiming: "It is in fulfilling the duties of husband and father that one learns to fulfill those of citizen. The sacred love of the *patrie* is able to embrace only hearts already filled with the sweet affection that provides the charm of the conjugal union. It is in making peace reign in the family that one feels the necessity to obey the laws that establish a vast empire."[84] Finally, the president of the municipality of Douai explained that "the inseparable qualities of a republican... are none other than those of an honorable man. In effect, can one be a good citizen if he is not a good father, good spouse, good friend? This principle has been so incontestably felt and recognized that it is consecrated in our social contract."[85]

In addition to the speeches, the *fête des époux* usually included a parade to a *place républicaine* or an altar to the *patrie,* as well as awards and sometimes music. The festival in the commune of Lorgues (Var) in the year 6 (1798) began with a procession to the Temple of Reason, hymns, and a reading of government proclamations. Then the commune presented a civic crown (a wreath of flowers) to Jacques Bonnet, a carpenter who had demonstrated civic loyalty by abandoning his craft in order to collect and process saltpeter for gunpowder. A second award went to Jean-Baptiste Vouse, who had adopted two orphans to rear along with his own large family.[86] Sometimes the festivities included public games and fireworks.[87]

Still another effort on the part of the Executive Directory to enhance and popularize civil marriage began with a proposal by the deputy of the Council of Five Hundred, Jean-Baptiste Leclerc, to require that marriages be celebrated and births and deaths reg-

83. Departmental administration of Seine-Inférieur to cantonal administrators, 3 *floréal* Yr. 6 (April 22, 1798), Archives Départementales (hereafter cited as AD), Seine-Inférieur, L 359.

84. Minister of the interior to central and municipal administrations, 21 *germinal* Yr. 7 (April 10, 1799), AD, Nord, L 1260.

85. Quoted in Benjamin Bois, *Les fêtes révolutionnaires à Angers de l'an II à l'an VIII (1793–1799)* (Paris: Félix Alcan, 1929), p. 89.

86. Report of the *fête des époux,* canton of Lorgues, 20 *floréal* Yr. 6 (May 9, 1798), AD, Var, L 451.

87. Traer, "Youth, Marriage, Patrie," pp. 10–12.

istered only on the *décadi,* or tenth day, of the revolutionary calendar. Leclerc proposed elaborate festivities to be held in republican temples. In the case of marriage, spouses were to purchase an ornate book called a *livre de famille* as a repository for the records of their marriage. Wealthy spouses would pay a high price for the *livre de famille,* thus subsidizing both the public marriage celebration and the cost of the book for poorer couples.[88] The proposal ultimately became law on 13 *fructidor* Yr. 6 (August 30, 1798) in a decree that stipulated that the public celebration of the *décadi* should include performance of marriage and registration of births, adoptions, marriages, divorces, and deaths.[89] The law omitted the flowers, songs, orations, and corteges desired by Leclerc, but the provisions ensured that at least a few persons would attend the tenth-day celebration. Despite official efforts, the *fête décadaire* never became a popular institution, and it was abolished by the decree of 3 *nivôse* Yr. 8 (December 24, 1799).[90]

The volume of correspondence, proclamations, and debate concerning marriage and the acts of civil status grows in the years after 1792. This fact, together with the family festivals and tenth-day celebrations, indicates that legislators and administrators of the central government were expending increasing energy in attempts to make the system of civil marriage and civil registration of vital statistics work. They met with some success, despite the obstacles of "fanaticism," ignorance, and attachment to old habits, but full observance of the law of September 20, 1792, was not achieved until after the Napoleonic Concordat had ended the nation's religious division.

The law of September 20, 1792, establishing the requirements for the records of civil status and for marriage, was not revolutionary in the sense of introducing totally new principles or procedures. Rather, it completed a process of change begun about the time of the Council of Trent and considerably advanced by 1789. For pur-

88. Jean-Baptiste Leclerc, *Rapport sur les institutions relatives à l'état civil des citoyens* (Paris: Imprimerie Nationale, Yr. 6), pp. 1–59.
89. Duvergier, *Collection complète des lois,* 10:398.
90. James Friguglietti, "The Social and Religious Consequences of the French Revolutionary Calendar," Ph.D. dissertation, Harvard University, 1966, pp. 91–127. I am indebted to Professor Friguglietti for letting me use his thesis.

poses of the law and civil society, marriage now became a wholly state-controlled institution. The provisions of the law of 1792 for the maintenance of the records of civil status reproduced in simplified form the rules of the Edict of Blois and subsequent royal ordinances.[91]

In part, the new legislation resulted from changing circumstances during the moderate phase of the revolution: the religious conflict stemming from the application of the Civil Constitution of the Clergy, the breakdown of record-keeping functions in society, and instances of civil marriage before it had been fully authorized by law. In part, the statute derived from the desire of revolutionary legislators to end such clerical abuses as those involving impediments to marriage, to enhance citizenship by emphasizing the duties of the married couple to the *patrie,* and to create a modern marriage and family. According to their conception, marriage would now be founded on the free choice of husband and wife rather than the coercive power of the parents. They believed that freedom to marry at age twenty-one would encourage unions based on personal inclination, thus furthering society's goals of good public morals and population growth as well as the individual's desire for happiness. The modern conception of marriage and the family that appeared in the law creating civil marriage and the records of civil status was developed more fully in the legislation governing divorce, the family court, and successions.

91. In *Les conséquences religieuses de la journée du 10 août 1792: La déportation des prêtres et la sécularisation de l'état civil* (Paris: Ernest Leroux, 1911), pp. 1–18, Albert Mathiez argued that a desire to subdue the Catholic church prompted the law of 1792. To be sure, the struggle with the refractory clergy provided the occasion for the legislation and helped to make it necessary, but Mathiez's interpretation ignores the work of Gallican churchmen and royal jurists before the revolution and the views of such legislators as Durand de Maillane, Treilhard, Bouchotte, Muraire, Vergniaud, and others who advocated civil marriage and civil control of vital records as a matter of principle rather than simply as a response to a conflict with the church.

4

The Law of Divorce

IN ADDITION to the statute creating civil marriage and the records of civil status, a second law of September 20, 1792, introduced into France the institution of divorce. Educated opinion had long been familiar with divorce in the context of Enlightenment thought on marriage and the family. As in the case of civil marriage, it was not a major demand at the beginning of the revolution, but it became the subject of a growing number of essays, pamphlets, and petitions advocating its adoption. The conflict engendered by the Civil Constitution of the Clergy undoubtedly contributed to public and legislative willingness to approve a measure repugnant to the Catholic church. But since divorce was not so immediately necessary to civil society as was the maintenance of public records, the debate about it was prompted less by pressing administrative necessities than by questions of principle and public policy. This debate constitutes an excellent vehicle with which to study revolutionary attitudes toward marriage and the family.

The most important argument on behalf of divorce contended, paradoxically, that it would serve as a means to both human liberty and happiness in marriage. The purpose of divorce was not to destroy marriages, except in those instances in which the spouses were badly matched (*mal assorti*) and unhappy with one another. Such loveless unions were usually marriages of convenience, the products of parental ambition and avarice imposed upon sons and daughters whose youth and inexperience made them powerless to resist. Critics condemned the judicial separation, the ancien régime's remedy for marital discord, as unhappy, unnatural, and unproductive for society. Since the spouses remained married, although living apart, the separation required either that they deny their legitimate sexual impulses or that they "give themselves over" (the usual phrase) to corruption of morals and even debauchery. Thus separations cost individuals untold unhappiness while denying the state the services of the legitimate children whom divorce and remarriage might have produced.[1]

Almost all writings favoring divorce link it with the ideal of a happy, loving, freely chosen marriage. Thus the count of Antraigues urged young persons to marry in their youth, at the age when they are closest to nature and able to respond to the voice of sentiment rather than the material considerations of the world.[2] Hubert de Matigny argued that happy marriages are based on love and the equality of husband and wife, while unions concluded by the vanity and greed of parents soon see indifference degenerate into hatred or discord and may legitimately be broken by divorce.[3] A pamphleteer named Jean Laporte contended that everyone should know the joy, sweetness, and peace that arise in marriage, but that men and women who have been deceived by false promises and disappointed hopes should be able to end their unions so that they may seek other partners.[4]

Numerous writers contended that divorce would protect women's equality and dignity.[5] The deputy Pierre Bouchotte asserted that in place of the law's past unequal treatment of women, especially in the case of adultery, divorce ought to be permitted to both sexes on the same grounds.[6] Hubert de Matigny echoed the same sentiments, and both men suggested that requests for divorce might

---

1. *Du divorce: Adresse à un grand prince qui s'est fait homme* (n.p., 1789), pp. 3–11; *Le divorce ou l'art de rendre les ménages heureux* (n.p., P. Devaux, 1790), pp. 10–16.

2. Emmanuel-Louis-Henri de Launay, comte d'Antraigues, *Observations sur le divorce* (Paris: Imprimerie Nationale, 1789), pp. 9–28.

3. Hilaire-Joseph-Hubert de Matigny, *Traité philosophique, théologique et politique de la loi du divorce...* (n.p., 1789), pp. 70–134.

4. Jean Laporte, *Essai sur la législation et les finances de la France* (Paris: Gastellier, 1789), pp. 113–14.

5. For other issues relating to women, see Jane Abray, "Feminism in the French Revolution," *American Historical Review* 80, no. 1 (February 1975):43–62.

6. Pierre-Paul-Alexandre Bouchotte, *Observations sur l'accord de la raison et de la religion pour le rétablissement du divorce...* (Paris: Imprimerie Nationale, 1790), pp. 7–97.

be heard by a marital court staffed by heads of families and meeting in closed sessions to protect a family's privacy.[7] Other critics urged legislation to protect a wife's property during divorce.[8] One denounced indissolubility as part of the ancien régime's "monstrous edifice of Gothic institutions."[9] Another proposed a court of women to deal with matters of divorce and cited Rousseau as condemning indissolubility as contrary to nature and therefore worthless.[10]

Another argument in favor of divorce maintained that with it France might hope to match the population growth enjoyed by such Protestant countries as the Netherlands, many German states, and Swiss cantons that permitted dissolution of marriage.[11] The journalist and advocate Linguet, who had previously been involved with questions of both Jewish divorce and Protestant marriage, published a pamphlet in 1789 arguing that divorce was wholly compatible with the Catholic religion.[12] Those writers who were concerned with the welfare of children reasoned that parental love of children would prevent abuse of divorce, but that in cases of total incompatibility of the spouses, the children's interest would be best served by divorce and remarriage of the parents.[13] Finally, the issue of divorce was sometimes treated lightly, as in a petition from the Assembly of the Most Numerous Order of the Realm (discontented husbands) which urged replacement of separation by divorce and early freedom of marriage for young persons, as well as abolition of the dowry so that wives would have to work harder to please their

7. Matigny, *Traité philosophique*, p. 130.

8. *Mémoire sur le divorce* (n.p., 1790), pp. 7–19; Cailly, *Griefs et plaintes des femmes mal mariées* (n.p., 1790), pp. 9–25, Archive Nationales, AD II 33 and AD XVIII 162, 163. Hereafter cited as AN.

9. *Le divorce par le meilleur ami des femmes, suivi d'une adresse au clergé* (n.p., P. Gueffier, 1790), p. 3.

10. Mademoiselle Jodin, *Vues législatives sur les femmes adressées à l'Assemblée Nationale* (Angers, 1790), pp. 47–56.

11. *Réflexions d'un bon citoyen en faveur du divorce* (Paris, 1789), pp. 2–6.

12. Simon-Nicolas-Henri Linguet, *Légitimité du divorce justifiée par les Saintes Ecritures, par les Conciles, etc. aux Etats Généraux de 1789* (Brussels, 1789), pp. 1–40.

13. Jean-René Loyseau, *Les états provinciaux comparés avec les administrations provinciales...* (Paris, 1789), pp. 399–408; *La nécessité du divorce* (Paris: Boulard, 1790), pp. 16–39; *L'ami des enfants: Motion en faveur du divorce* (n.p., Devaux, 1790), pp. 1–7, AN, AD II 33, AD XVIII 163.

husbands.[14] An assembly of "*honnêtes citoyennes*" responded that divorce would be useful in situations in which love has fled from marriage and urged that the law require husbands to observe the same fidelity they demanded from their wives, or allow the wives to take lovers.[15]

The most important and controversial pamphlet favoring divorce during the early years of the revolution was Hennet's *Du divorce*, which was widely circulated and reprinted and which drew rejoinders from clerical spokesmen such as the abbés Barruel and Chapt de Rastignac. Hennet began by regretting that the rule of marital indissolubility had not been abolished during the Night of August 4, when the French nation had destroyed so many other outdated customs. With regard to the objection that divorce is prohibited by the Catholic religion, Hennet replied that given the disagreements among the Holy Scriptures, the church fathers, and the councils, man should use his reason, "that torch which God has given to all men to enlighten them."

Divorce should be tested by its utility. Nature's two major goals for mankind are reproduction and happiness, and divorce furthers both of these ends, whereas separation leaves the partners with the choice of adultery or sterility. Society's goal should be the happy, loving marriage, which is productive and which offers the proper environment for the rearing of children: "Happy the child who receives life from two spouses united by tenderness. The blossoms of love shadow his cradle; friendship, confidence, and indulgence spread flowers under his first steps. He mixes his childish caresses with the loving embraces of the authors of his days."[16] But pity the child who is born to an unhappy marriage; he should be removed from the spectacle of parental dissension as quickly as possible. It would be better for the child to be reared by a loving stepparent in a second marriage than to suffer the effects of the union of an inno-

14. *Procès-verbal et protestations de l'Assemblée de l'Ordre le plus Nombreux du Royaume* (n.p., 1789), pp. 11–14.

15. *Délibérations et protestations de l'Assemblée des Honnêtes Citoyennes compromises dans le procès-verbal de celle de l'Ordre le plus Nombreux du Royaume* (n.p., 1789), pp. 21–24.

16. Albert-Joseph-Ulpien Hennet, *Du divorce* (Paris: Monsieur, 1789), pp. 134–35.

cent spouse linked to an adulterous wife or a cruel husband and father.

Hennet argued that the law should permit divorce by either spouse for a variety of grounds, including penal sentences and other forms of punishment, exile, absence, sterility, and disease preventing procreation. For instances in which the existence or nature of the ground had to be determined, such as adultery or incompatibility of character, he recommended use of an assembly of relatives. This institution composed of relatives of both husband and wife would resolve the issue without scandal or wrong to either party and would present its decision to a judge in a formal recommendation. The assembly of relatives would also make suggestions to the magistrate as to custody of the children and arrangements to protect their property rights. Thus Hennet would permit divorce on a liberal basis, but always with the goal of furthering loving, productive marriages. His argument rested on the belief that legislation informed by reason and philosophy could improve social institutions and advance the cause of human happiness.

On January 1, 1790, a copy of the second edition of Du divorce was formally presented to the National Assembly, and extracts and a favorable comment were printed in that day's issue of Le moniteur.[17] Clerical writers were quick to respond with lengthy refutations. The abbé Barruel, an outspoken critic of Durand de Maillane and the Ecclesiastical Committee, issued a collection of four letters condemning Hennet's interpretation of the history of divorce and insisting that questions of Catholic doctrine must be left to the competence of theologians. He argued that divorce would be disastrous for children and would only encourage men and women to chase after ephemeral, worldly happiness instead of placing their confidence in the eternal truths of religion.[18] Another opponent, the abbé Chapt de Rastignac, presented a detailed ac-

17. *Moniteur universel*, reprint (Paris: H. Plon, 1858–70), 3:4–5. One critic charged that every member of the National Assembly had been given a copy of the book (Abbé Nicholas-Sylvestre Bergier, *Observations sur le divorce* [Paris: Imprimerie Nationale, 1790], p. 3).

18. Abbé Augustin de Barruel, *Lettres sur le divorce à un député de l'Assemblée Nationale; ou bien, réfutation d'un ouvrage ayant pour titre: Du divorce* (Paris: Crapart, 1789), pp. 1–36.

count of the church's doctrinal position and warned that divorce would weaken conjugal affection and encourage human inconstancy.[19] Still another author contended that the demands of nature make marriage indissoluble because the goal of marriage is the rearing of children—a task that requires the energy and devotion of both parents for most of their adult lives.[20]

Prior to the controversy generated by pamphlets and brochures, the *cahiers* of 1789 had contained little mention of divorce, with only two statements of grievances from the third estate favoring it and four from the clergy opposing it. The third estate of the *prévôté* of Fleury-Merogis (Châtellenie de Corbeil, Oise) suggested it would be useful to avoid scandal and proposed that marriage might be dissolved by a simple assembly of relatives and the spouses before a royal judge. The judge would safeguard the rights of the children of the marriage by reserving part of the couple's common property for them.[21] The third estate of the district of the Eglise des Théatins in Paris affirmed that divorce should be permitted because an indissoluble contract is contrary to the inconstant nature of man. It also urged that priests be permitted to marry and that dispensations for marriage be abolished, for "if a thing is bad in itself, it must not be permitted for money."[22]

On the other hand, *cahiers* from the clergy of Orange and the *vicomté* of Soule and from the parishes of Aulnay-les-Bondis and Stains (both neighboring Paris) called for opposition, should divorce be proposed to the Estates General.[23] That only two *cahiers* should contain comments favorable to divorce is somewhat surpris-

---

19. Abbé Armand de Chapt de Rastignac, *Accord de la révélation et de la raison contre le divorce* (Paris: P. Clousier, 1790), pp. 320–64.

20. Gaetin de Raxis de Flassin, *La question du divorce discutée sous les rapports du droit naturel*... (Paris, P. Prévost, 1790), pp. 9–16. Other works responding to Hennet include *L'indissolubilité vengée: Lettre à M. * * * député à l'Assemblée Nationale* (Paris, 1789), AN, AD XVIII 169, and *L'homme mal marié, ou questions à l'auteur du divorce* (Paris, 1790).

21. Jérôme Mavidal and Emile Laurent, eds., *Archives parlementaires de 1787 à 1860: Recueil complet des débats législatifs et politiques des chambres françaises*, 1st ser. (1787–99), 2d ed. (Paris: Paul Dupont, 1879–), 4:549. Hereafter cited as *AP*.

22. *AP*, 5:361, arts. 25–27.

23. *AP*, 4:267 (Orange) and 325, art. 17 (Aulnay-les-Bondis); 5:124, art. 12 (Stains), and 775, art. 42 (Soule).

ing, since the duke of Orléans, Louis XVI's cousin, had recommended this reform to the assemblies of the numerous districts where he possessed property.[24] The duke's instructions were widely circulated but did not achieve their goal.[25]

The first legislative proposal on the subject of divorce appeared on August 5, 1790. The legislature was discussing measures for the judicial reorganization of France, including an institution called the family court, which would supervise the discipline of children and resolve other conflicts within the family. In the midst of the debate, the deputy Gossin offered an amendment to modify judicial separation. The amendment would have introduced divorce in an indirect manner, for it proposed that persons separated by judicial decree be permitted to remarry. While the country was awaiting a complete reform of the civil law, relations between separated spouses who wished to marry again and questions concerning their children would be controlled by the laws governing separation and the remarriage of widows. Gossin introduced the amendment with enthusiastic rhetoric about "liberty breaking the chains of despotism," but the assembly was unmoved and refused to allot any time for consideration of the proposal.[26]

The National Assembly again considered divorce briefly in 1790 in connection with the claims of Alsatian Lutherans. According to the treaties of the Peace of Westphalia, these Protestants had been guaranteed the right to observe their own religious practices within the French state. The Lutheran faith permitted divorce for adultery and on several other grounds, and until forbidden by royal order in 1722, the consistories of the Lutheran church had regularly adjudicated divorce proceedings. The representatives of the Protestant communities in Alsace, Professor Koch of the University of Stras-

---

24. *Instructions données par S.A.S. mgr. le duc d'Orléans à ses représentants au bailliages . . .* (n.p., 1789), p. 6. The work has been attributed to Sieyès, Choderlos de Laclos, Geoffroy de Limon, and others, but without any conclusive evidence of its authorship.

25. Beatrice Fry Hyslop, *A Guide to the General Cahiers of 1789* (New York: Columbia University Press, 1936), pp. 57–61. For more information on the role of the duke of Orléans, see Hyslop, *L'apanage de Philippe Egalité, duc d'Orléans, 1785–1791* (Paris: Société des Etudes Robespierristes, 1965).

26. *AP*, 17:616–18. See also Pierre-François Gossin, *Motion sur l'article XII du titre 9 du projet sur l'ordre judiciaire* (Paris: Baudouin, 1790), pp. 1–7.

bourg and Mayor Sandherr of Colmar, published a list of Lutheran demands, first among them being the restoration of the institution of divorce. In support of their position, they argued that the law permitted divorce to the Jews of Alsace and the Catholics of Poland. All manner of scandals resulted from the rule of indissolubility, they maintained, and these scandals "are much more troublesome for Protestants, who do not have the resource of convents in which to confine their debauched and adulterous wives. The known rule, 'The father is that one indicated by the marriage,' causes ruinous litigation, which often results in great losses to families."[27]

Another petition proposed a civil constitution of the churches of the Confession of Augsburg. The author of the project admitted the right of the state to supervise these churches within the limits of the Scriptures, but his proposal left regulation of their internal affairs in the hands of the consistories. In order to ensure the equality founded on the constitution, all limitations on natural or religious rights, such as prohibition of divorce to Lutherans, would be removed immediately.[28] The Lutheran congregations of Doubs and Haute-Saône presented similar demands in a letter sent to the National Assembly.[29]

The assembly discussed these and similar requests on August 17, 1790. Speaking for the Legislative Committee, Le Chapelier called divorce a "sensible institution," and after a short debate the deputies approved a decree providing that "Protestants of the two Confessions of Augsburg and Switzerland, inhabitants of Alsace, would continue to enjoy the same rights, liberties, and advantages

27. *Très-humble et très-respectueuse adresse, présentée à l'Assemblée Nationale par les habitants de la Confession d'Ausbourg* [sic] *des villes de Strasbourg, Colmar, Wissembourg, et Munster en Alsace* (Paris: Société Typographique, n.d.), pp. 12–13, AN, AD XVIII 48. A similar petition, also signed by Koch and Sandherr and dated May 22, 1790, may be found in the records of the Ministry of Justice, AN, BB³⁰ 88.

28. *Principes généraux des protestants de la Confession d'Augsbourg et leur incompatibilité avec le Constitution Civile du Clergé* (n.p., n.d.), pp. 8–29. The copy in AN (XVII 48) is inscribed "For Monsieur Camus, deputy to the National Assembly, from Monsieur Koch, Professor."

29. *Très-humble et très-respectueuse adresse présentée à l'Assemblée Nationale par les citoyens de la Confession d'Augsbourg, habitants des quatres Terres de Blamont, Clemont, Hericourt et Chatelot, départements du Doubs et de la Haute-Saône* (n.p., n.d.), signed Kilg, Pastor of Blamont, AN, AD XVII 48.

that they had enjoyed and had the right to enjoy, and that the restrictions that had been imposed against them would be considered as null and of no effect."[30] The assembly's decision cannot be construed as approval of divorce generally, however, for it confined its attention to Alsatian Lutherans and decided to permit them divorce only on the grounds of religious liberty and ancient treaty rights.[31]

New pamphlets published in 1790 continued to present arguments in favor of divorce. A work purporting to be the letters of a nobleman opposing divorce vividly illustrated the dangers of an indissoluble marriage. The correspondent related to a friend how he had won the hand of a young heiress by feigning love for her and how he had used her fortune in the pursuit of other women. His only fear was that a law of divorce might permit his wife to escape from his control.[32] One bachelor argued that indissolubility was one of the chief reasons that celibacy was so common in society. To reduce it, he offered a projected law whereby separations might be converted into divorces after a waiting period.[33] Similar provisions appeared in Le Noble's extensive treatise on civil marriage.[34] Diderot's Swiss friend Jacob Meister argued that divorce was neces-

---

30. *AP*, 18:126–28. The debate as recorded in the *Archives parlementaires* made no specific mention of divorce, but the deputy Bouchotte later noted that Le Chapelier had discussed divorce in connection with Lutheran demands. See Bouchotte, *Observations sur l'accord*, p 35.

31. Although divorce was demanded by French Lutherans, the more numerous French Calvinists seem to have remained silent on the issue. One explanation suggests they did not wish to endanger the gains they had recently won with the Edict of 1787, but this view overlooks the proposals of Rabaut Saint-Etienne and others for modifications and improvements in the edict. See Burdette C. Poland, *French Protestantism and the French Revolution* (Princeton: Princeton University Press, 1957), pp. 83–105. A better explanation is the strict doctrine of the French Reformed Church, which permitted dissolution of marriage only for adultery. Marriage was not to be contracted lightly and church rules even forbade breaking of engagements without good cause. See J. Faurey, "Le protestantisme français et le mariage," *Revue générale du droit* (1924), pp. 265–74.

32. *Lettre du marquis de C * * * au comte de F * * * contre le divorce* (Paris: Desenne, 1790), pp. 1–7; AN, AD II 33, AD XVIII 163.

33. *Réflexions d'un célibataire en faveur de ceux qui ne le sont pas* (Paris: Guillaume, 1790), pp. 7–10; AN, AD II 35.

34. Pierre-Madeleine Le Noble, *Projet de loi pour les mariages* (Paris: Garnery, Yr. 2 [1794]), p. 49.

sary for the regeneration of public morals.[35] In addition to the numerous pamphlets published during the year, divorce received frequent mention in the revolutionary press, with articles or letters appearing in *Le moniteur, Spectateur nationale, Feuille du jour, Les petites affiches, Le courrier nationale, Annales patriotiques, Révolutions de Paris,* and other journals.[36]

Private petitions urging the National Assembly to enact a law of divorce began to appear in 1791. One demanded temporary legislation against the abuses of judicial separation, specifically a rule requiring an inventory and the placing of seals on community property at the moment either spouse filed for a separation. The petitioner stated that as things stood, by the time a wife obtained a separation, she often found that her husband had dissembled or disposed of their community property, thus leaving her penniless.[37] Another writer claimed that divorce would encourage marriages of inclination and permit the spouses to remain lovers.[38] Still another petitioner, who signed himself "*citoyen philosophe,*" complained that while the National Assembly no longer recognized religious vows or engagements contrary to the natural rights of man, it still failed to abolish clerical celibacy and the rule of indissolubility.[39] A letter from Benoist La Mothe of Château-du-Loire recounted a sad incident near Le Mans in which an unhappily married woman had hanged herself. He argued that it was the rule of indissolubility that often reduced married persons to despair and such extreme action.[40]

In 1791, Hennet published another pamphlet that included exerpts from the favorable comments on divorce of Montaigne,

---

35. Jacob Heinrich Meister, *Des premiers principes du système social* (Paris: Guerbart, 1790), p. 87. Another work, entitled *Essais sur les moeurs, ou point de constitution sans moeurs* (Paris: Grégoire, 1790), pp. 77–82, makes the same point.

36. *Moniteur universel,* 7:111–12; 10:271. Pierre Damas, *Les origines du divorce en France* (Bordeaux: G. Gounouilhou, 1897), pp. 93–95, discusses the agitation for divorce in the popular press, as does Maurice d'Auteville's essay "Le divorce pendant la Révolution," *Revue de la Révolution Française* 2 (1883):206–13.

37. *Petition adressée à l'Assemblée Nationale* (n.p., Cercle Sociale, n.d.), pp. 1–17. A provision to this effect was adopted after passage of divorce legislation by the National Convention (AN, AD II 33).

38. *Loi du divorce* (n.p., n.d.), pp. 1–8, AN, AD II 33.

39. Petition dated October 4, 1791, in AN, AD II 33.

40. Committee on Petitions to Legislative Committee, October 1791, AN, D III 361.

Montesquieu, Voltaire, and others. The final part of the brochure presented a detailed analysis of the law of divorce in Catholic Poland and in the Protestant cantons of Switzerland in parallel columns, with a third column left blank for readers to add their own ideas. The novel form of presentation undoubtedly made it easier for a reader untrained in the law to understand how a law of divorce might work.[41] Another work by Bouchotte continued his battle with the abbé Barruel over the competence of the National Assembly to legislate on marriage, and argued that the law should provide equal treatment of both sexes and ensure freedom of marital choice.[42] Charles-Louis Rousseau's essay on education and the civil life of women insisted that marriage must be founded on love, that feeling which "nourishes itself on sacrifices, feeds upon obstacles, heightens existence, instructs courage, carries [one] to heroic actions, inspires sublime sentiments and the enthusiasm of virtue."[43] He concluded that divorce would protect the dignity of marriage undertaken for love by the free choice of the spouses. With it, the words *wife* and *mother* would become objects of public veneration.

The themes of divorce and the marriage of priests provided the basis for Louvet de Couvrai's novel *Emilie de Varmont*, which appeared in 1791. The work consisted of a series of letters written

41. Albert-Joseph-Ulpien Hennet, *Pétition à l'Assemblée Nationale par Montaigne, Charron, Montesquieu et suivi d'une consultation en Pologne et en Suisse* (n.p., P. Desenne, 1791). The work includes a bibliography of other pamphlets and newspaper articles on the subject of divorce.

42. Pierre-Paul-Alexandre Bouchotte, *Dernières observations sur l'accord de la raison et de la religion pour le rétablissement du divorce . . .* (Paris: Imprimerie Nationale, 1791), pp. 1–47.

43. Charles-Louis Rousseau, *Essai sur l'éducation et l'existence civile et politique des femmes dans la constitution française* (Paris: Girouard, n.d.), pp. 15–16. Another pamphlet published during 1791, *Un mot sur le divorce, suivi d'un projet de loi, et d'un tableau des usages de tous les pays de la terre sur le mariage* (Paris: P. Fr. Didot, 1791), emphasized the marriage and divorce practices of exotic Eastern societies. *Il est temps de donner aux époux qui ne peuvent vivre ensemble la faculté de former de nouveaux liens* (Paris, 1791) offered a draft statute of divorce with provisions governing the property rights of children, whereas *Sermon capucino-philosophique par M * * * ci-devant cordelier* (Paris: Monory, 1791) connected the rule of indissolubility with that of clerical celibacy, both representing "Gothic and feudal" abuses of the church. Félix Faulcon's *Extraits de mon journal* (Paris: Cusac, 1791), pp. 41–48, commented on the growing public demand for a divorce law.

by the principal characters to one another, recounting the unhappy marriages of a mother and her two daughters. In the end, the mother's despair drives her to suicide while the two daughters impatiently await action on a law of divorce by the National Assembly. Emilie, writing to her sister, prays that God will aid France to overcome its prejudices, ignorance, and superstition:

> Then the open cloisters will be forced to let their victims escape; then this poor Monsieur Sevin, now so unhappy, will be able to find some consolation on earth for celibacy.... Then, especially, one will no longer hear our courts resound with these demands for separation, pursued with such great scandal and obtained at the price of so much dishonesty, and of which the sole effect is to condemn young persons separated but not disunited to drag themselves to their tombs, [trapped] between the evils of celibacy and the crimes of adultery.[44]

Although it was not the major focus of the play, the divorce theme also appeared in Beaumarchais's *L'autre Tartuffe ou la mère coupable,* presented in June 1792, in which the villain sought to exploit and destroy a happily married family by disclosing youthful indiscretions of both husband and wife.[45]

In the early months of 1792, more petitions and letters urged the Legislative Assembly to approve divorce.[46] At the same time, even constitutional clerics found divorce too radical. Bishop Flavigny of Haute-Saône argued that rumors of a possible divorce decree would only arouse opposition among the enemies of the revolution, while the bishop of Puy-de-Dôme insisted that such a law would alienate many clerics who had loyally supported the Civil Constitution of the Clergy.[47] An article in *Le moniteur* for March 21, 1792, ex-

---

44. Jean-Baptiste Louvet de Couvrai, *Emilie de Varmont ou le divorce nécessaire et les amours du curé Sevin* (Paris: Bailly, 1791), 3:166–67.

45. Pierre-Augustin Caron de Beaumarchais, *L'autre Tartuffe ou la mère coupable* (Paris: Maradan, 1792), pp. 1–100.

46. On February 13, 1792, a group of Parisian women addressed a statement to the Legislative Assembly urging adoption of divorce to force husbands to respect the equality and dignity of their wives (AP, 38:466). Other petitions came from separated women who sought the opportunity to remarry (petition of Catherine Joseph Waterlot Bagot, February 3, 1792, AN, D III 361; Madame de Lespinasse to president of Legislative Assembly, March 1, 1792, AN, AA 45 [doss. 1351]). On March 17, 1792, one Monsieur Demati formally presented the assembly with a two-volume work on divorce and clerical celibacy (AP, 40:138). Three days later it received a lengthy memoir from an English jurist named William Williams (AN, D III 361).

47. Bishop Flavigny of Haute-Saône to Legislative Assembly, February 29,

plained that demands for divorce were reaching the assembly from all parts of France. The author went on to discuss possible means of caring for the children of divorce and protecting their property rights.[48]

On the first of April, a group of women led by a Dutchwoman named Etta Palm, the former baroness d'Aelders, appeared at the bar of the assembly to petition for women's rights, including state education for girls, majority at age twenty-one, equality of rights for the two sexes, and divorce.[49] Later in the month, Lenglet's *Essai sur la législation du mariage* reached the legislature. Lenglet would permit divorce under some circumstances, but with waiting periods to guard against the "inconstancy and lightness of French morals."[50] Nicholas de Bonneville believed that a new marital law should permit divorce, but only after extensive opportunities for reconciliation and with the action being governed by the arbitration of friends and relatives.[51] The abbé Chapt de Rastignac repeated that, contrary to Hennet's statements, divorce did not exist in Poland. Instead, actions for nullity of marriage were common and similar in form and effect. While the abbé won the technical aspect of the dispute, his argument emphasized that the rule of indissolubility was little respected in Poland.[52]

As had been the case with civil marriage, instances of divorce preceded passage of the divorce law. In November 1791 a citizen named Espinay divorced his wife by an authenticated act prepared by a notary and executed before witnesses. He remarried almost immediately.[53] In May 1792 a mayor in the department of Eure who had been judicially separated from his wife sought to

1792; bishop of Puy-de-Dôme to Legislative Assembly, Clermont, March 4, 1792; both in AN, AA 62 (doss. 1350).

48. *Moniteur universel*, 11:681–83.

49. *AP*, 41:63–64.

50. Etienne-Géry Lenglet, *Essai sur la législation du mariage*, 2d ed (Paris: Moutardier, Yr. 5 [1797]), pp. 46–55. Lenglet was a municipal judge from Pas-de-Calais.

51. Bonneville, *Nouveau code conjugal*, pp. 40–65.

52. Abbé Armand de Chapt de Rastignac, *Questions envoyées de France en Pologne, et réponses envoyées de Pologne sur le divorce en Pologne* (Paris, 1792), pp. 1–99; AN, AD II 33.

53. Espinay's first wife sought confirmation of the divorce after the passage of the law of September 20, 1792 (AN, D III 361).

convert the separation into a divorce and simultaneously to publish banns for a second marriage. The mayor's cousin, who was evidently scandalized by the action, filed a formal opposition, but the court that heard the dispute not only dismissed the cousin's objection but fined him 3,000 livres for unwarranted interference with the marriage.[54] De facto divorces became more frequent as the summer progressed and passage of a divorce law became more probable.[55]

The Legislative Assembly did not begin to debate the issue of divorce until after the Revolution of August 10, 1792, had deprived it of independent authority. By then, conservative deputies who had taken their stand on the issue of civil marriage had fled or fallen silent. On August 20, the receipt of a petition favoring divorce moved the assembly to urge the Legislative Committee to greater speed in preparing a draft law.[56] On August 30, Deputy Aubert-Dubayet interrupted the discussion of legislation governing the registration of births, deaths, and marriages to propose that the assembly approve in principle the institution of divorce. He urged that the assembly act to reaffirm its commitment to individual liberty and equal justice for both men and women, leaving the Legislative Committee to work out the details of the law later. The proposition won support from Cambon, who argued that divorce was already permitted implicitly by the Declaration of the Rights of Man. Other deputies voiced favorable sentiments. The assembly concluded that debate by affirming that "marriage is a contract that is dissoluble by divorce," and instructing the Legislative Committee to draw up legislation establishing procedures for dissolving mar-

54. Jean Sourdois, "Le mariage et le divorce sous la législation intermédiaire (1789–1804)," *Revue générale de droit, de la législation et de la jurisprudence* 34 (1910):22.

55. For example, a document entitled *Premier jugement de divorce prononcé par M. le juge de paix de la section de mil sept cent quatre-vingt-douze*, September 12, 1792, recorded that Joseph Bouchez, a tailor, and his wife, Cécile-Hélène Caux, obtained a divorce on the ground that they had been married twelve years without issue and that their humors and characters were not compatible. The justice of the peace pronounced the parties' divorce in the name of the constitutional provision making marriage only a civil contract, and he approved the property settlement they had worked out privately (AN, AD II 33).

56. *AP,* 48:400.

riages and protecting the rights and upbringing of the children of divorce.[57]

After having approved divorce in principle, the assembly received a report and draft law from the Legislative Committee on September 7, 1792. Speaking for the committee, Léonard Robin explained that it had sought to accord the greatest latitude to divorce because the contract of marriage rests on the consent of the spouses and because individual liberty may never be alienated in an indissoluble manner. While following these principles in the Declaration of the Rights of Man and in the constitution, the committee nevertheless sought to protect the interests of children and society at large by provisions preventing spouses from dissolving their marriages lightly, without time for careful reflection.[58]

At the beginning of the discussion of the committee's proposal, Deputy Sédillez sought to substitute his own version, which he claimed would afford greater protection to women. Sédillez defined divorce narrowly, as based solely on the mutual consent of the parties, and in the case of repudiation of one spouse by the other, he would require that the complaining spouse submit his or her demand to a jury of repudiation composed of members of the opposite sex. Some deputies were intrigued by Sédillez's proposed jury of repudiation, but most voted to direct their consideration to the committee's projected law.[59] In fact, that consideration proved quite perfunctory, with the assembly's only change being the addition of emigration under the terms of the law of April 8, 1792, to the grounds for divorce. A few deputies voiced concern that the liberal provisions permitting divorce would be harmful to society, but the majority approved the law article by article without much further comment or inquiry.[60] As in the case of the legislation on civil marriage and the registration of vital statistics, the assembly promulgated the divorce law on September 20, 1792.

57. AP, 49:117–18.
58. Ibid., pp. 433–36. A copy of the committee's report may also be found in AN, AD XVIII 192. The records of the Legislative Committee in series D III in the Archives Nationales include many petitions and letters, but they do not explain how the divorce law was drafted.
59. AP, 49:612–13. Printed copies of Sédillez's report may be found in AN, AD XVIII 192, 325.
60. AP, 49:643, 678–79; 50:113–14, 149, 172, 188–94.

Although the revolutionary legislators had proclaimed that marriage was simply a civil contract, the new statute warned that the union might be dissolved only in conformity with the law of divorce. Furthermore, the divorce law abolished the institution of judicial separation, giving spouses who were presently separated by judicial decree the opportunity to convert that decree to one of divorce.

The law provided for three basic types of divorce. First, the parties might decide to terminate their marriage by mutual consent, in which case they would explain their decision before a family council or court composed of relatives or friends and listen to any efforts at arbitration it might offer.[61] If reconciliation did not result after a delay of no less than one month and no more than six, the parties would present a document attesting to the meeting of the family council to the public officer who recorded acts of civil status, and receive their divorce decree.

Second, a spouse might obtain divorce by reason of incompatibility of temperament or character, in which case he or she would also use the family court, but with the requirement of three separate meetings held at specified intervals. If a spouse persisted after the third meeting, divorce would be granted by the public officer.

Third, divorce might be granted on the specified grounds of mental illness, condemnation to an infamous punishment, cruelty or serious injury, notorious disorder of morals, abandonment of at least two years, absence without news for at least five years, or emigration. In this case also the family court would determine the validity of the complaint, with appeal from its decision running to the district court.

Once divorced, both parties were free to remarry whomever they wished, with the stipulation that those divorcing by mutual consent or for incompatibility had to wait one year. Property rights between divorced spouses were to be regulated by prior arrangements, determined either by contract or by the law, with the exception that if a husband divorced his wife for a specified ground other than mental illness, she lost her community property rights.[62] In addition to

61. For a complete discussion of the family court, see Chapter 5.
62. The law's lack of clarity on the division of community property undoubtedly caused much confusion and litigation. Soon after its passage, Parisian notaries began

evaluating the justification for divorce, the family arbiters might decree indemnities and support payments (*pensions alimentaires*) and regulate disputes over division of community property. With regard to children, the law provided that in the case of divorce by mutual consent or incompatibility, the mother would be awarded custody of all girls and any boys under seven years of age, with the father caring for boys over seven. The family court would determine custody arrangements in the case of divorce for specified cause. When a divorced spouse remarried, the children of the first marriage retained succession rights, to be regulated by the same provisions governing children's rights in remarriage by widows or widowers.[63]

The law of September 20, 1792, was a liberal statute, providing a number of means of access to divorce and relying heavily on the goodwill of the spouses and their families in matters concerning division of community property and care of minor children. Several proposals during the period of the radical republic (1793–94) sought to render divorce easier to obtain. The first draft of a civil code prepared by Cambacérès and submitted to the National Convention on August 9, 1793, viewed divorce in the light of the ideal of individual liberty. According to the document, since marriage is simply the agreement of a man and a woman to live together and raise children, the union could be dissolved by the will of either spouse. Divorce might be accomplished within a month, after two brief meetings of a family council. Although the draft code contained provisions governing custody and support for children of divorced parents, the law's emphasis clearly fell on the right of individuals to end their marriages as they wished.[64]

Another undated proposal for revision of the divorce law prepared by the Legislative Committee sought to limit individual lib-

---

to include provisions governing the eventuality of divorce in marriage contracts. See Jacques Lelievre, *La pratique des contrats de mariage chez les notaires au Châtelet de Paris de 1769 à 1804* (Paris: Cujas, 1959), pp. 189–92.

63. Jean-Baptiste Duvergier, *Collection complète des lois, décrets, ordonnances, règlements, et avis du Conseil d'état* (Paris: A. Guyot, 1825–), 44:556–62.

64. P. A. Fenet, *Recueil complet des travaux préparatoires du code civil* (Paris, 1827–28), 1:18–29. A second draft presented to the convention by Cambacérès on 23 *fructidor* Yr. 2 (September 9, 1794) contained the same emphasis on individual liberty (ibid., pp. 113–15).

erty primarily by the claims of sentiment. It would have maintained the liberal provisions permitting divorce by mutual consent or for a variety of specified grounds, with the suit being tried before a family council or assembly. The projected law required that a couple's children be present at all meetings of the family council considering a request for divorce, and that these children should pass alternately from the arms of their mother to those of their father during the discussion. The relatives, friends, or neighbors should not fail to encourage expressions of filial piety or parental love and the children might at any time request their parents to cease their effort to destroy their home and family. Finally, if the family council refused to consent to a divorce demanded by one spouse, the presiding officer was to address to that spouse an exhortation (which was doubtless unwelcome) praising "the reciprocal duties and sentiments of affection and generosity that create happy marriages and prosperous families."[65]

The National Convention enacted two statutes further liberalizing the law of divorce: one concerning remarriage of divorced persons and the other governing grounds for divorce. By a decree of 8 *nivôse* Yr. 2 (December 28, 1793) the Convention adopted the suggestion made by a petitioner that a husband should be able to remarry immediately after divorce. A wife had to wait ten months to avoid possible confusion over the paternity of her children. If the wife had obtained a divorce with proof of her husband's absence, however, she might remarry immediately after the action became final.[66] The second law, dated 4 *floréal* Yr. 2 (April 23, 1794), marked the high point of legislative concern for individual freedom. The deputy Oudot proposed it on behalf of the Legislative Committee, noting that the revolution had created political differences in many families which made speedy divorce necessary:

> Divorce is a consequence of the first of the rights of man; it is incontestable that one may not constrain any individual to remain

65. AN, D III 362–65. Durand de Maillane offered a more realistic document to the Legislative Committee on July 8, 1793. It unified and combined the various decrees on marriage and divorce without making any substantive changes in them.

66. Duvergier, *Collection complète des lois*, 6:442–43. The law of 8 *nivôse* Yr. 2 also expanded the jurisdiction of the family court and provided for appeals from it to the regular courts in cases of delay.

attached in his destiny to another, and that the will of one of the spouses is sufficient to break their ties; however, marriage is too important an institution for the happiness of families and the maintenance of morals to permit one to dissolve it without formalities.[67]

The law of 4 *floréal* Yr. 2 provided that divorce might be obtained by a husband or wife who could produce authenticated evidence that he or she had in fact been separated from his or her spouse for six months. The authenticated evidence—statements of six witnesses attesting to six months' separation—was easy to obtain or to falsify. Only wives of soldiers and officials absent in the service of the government were forbidden to take advantage of the rule. Another article prohibited attack on a divorce decree on the ground that the party obtaining it had failed to meet the statutory waiting period. The act stipulated that time cured such a fault. Finally, the law confirmed all divorces concluded by declarations before municipal officers, justices of the peace, or notaries during the period between declaration of the principle that marriage was only a civil contract in the Constitution of 1791 and the law of September 29, 1792.[68]

Divorce as a symbol of individual liberty received favorable treatment in the Parisian theater of the period, at least when it was employed to permit marriage for love. Brienne's *La liberté des femmes,* produced in the summer of 1793, depicts a hastily married

67. Charles-François Oudot, *Rapport et projet d'articles additionnels sur le divorce* (Paris: Imprimerie Nationale, 1793), p. 3. See also his *Essai sur les principes de la législation des mariages privés et solennels...* (Paris: Imprimerie Nationale, 1793), pp. 1–11.

68. Duvergier, *Collection complète des lois,* 7:183–84. Most of the less important laws concerning divorce passed during the convention also related to émigrés or persons who might be suspected of being enemies of the Republic. By the act of October 19, 1793, the convention determined that divorced wives of émigrés were not to be included in the categories of suspected persons under the law of suspects of September 17, 1793. In other words, a divorce was sufficient to obtain at least temporary security for the wife of an émigré (AP, 7:23).

A decree of 23 *thermidor* Yr. 2 (August 10, 1794) permitted nonnoble wives of former nobles to return to Paris for purposes of pursuing divorce suits, and a similar law of 8 *vendémiaire* Yr. 3 (September 29, 1794) allowed all persons who had been proscribed from Paris or from frontier or maritime areas to return for purposes of celebrating marriages or obtaining divorces. Finally, the act of 24 *vendémiaire* Yr. 3 (October 15, 1794) declared that persons suing for divorce on the ground that their spouses were émigrés or were absent in a foreign country were relieved of having to establish the spouses' domicile (AN, AD II 33).

couple who fall in love with others and resort to divorce to end their union.[69] Nicholas Forgeot's *Le bienfait de la loi* develops the same theme. The drama focuses on two young persons, each married to older spouses, who ultimately divorce their partners and marry one another. It condemns marriages of convenience while praising unions based on love and mutual inclination. When the youthful Cécile hesitates to begin a divorce action against her husband out of a misguided sense of duty, her friend Lucinde urges her to act at once:

> Profit immediately when happiness dawns for you.
> Especially don't speak any longer of a sad marriage,
> Authority made it and the law destroys it:
> Divorce is the right escape from slavery.
> Love and virtue must choose for themselves.
> Soon undoubtedly all spouses will feel them.
> Then we will know the road to true happiness.
> Our bliss will be born from our choice.[70]

Desfontaines de la Vallée's *Le divorce* enjoyed a good reception at a new theater, the Vaudeville.[71] The husband and wife in this play, Germeuil and Isabelle, have chosen one another freely and married for love. Germeuil adores their little daughter, Angélique, but he has grown distant from his wife without knowing how to correct the situation. Isabelle, meanwhile, has been courted by a former abbé whom she hopes to marry as soon as she has divorced her husband. The plot centers on Germeuil's efforts to win back his wife's love with the aid and instruction of Suzanne, the family's nurse, and Cécile, the maid. Ultimately Germeuil succeeds in reviving his wife's affection, while frightening off the abbé with tales of her expensive tastes and her fondness for theatergoing. In the last scene, the husband and wife and the two servants end the play singing:

---

69. Marvin Carlson, *The Theater of the French Revolution* (Ithaca: Cornell University Press, 1966), p. 157.

70. Nicholas Forgeot, *Le bienfait de la loi ou le double divorce* (Paris: Prault, Yr. 3), p. 20.

71. The production played almost continuously from August to December 1794, first at the Vaudeville and later at the Cité-Variétés (François-Alphonse Aulard, *Paris pendant la Réaction thermidorienne et sous le Directoire* (Paris: Léopold Cerf, 1901), 4:835.

> One applauds a happy couple
> Who still love each other in marriage;
> One applauds a happy couple
> Whose friendship tightens their marital bonds.[72]

Popular songs also praised divorce, insisting that it was quite legitimate:

> When an attractive woman,
> Overwhelmed by the vows of a seducer
> And languishing on her [marital] chain,
> Finds its weight too heavy . . .[73]

"Bless divorce," declared another, "the generous law that is able to make you happy while your spouse grumbles like a dried-up hollow willow tree."[74] Finally, in the amusing and vulgar "Dialogue between Madame Engeule and Madame Saumon, Fishwives," the latter declares that with divorce, her husband will no longer dare carry off to his slut all that she earns, while the former announces:

> With divorce that dog of a husband
> Will not be able to embarrass me so much;
> He will no longer sell everything up to our sheets
> In order to pay for his bottles of spirits.[75]

72. Guillaume François Desfontaines de la Vallée, *Le divorce, comédie en un acte et en vaudevilles* (Paris, Yr. 2), p. 51.
73. Lorsqu'une femme intéressante
    D'un séducteur comble des voeux
    Et de sa chaine languissante
    Porte le poids trop douloureux . . .
    [Henri d'Alméras, *La vie parisienne sous la Révolution et le Directoire* (Paris: Albin Michel, n.d.), p. 239]
74. . . . n'aimez-vous pas vraiment
    Cette loi généreuse
    Qui par un heureux changement,
    Pourra vous rendre heureuse?
    Semblable au vieux saule-pleureur
    Qui n'a plus que l'écorce,
    Votre époux est toujours grondeur!
    Bénissez le Divorce.
    [Ibid., p. 238]
75. Avec le divorce mon chien d'homme
    N'me f'ra pu tant son embarras;
    Il n'vendra plus jusqu'à nos draps
    Pour payer ses d'misquies d'rogome.
    [Louis Damade, *Histoire chantée de la Première République* (Paris: Paul Schmidt, 1892), pp. 156–58]

Thus during the radical phase of the revolution, legislators and social critics viewed divorce primarily as an instrument of individual liberty. To be sure, they hoped that the force of sentiment would help to resolve marital difficulties and strengthen family unity. But their major emphasis fell on the right of a man or woman to gain liberty and happiness, regardless of the demands of spouse, children, family, society, or the state. Popular songs extolled freedom, and the law of 4 *floréal* Yr. 2 no longer sought to regulate divorce, but merely provided a means for recording it, leaving to individuals the decision to end a marriage whenever they wished.

The sympathy for divorce as the symbol of individual liberty under the Radical Republic rapidly gave way during the period of the Thermidorian Reaction and the Executive Directory to condemnation of divorce as a device permitting social irresponsibility. Instead of glorifying freedom to seek happiness, critics and social theorists reemphasized the responsibilities of marriage and the family. Legislators and administrators sought to prevent casual divorces, justifying their measures on the ground that they were righting the balance between individual liberty and the needs of family and society, but without returning to the errors and prejudices of the ancien régime.

In 1795, several members of the Convention attacked the decrees that had been passed during the Terror and proposed suspension of the laws of 8 *nivôse* and 4 *floréal* Yr. 2 indefinitely while the Legislative Committee undertook a revision of the law of divorce.[76] Oudot and Merlin de Douai defended the earlier legislation, but the Convention approved the suspension with a decree of 15 *thermidor* Yr. 3 (August 2, 1795).[77] The end of the Terror brought greater freedom of public expression, including a number of pamphlets criticizing divorce. One writer contended that since marriage was the basis of the social order, it should not be dissoluble after the manner of the most ordinary of human contracts.[78] Another argued

76. *Moniteur universel*, 24:488; 25:291.
77. Ibid., pp. 403–4. The decree may be found in Duvergier, *Collection complète des lois*, 8:254.
78. J. Girard, *Considérations sur le mariage et sur le divorce* (Paris: Deltufo et Everat, 1797), p. 9.

that the family was by nature essentially monarchic, with the husband as its king or chief.[79] Writing from Switzerland, Suzanne Necker, wife of Louis XVI's former minister of finance and mother of Madame de Staël, argued against divorce on the ground that it precluded the primary end of marriage—the dedication of the spouses to the rearing of their children.[80]

The constitutional church, which had been greatly weakened during the Terror by loss of personnel and hostility toward any form of Catholicism, condemned divorce in its last national council. On 22 *brumaire* Yr. 6 (November 12, 1797), the church declared itself "inviolably attached to the doctrine ... of the perpetuity and the indissolubility of marriage." It instructed priests not to perform the sacrament of marriage for persons who had been divorced.[81] Individual clerics had already adopted a similar position. In a letter written to a friend in 1795, the constitutional bishop Emery explained that compliance with the civil laws did not necessarily mean acceptance of them:

> Take, for instance, the law of divorce. I submit to this law myself; that is to say, I do not employ violence to prevent its execution. But that does not prevent me from saying openly that the law is contrary to good morals and the Gospel. If a man who is divorced and married to another woman comes to me to obtain religious succor, I am not prevented from saying that he must begin by recognizing and repenting his fault and accompany this by sending away his second wife and recalling the first.[82]

The adherents of liberal divorce legislation—the *divorçaires,* as contemporaries sometimes called them—failed to respond effectively. Cambacérès included all the liberal provisions of the law of 1792 in his third projected draft of the civil code and he defended them in his report to the Convention as necessary guarantees of

79. Charles-Phillippe-Toussaint Guiraudet, *De la famille considérée comme l'élément des sociétés* (Paris: Desenne, Yr. 5), pp. 1–86.

80. Suzanne Churchod Necker, *Réflexions sur le divorce* (Lausanne: Durand Ravanel, 1794), pp. 5–43.

81. Jules Basdevant, *Des rapports de l'église et de l'état dans la législation du mariage du Concile de Trente au code civil* (Paris: Sirey, 1900), pp. 193–95.

82. J. E. A. Gosselin, *Vie de M. Emery* (Paris, 1861), 1:371–72, as quoted in Henry Horace Walsh, *The Concordat of 1801: A Study in the Problem of Nationalism in the Relations of Church and State* (New York: Columbia University Press, 1933), p. 156.

individual freedom.[83] But the Convention was unsympathetic and it gave the projected code less attention than it had the earlier drafts of 1793 and 1794. Etienne-Géry Lenglet, now a member of the Council of Five Hundred, revised his *Essai sur la législation du mariage,* replacing extravagant praise of divorce with proposals for longer waiting periods and other safeguards against hasty action in divorce.[84] A fervent but rather incoherent *Adresse aux républicains* insisted that divorce was necessary to protect the "new marriage" created by the revolution and then reverted to a long critique of marriage under the ancien régime.[85]

A growing number of private petitions, letters, and *mémoires* reached the files of the Legislative Committee, the Committee for Classification of Laws, and the ministries of Justice and the Interior during the years 1795 to 1799.[86] Some public officials inevitably misunderstood the decree of 15 *thermidor* Yr. 3, thinking that it had suspended all suits for divorce, and they had to be corrected by the minister of the interior.[87] Most of the correspondents who wrote to the National Convention, the councils of the Directory, or a minister were hostile to divorce, and particularly to incompatibility of temperament or character as a ground for divorce.[88] These persons complained that the ease with which divorce might be obtained on the ground of incompatibility was an invitation to human inconstancy and immorality. Often the petitioners appear to have been frustrated wives or husbands who had been divorced on the

83. Fenet, *Recueil complet,* 1:157–58, 230–37.
84. Lenglet, *Essai sur la législation,* p. 76.
85. *Adresse aux républicains sur le divorce considéré dans ses rapports moraux et politiques* (Paris: Bureau Général des Journaux, Yr. 4), pp. 1–22.
86. The largest collection of documents is the archives of the Ministry of Justice, BB[16], consisting of more than 900 cartons of correspondence organized by department of origin. The only inventory, covering materials from the department of the Seine, is very inaccurate and incomplete. I have sifted through more than 100 cartons from the department of the Seine and all of those listed alphabetically from Ain through Cher.
87. Minister of the interior to public officer of Valence, 18 *nivôse* Yr. 4 (January 8, 1796), AN, F[2] I 389.
88. Lawyers contend that there exists a kind of Gresham's law governing the grounds for divorce: that ground which is the most general and least susceptible of definite proof will inevitably form the basis for the largest number of complaints. If the formulation is correct, incompatibility would have been the most commonly used ground under the 1792 law. Comments in correspondence tend to support this conclusion, but no statistical evidence on the point is available.

ground of incompatibility of temperament, sometimes while they were imprisoned or absent in military or governmental service. An occasional writer adopted the position that divorce had to be restricted in the interest of protecting the larger social and political order, but most voiced personal complaints and criticisms founded on very human frustrations and disappointments.[89]

The legislators of the Directory considered motions to suspend or abolish the ground of incompatibility almost daily from 5 nivôse Yr. 5 (December 26, 1796), when the Council of Five Hundred appointed a committee to consider the matter, until the first complementary day of the year 5 (September 17, 1797).[90] Conservatives accused divorce of giving free reign to human passions, violating the laws of God, and confusing a sacred engagement with the most ordinary of human contracts.[91] Defenders of the existing law of divorce, mainly former Jacobin members of the National Convention, attacked divorce's critics as giving aid to fanaticism and suggesting the country should return to the evils of the ancien régime.[92] In the eyes of both, divorce had become a political symbol, rather than simply one aspect of marriage and family law.

89. One example of the former category is a letter from one Arthon, an *instituteur* in Lille, dated 5 *thermidor* Yr. 4 (July 23, 1796) to the Council of Five Hundred, in which he asserted that only persons who were devoted spouses and loving parents could fulfill the duties of citizenship and help to restore good order in government (AN, D XXXIX 4).

90. *Moniteur universel*, 28:154. The bound reprint of *Le moniteur* covering the period of the Directory has been heavily edited and does not present a complete record of the debates on incompatibility. The reprint published on microfilm by the Bibliothèque Nationale does include the complete debates. A detailed account of the debate over incompatibility may be found in Gérard Thibault-Laurent, *La première introduction du divorce en France sous la Révolution et d'Empire* (Clermont-Ferrand: Imprimerie Moderne, 1938), pp. 130–42, and in François Olivier-Martin, *La crise du mariage dans la législation intermédiaire, 1789–1804* (Paris: A. Rousseau, 1901), pp. 133–39. Many legislators had their opinions published in separate pamphlets.

91. Guillaume-Jean Favard de Langlade, *Rapport sur le divorce*... (Paris: Imprimerie Nationale, Yr. 5 [1797]), p. 8 (AN, AD XVIII^C 325); Jean-Henry Bancal, *Opinion sur le divorce* (Paris: Baudouin, Yr. 5 [1797]), pp. 6–14. A suggestion by Debonnières to the Council of Five Hundred that marriage should become indissoluble was greeted by grumbling and muttering (*murmures*) (*Moniteur universel*, 28:726).

92. Michel-Mathieu Lecointre-Puyraveau, *Opinion sur le projet de suspension de l'article III de la loi du 20 septembre 1792, qui permet le divorce pour cause d'incompatibilité d'humeur ou de caractère* (Paris: Imprimerie Nationale, Yr. 5

At the close of several months of debate, Portalis presented a report to the Council of Ancients which sought to resolve the conflict. He contended that marriage is of great importance to society and that therefore society should regulate it carefully. If marriage is to be viewed as a contract, it must be considered as a special kind in which the parties make promises for the benefit of other persons (their children, society) as well as themselves. Such a contract should not be dissolved lightly, but neither can it be indissoluble in a state that recognizes religions that permit divorce. Since divorce for incompatibility may lead to arbitrary or capricious dissolution of marriage, it should not be permitted.[93] In spite of Portalis's carefully reasoned analysis, the Council of Ancients rejected his proposal and the two councils ultimately settled on an amendment that, in the case of divorce for incompatibility, would extend the waiting period before divorce became final for six additional months after the last meeting of the family assembly.[94] This slight modification of the law of 1792 was the only result of all the legislative energy expended by the Directory's legislative body on the question of divorce.

Legislators and others who were opposed to divorce, or at least to the ground of incompatibility, charged the law of 1792 and its subsequent amendments with initiating a period of pervasive immorality. Conservative historians have adopted the same conclusion, alleging that a tremendous number of divorces were recorded during the Terror and immediately following it.[95] The Goncourt brothers spoke of a time of "legalized prostitution," and cited a poem entitled *Le rabachage de père Luron* to illustrate their point:

> I had only one wife, and sometimes
> That was too many in the household.
> I will have two of them, I will have three,

[1797]), pp. 1–16; Félix Faulcon, *Opinion relative à la suspension du divorce pour cause d'incompatibilité* (Paris: Imprimerie Nationale, Yr. 5 [1797]), pp. 2–3.

93. Jean-Etienne-Marie Portalis, *Rapport sur la résolution du 29 prairial dernier, relative au divorce* (Paris: Imprimerie Nationale, Yr. 5 [1797]), pp. 1–40.

94. Duvergier, *Collection complète des lois,* 10:60.

95. Works presenting this interpretation include Olivier-Martin's *Crise du mariage* and Thibault-Laurent's more recent *Première introduction du divorce.*

What a delight! What chattering!
Now that one may divorce,
What pleasure to marry every year again!
Like children going to make merry with a game,
After the fashion of barbarians, my friend![96]

Another author declared that with divorce by mutual consent and especially for incompatibility of temperament, one had arrived at a "true legal concubinage, a successive polygamy, a type of community of women which led fatally to the ruin of society."[97] Even the usually cautious Philippe Sagnac identified divorce with the "torrent of corruption that invaded the cities and especially Paris" during the Terror and the months following it.[98]

The statistical evidence of marriage and divorce in the decade after 1792 supports two important conclusions regarding the frequency of divorce. First, divorce was predominantly an urban phenomenon. While it is not true that divorce left the countryside untouched, as some historians have asserted, it was most frequent in Paris and other large cities and in such maritime centers as Marseilles, Rouen, Toulon, Nancy, Lyons, and Troyes. In Paris, the ratio of divorces to marriages during the ten-year period ran about 1 to 4; in these other large cities, it was about 1 to 10. Second, whether in large cities or in the countryside, divorce was more frequent during the 1792–96 period than in the years that followed. In Paris during the revolutionary years 2 (1793–94) and 3 (1794–95), the records show one divorce for every three marriages, with the total number of both marriages and divorces much higher than

96. Je n'avions qu'une femme, et queuqu'fois
    C'était trop dans le ménage.
    J'en aurons deux, j'en aurons trois.
    Queu délic! Queu ramage!
    Maintenant qu'on peut divorcer,
    Queu plaisir tous les ans de se remarier!
    Comme les enfants vont s'rejouir biribi,
    A la façon de Barbari, mon ami!
    [Jules de Goncourt and Edmond de Goncourt, *Histoire de la société française pendant le Directoire* (Paris: Charpentier, 1914), p. 358]
97. Georges Mallet, *Le divorce durant la period du droit intermédiaire (1789–1804)* (Paris: Sirey, 1899), p. 133. Mallet cites Taine frequently and shares his interpretation of the revolution.
98. Philippe Sagnac, *La législation civile de la Révolution française* (Paris: Hachette, 1898), p. 293.

in subsequent years.[99] Read by themselves, the statistics would seem to indicate a period of widespread breakdown of marriage. A number of qualifying factors, however, suggest that this conclusion is not warranted. For example, in the first year or two after 1792 many persons converted judicial separations obtained under the ancien régime into divorces. The law of 1792 encouraged such action, and letters in the archives of the ministries of Justice and the Interior indicate that it was common. Leaving aside the question of whether dissolution of marriage is necessarily immoral, these divorces could hardly be said to represent destruction of marriages during the revolution. Also, official republican doctrine made marriage a patriotic act by which a couple dedicated themselves and their children to the service of the *patrie*. Hence marriage offered a good way of escaping suspicion, especially for former ecclesiastics, but men or women who entered into such marriages did not necessarily intend them to be permanent. A petitioner writing the Council of Five Hundred in 1796 urged that divorce not be limited, for many marriages made during the Terror were intended only "as an infallible means of security against deportation or the guillotine."[100]

More important, wives of émigrés frequently used divorce to protect their own person and the family's property. The law included emigration as a ground for divorce, and as early as October 1792 the minister of the interior, Roland, warned the convention that many women were using it to secure property that ought to be confiscated by the state.[101] Although the law did not specify that the wife should obtain full control of community property in case of divorce for emigration, courts usually reached this conclusion.

99. This paragraph summarizes the statistical conclusions reached by Thibault-Laurent in *Première introduction du divorce*, pp. 149–64. Since the vital records for the city of Paris were destroyed in 1871, he reconstructed them from the totals of marriages and divorces appearing in *Le moniteur* and a newspaper entitled *La décade*, and from estimates for the years 1800–1802 made by the civil code draftsman Maleville and by a member of the Tribunate, Carion-Nisas. Thibault-Laurent also undertook detailed research in departments located mainly in the regions of Provence and Auvergne and used published figures for many large cities.

100. Daubian to Council of Five Hundred, 8 *frimaire* Yr. 5 (November 28, 1796), AN, D XXXIX 5.

101. Minister of the interior to National Convention, October 16, 1792, AN, D III 361.

Revolutionary administrators were certainly not pleased at the thought of losing property that would otherwise go to the state, but on the other hand persons divorcing émigrés usually swore loyalty to the Republic, and one could hardly confiscate the property of patriots.[102]

A study of divorces by wives of émigrés living in Limoges revealed that most of these women were under close surveillance or house arrest at the time they obtained their divorces. While they usually managed to protect their own property, they were sometimes less successful in retaining community property or property that had been held solely by their husbands. Of the twelve divorced women studied, one promptly contracted a union with a person described only as a "*sans-culotte*," while three later remarried their former husbands and the rest remained single.[103] When émigrés returned to France in large numbers after the coup of 18 *brumaire*, the Ministry of the Interior received numerous reports of remarriages between persons who had been divorced at earlier stages of the revolution.[104] Wives of political figures also frequently used divorce to dissociate themselves from their husbands when the latter had been declared enemies of the Republic. A former member of the National Convention, Lanjuinais, later recounted how he had instructed his wife to divorce him at a time when his life had been in danger.[105] During the Thermidorian Reaction, the wife of Billaud-Varenne wrote to the minister of justice inquiring whether her husband's deportation was an "infamous punishment" within the meaning of the statute authorizing divorce.[106]

Divorce also proved useful in cases in which one party to a marriage disappeared, often during military or governmental service. The law required five years' absence without news to establish

102. The ministers of the interior and of justice thrashed out this issue in a series of letters to one another in 1792 and early 1793 (AN, BB¹⁶ 122 [Cantal]).

103. Joseph Boulaud, *Douze femmes d'émigrés divorcées à Limoges sous la Terreur (1793–1794)* (Limoges: Ducourtieux et Gout, 1913), pp. 1–197.

104. For example, see mayor of Calais to minister of the interior, 3d complementary day Yr. 9 (September 20, 1801), AN, F² I 399.

105. Jean-Denis Lanjuinais, *Opinion sur le projet de loi relative aux suites du divorce* (Paris: Plassan, n.d.), pp. 6–7.

106. Anne-Angélique Doize (wife of Billaud-Varenne) to minister of justice, *frimaire* Yr. 5 (November–December 1796), AN, BB¹⁶ 709 (Seine).

death and the right to remarry, but divorce permitted a spouse to achieve the same result in a much shorter time.[107] For example, numerous letters to the minister of the interior from Bordeaux, La Rochelle, and other Atlantic ports discuss the plight of women whose husbands had remained on the island of Hispaniola or had been sent there to repress the rebellion led by Toussaint L'Ouverture. By 1795 or 1796 they were presumed dead, but for purposes of remarriage it proved easier for these women to divorce their husbands than to try to establish their deaths.[108] Letters and complaints from the Ministry of the Interior also reveal that divorce was commonly employed for the same purpose by wives of soldiers missing in action.[109]

The use of divorce to establish probable death or permanent absence, to protect persons and property by dissolving a marriage with an émigré or an individual under suspicion, or to transform a judicial separation obtained under the ancien régime all contributed to the relatively large number of divorces and remarriages in the first years after 1792. Given these factors, the divorce statistics do not necessarily establish a greater degree of marital breakdown or moral looseness during the period than at earlier or later times.

The subject of divorce underlines many of the fundamental assumptions of the eighteenth century, as revealed in the debates of critics and legislators. These men saw individual happiness as a primary human goal, exalted above duty to family, society, and the state. Furthermore, most proponents of divorce assumed that freedom—here freedom of choice in marriage—would automatically produce happiness. Unhappy marriages had to be the badly joined products of parental coercion, youthful ignorance, or the evil designs of one partner, usually an individual identified with the

107. Minister of the interior to commissioner of Executive Directory, municipal administration of Luynes, 2 *thermidor* Yr. 4 (July 20, 1796), AN, F² I 391.

108. Municipal administration of canton of Nantes to minister of the interior, 29 *floréal* Yr. 6 (May 18, 1798), AN, F² I 393.

109. By 1799 the minister of the interior had ordered courts to cease granting divorces on any ground whatsoever to wives of men absent on military service (minister of the interior to departmental administration of Somme, 6 *brumaire* Yr 8 [October 28, 1799]), AN, F² I 406).

ancien régime. A second major theme in the debate reversed a tradition of centuries, which saw love and marriage as antithetical. The
revolutionaries contended that human love must be the very basis
of marriage; it was inconceivable to them that marriage might be
freely chosen for some other reason, such as financial gain, social
position, or personal security. The modern marriage was the fruit of
love, sentiment, nature, affection, the inclinations of the heart—to
use the phrases of the time. Finally, the debates emphasized sentiment as a means of strengthening and regulating human relationships in the family. The family court or assembly received important functions under the divorce law of 1792 precisely because
legislators believed that family feeling could reconcile unhappy
spouses or, if necessary, oversee the care of their children.

These assumptions might have remained the intellectual property
of a small group of individuals had not the French Revolution
intervened to give their ideas weight and political authority. A variety of factors led to passage of the law of September 20, 1792.
Divorce was a logical consequence of the contractual theory of
marriage developed under the ancien régime and written into the
nation's new constitution. The contractual theory emphasized the
individual's, rather than society's, interest in marriage and identified the marriage contract with the general theory of contracts,
which permitted the participants to modify or terminate an agreement as they wished. The claims for toleration of minority rights,
including Protestant and Jewish practices permitting divorce, were
also influential. The growing deterioration of relations between the
revolutionary government and the nation's nonjurant clergy made
many legislators ready to strike a blow against the fanaticism of
Catholic doctrine and the disloyalty of its adherents. Finally, the
Revolution of August 10, 1792, silenced conservative opposition
and made passage of the law easy.

The decade after 1792 witnessed the widespread use of divorce,
particularly in the years of the radical revolution. Many a spouse
converted an earlier separation into a divorce or employed it to
protect property and person in instances of emigration or arrest.
Divorce became not only a guarantee of a new kind of marriage but
a political symbol of liberty, and as such it came under increasing

attack during the period of the Executive Directory. The passage of time eroded the comfortable assumption that freedom of choice would invariably yield marital happiness.

In 1796, a petitioner to the Councils of Five Hundred and of Ancients of the Directory summarized part of the decade's experience. Suzanne Rauly of Toulouse explained in puzzled and hurt tones that although she and her husband had founded their marriage on mutual inclination rather than considerations of wealth, her husband had not hesitated to desert her for another woman.[110] Thus romantic love did not invariably yield marital happiness. But other citizens praised the blessing of divorce. Joseph Larthe of Angoulême wrote to the minister of justice explaining that he had fled an unhappy marriage of convenience in his youth and had later dissolved it in order to wed a companion whom he truly loved and who had borne him two children.[111] If freedom of choice and marriage for love could not guarantee marital contentment, as revolutionary legislators had assumed, divorce could at least offer disappointed spouses another chance at happiness.

110. Petition of Suzanne Rauly to the Councils of Five Hundred and of Ancients, 30 *floréal* Yr. 4 (May 19, 1796), AN, D XXXIX 4.
111. Petition of Joseph Larthe to the minister of justice, forwarded to the minister of the interior, 28 *thermidor* Yr. 7 (August 15, 1799), AN, F² I 384.

5

Reorganization of the Family: The Family Court, Majority, Adoption, Illegitimacy, and Successions

A THIRD MAJOR area of revolutionary legislation concerning marriage and the family created a new institution, the family court or *tribunal de famille*, and changed relationships of family members with statutes governing majority, adoption, illegitimacy, and successions. The court provided a mechanism for resolving disputes by arbitration within the family while reserving to the parties the right to appeal its decisions to the district court, the court of first instance in the regular judicial system. Initially, creation of the court stemmed from the abolition of the *lettre de cachet* and the apparent need for another means to enforce parental authority over children. But the law extended its jurisdiction to disputes between spouses and other adult family members, with the result that regulating these relationships became its primary business.

Just as legislators had sought to create a new kind of marriage with the laws of secularization and divorce, so they intended that the family court should change relationships within the family. In place of the ancien régime's traditional family, dominated by the husband and father, they hoped to substitute a democratic form of family organization, providing more nearly equal rights for all family members. In so doing, they gave legal substance to Enlightenment thought, which emphasized the role of sentiment in family life and sought for women and children greater dignity, liberty, and equality with men.

Those writers who urged changes in marriage and family law that would protect and benefit women were not, in most cases, feminists. They idealized the roles of wife and mother and urged the importance of happiness in the modern marriage and family. But they did not advocate the extension of civil and political rights to females or propose expansion of the kinds of employment available to women. Of the great figures of the Enlightenment, only Condorcet could be described as an active proponent of women's rights. Pamphlets and writings by less well-known authors seem to have made little impression, while feminist leaders during the revolution—such women as Olympe de Gouges, Téroigne de Méricourt, Etta Palm (baroness d'Aelders), Claire Lacombe, and Pauline Léon—met indifference or ciriticism for having abandoned the duties and demeanor generally regarded as appropriate to their sex.[1]

How, then, is one to explain the changes in private law that drastically, although briefly, improved women's personal and property rights? Not only could women marry and divorce under the same rules as men after September 20, 1792, but abolition of the *lettre de cachet* and the creation of a family court afforded them nearly equal rights with their husbands in the supervision of children. Finally, a series of modifications in succession law, to be discussed later in this chapter, guaranteed them equality of inheritance with their brothers and other male relatives. Part of the explanation is surely widespread acceptance of the slogan of "equality," which appears so frequently in the revolutionary debates on the new laws and which may have impelled legislators to decree equality in an abstract sense without desiring some of the practical results that the principle produced. In addition, the modern conception of marriage and the family, with its concern for happiness of the spouses and increased attention to the rearing of

1. See the works cited in Jane Abray, "Feminism in the French Revolution," *American Historical Review* 80, no. 1 (February 1975):43–62. Also Katherine B. Clinton, "Femme et Philosophe: Enlightenment Origins of Feminism," *Eighteenth-Century Studies* 8, no. 3 (Spring 1975):283–99, and Léon Abensour, *La femme et le feminisme avant la Révolution* (Paris: Ernest Leroux, 1923).

children, emphasized the importance and dignity of the wife and mother. While she might be denied political rights and other opportunities in the world, within the domestic circle she had earned new affection, equality, and respect.

Under the ancien régime the rules governing majority were both varied and complicated. Women of any age were, with a few exceptions, legally incapable of independent acts concerning property and hence they lived in a sort of permanent minority, under the authority of father, husband, or other male relative. Only as independent merchants or as widows did they acquire a measure of independent legal capacity.[2] Both customary and written French law before 1789 had been heavily influenced by Roman notions of *patria potestas*, the father's virtually unlimited power over his children and their property until emancipation by marriage, establishment of a separate household, or other formal act. In most regions a son was under the authority of his father until he reached age twenty-five, at which time he could make a will or contract or incur other forms of legal liability.[3] But as previously noted, the requirement of paternal consent to marriage had been extended by royal statute to age thirty for sons and twenty-five for daughters, with the father usually retaining the power to disinherit an adult son or daughter whose marriage or other action displeased him. Thus the significance and age of majority varied according to sex and the nature of the action in question.[4]

A father who wished to discipline his minor son or daughter

2. Paul Ourliac and J. de Malafosse, *Le droit familial*, vol. 3 of *Histoire du droit privé* (Paris: Presses Universitaires de France, 1968), pp. 126–59. Two older works on the legal capacity of women are E. Laboulaye, *Recherches sur la condition civile et politique des femmes* (Paris: Durand, 1843), and Paul Gide, *Etude sur la condition privée de la femme dans le droit ancien et moderne* (Paris: Durand et Pedone-Lauriel, 1867).

3. On the history of paternal power, see Emile Masson, *La puissance paternelle et la famille sous la Révolution* (Paris: A. Pedone, 1910); Marie-Paul Bernard, *Histoire de l'autorité paternelle en France* (Paris: Montdidier, 1863); and J. Duplessis de Grenedan, *Histoire de l'autorité paternelle en France* (Paris, 1900).

4. In criminal actions, the courts customarily considered fifteen or sixteen to be the age beyond which a youth assumed full adult responsibility for his acts. See André Abbiateci et al., *Crimes et criminalité en France sous l'ancien régime, 17ᵉ – 18ᵉ siècles* (Paris: Armand Colin, 1971).

could employ the useful weapon of the *lettre de cachet,* a royal order directing the arrest and imprisonment of the person named in it. *Lettres de cachet* were available at the pleasure of the king or his servants, and in addition to punishing rebellious or unruly children, they might be used to obtain detention of mentally ill persons, adulterous wives, or any family members whose actions threatened the honor or security of the family. The law provided no established judicial procedures for determining the validity of the complaint that formed the basis of a *lettre de cachet,* and hence young persons were often incarcerated for failure to marry a person chosen by the family or refusal to follow a given career. Sometimes the complaint alleged only a vague lack of discipline.[5]

The *lettre de cachet* was also, of course, an important instrument of political control, and its use against critics and enemies of the regime aroused widespread resentment before the revolution.[6] The general *cahiers* of all three estates are full of demands that it be abolished and replaced with safeguards against arbitrary arrest and guarantees of judicial due process. In the case of family difficulties with sons and daughters, however, a number of *cahiers* expressed reservations and proposed that a modified version of the instrument be retained to enforce a father's paternal power. The third estate of Angoulême explained that many fathers "are justly alarmed over the misconduct of their children," while representatives of the city of Limoux warned against abandoning the remedy of imprisonment for those youths who "abandon themselves to vices dishonoring their family."[7] These reservations arise as frequently in the *cahiers* of the third estate as in those of the nobility, thus refuting sugges-

5. André Chassaigne, *Des lettres de cachet sous l'ancien régime* (Paris: A. Rousseau, 1903), pp. 1–337; François-Xavier Emmanuelli, "'Ordres du roi' et lettres de cachet en Provence à la fin de l'Ancien Régime," *Revue historique* 512 (October-December 1974):357–92.

6. *Des lettres de cachet et des prisons d'état,* composed by Mirabeau while he was detained in Vincennes and published in Hamburg in 1782, is the best known expression of protest against this arbitrary exercise of royal power. Mirabeau's father had had the young man confined under a *lettre de cachet* several times before the son reached the age of thirty (Oliver J. Welch, *Mirabeau: A Study of a Democratic Monarchist* [London: Jonathan Cape, 1951], pp. 1–93).

7. Jérôme Mavidal and Emile Laurent, eds., *Archives parlementaires de 1787 à 1860: Recueil complet des débats législatifs et politiques des chambres françaises,* 1st ser. (1787–99), 2d ed. (Paris: Paul Dupont, 1879–), 2:11 (Angoulême); 3:580 (Limoux). Hereafter cited as *AP.*

tions that the *lettre de cachet* was identified exclusively with aristocratic family concerns.[8]

In the fall of 1789, the National Assembly appointed a special committee, which included the deputy Mirabeau, to consider abolition of the *lettre de cachet*.[9] Even before the committee had presented its proposal, the assembly had heard frequent petitions and speakers urging it to abolish this judicial practice, while others warned that emptying the prisons of all persons held by virtue of *lettres de cachet* would turn loose on Paris and other cities a flood of vagrants, lunatics, and criminals.[10] The assembly acted in March 1790 with a decree abolishing the *lettre de cachet* while providing for continued detention of persons who had been convicted by judicial process or who were detained on a basis of formal statements showing grave cause. The law provided that those persons imprisoned at the request of their families should be released unless they had been convicted of an offense by judicial process or unless their families could within three months show good cause before a court why they should continue to be detained.[11]

While the assembly focused on the abolition of the *lettre de cachet*, some deputies sought to create an alternative legal basis for relations between parents and minor children. They proposed to govern these relations through the institution of a family court, which they included as part of the scheme of judicial reorganization of France. Few records of the Judicial Committee of the National Assembly survive and hence it is impossible to determine with certainty the origin of the idea of the family court.[12] Some historians have argued that the institution derived from Roman law, while

---

8. The *cahiers* printed in the *Archives parlementaires* contain at least thirty-one requests that a modified form of the *lettre de cachet* be retained to serve the interests of families. These requests are distributed by estate as follows: clergy, 4; nobility, 10; third estate, 13; two or more orders sitting together, 4 (*AP*, 7:480–81).

9. *AP*, 10:249.

10. Shelby T. McCloy, *The Humanitarian Movement in Eighteenth-Century France* (Lexington: University of Kentucky, 1957), pp. 152–53.

11. Jean-Baptiste Duvergier, *Collection complète des lois, décrets, ordonnances, règlements, et avis du Conseil d'état* (Paris: A. Guyot, 1825–), p. 143.

12. The only relevant document in the Judicial Committee's files is a letter dated September 1, 1789, from a man named Gassaud living in Manosque, a city in Provence. Gassaud proposed to end costly and complicated lawsuits by means of a family assembly that would administer estates and settle all questions relating to successions (Archives Nationales, D XVII 5; hereafter cited as AN). For a compara-

others have seen a more likely antecedent in a fifteenth-century Provençal statute that required arbitration of disputes within families and which King Francis II attempted unsuccessfully to incorporate into royal legislation.[13] Several of the *cahiers* that favored limited retention of the *lettre de cachet* suggested that it be obtainable on the request of a family assembly.[14] And pamphleteers favoring divorce often included a family council or court in their proposed legislation.[15]

Whatever the origin of the institution, it appeared in two projected laws of judicial organization drafted by Bergasse and Sieyès, as well as in the document that finally emerged from the Judicial Committee.[16] During a session of February 7, 1790, an unidentified deputy interrupted the debate on the reorganization of local government to urge the assembly to come to the aid of families by creating a substitute for the abolished *lettre de cachet*. In support of

---

tive study of other forms of lay justice, see John P. Dawson, *A History of Lay Judges* (Cambridge: Harvard University Press, 1960).

13. R. de Fesquet, "Les tribunaux de famille à Rome," *Revue historique de droit français et étranger* 1 (1855):125–47; Lucien Darnis, *Des tribunaux de famille dans le droit intermédiaire* (Paris: H. Jouve, 1903), pp. 14–23. The Provençal statute is printed, together with an extensive gloss and commentary, in *Statuts et coutumes des pays de Provence avec les glosses de M. L. Masse . . .* (Aix: Jean Tholosan, 1620), pp. 73–111. It also appears with a discussion of later jurisprudence in Jean-Joseph Julien, *Nouveau commentaire sur les statuts de Provence* (Aix: A. David, 1778), 1:350–57.

14. *AP*, 1:697 (combined estates of Aix-en-Provence); 2:489 (nobility of Caen), 687 (nobility of Châlons-sur-Marne), 630 (third estate of Chartres), 702 (third estate of the *bailliage* of Montague, Châtillon-sur-Seine, Burgundy); 3:37 (nobility of the *sénéchaussée* of Condom, Gers), 308–9 (third estate of Beaumont-le-Roger, Evreux), 386 (third estate of Forex, Montbrison), 494 (third estate of the *sénéchaussée* of Lesneven, Brittany), 570 (nobility of Limoux), 634 (third estate of Macon); 4:63 (nobility of Montreuil-sur-mer, Picardy); 5:723 (third estate of Saumur), 760 (third estate of Sens), 788 (third estate of Toulon).

15. Hilaire-Joseph-Hubert de Matigny, *Traité philosophique, théologique et politique de la loi du divorce* (n.p., 1789), p. 131; Albert-Joseph-Ulpien Hennet, *Du divorce* (Paris: Monsieur, 1789), pp. 136–40, and *La nécessité du divorce* (Paris: Boulard, 1790), p. 36; Jean-René Loyseau, *Les états provinciaux comparés avec les administrations provinciales* (Paris, 1789), pp. 404–5; Pierre-Paul-Alexandre Bouchotte, *Observations sur l'accord de la raison et de la religion pour le rétablissement du divorce* (Paris: Imprimerie Nationale, 1790), p. 72.

16. Alfred Hiver de Beauvoir, *Histoire critique des institutions judiciaires de la France de 1789 à 1848* (Paris: Joubert, 1848), pp. 18–31; Abbé Sieyès, *Aperçu d'une nouvelle organisation de la justice et de la police en France* (Paris: Imprimerie Nationale, 1790), pp. 43–46.

his argument, the speaker related the unhappy story of a minor official of the Parlement of Nancy whose son had incurred huge debts, insulted his father, and subsequently shot him. Le Chapelier replied that the assembly could not occupy itself with individual situations, but that it should hurry to establish the family court as a means of resolving them. Similarly, Mirabeau insisted that having the assembly issue an order of imprisonment, as demanded by the deputy, would offer a dangerous example to all future legislatures, and he urged instead that the assembly act to establish the family court, preventing crimes by justice rather than by arbitrary action.[17]

On August 5, 1790, the deputy Thouret presented to the assembly those sections of the proposed law of judicial organization governing bureaus of peace and the family court.[18] The bureau of peace offered one possibility of reducing the likelihood of formal litigation. According to the proposed law, all disputes had to be submitted to a bureau composed of a justice of the peace and his assistants for conciliation and arbitration before suit could be begun in a regular court.[19] The reporter introduced the family court as another means of settling disputes without publicity (*éclat*) or expensive and time-consuming legal procedures. Also, the family court would make available a means for disciplining young persons still under the authority of their elders. The debate on the articles creating the court consisted of favorable comments and suggestions for changes in wording of the provisions, except for a few critical comments by Robespierre, who argued that it was ridiculous to expect relatives to render impartial justice in family quarrels. The deputies who spoke reacted favorably to the provisions governing the relations of parents and children, although some urged extension of the family's jurisdiction over a minor child to age twenty-five, instead of twenty or twenty-one.[20]

The law as finally passed provided that in cases of a dispute

17. *Moniteur universel*, reprint (Paris: H. Plon, 1858–70), 5:323–24.

18. For a discussion of the changes in the judicial reform, see James F. Traer, "The Search for Simple Justice: Judicial Reform and the Courts from the Old Regime through the French Revolution," paper delivered at the Annual Meeting of the American Society for Legal History, Philadelphia, October 1974.

19. Duvergier, *Collection complète des lois*, 1:373. Roderick Phillips of Oxford University is preparing a study of the bureaus of peace in Rouen.

20. *Moniteur universel*, 5:312–15.

between husband and wife, father and son, grandfather and grandson, brothers and sisters, nephews and uncles, or other persons within the same degrees of relationship, the parties were required to name relatives as arbiters.[21] The provisions also applied to disputes between wards and guardians over the guardianship relationship. Each party was to name two arbiters, and lacking relatives, he might name friends or neighbors. If the arbiters could not agree, they were to name a fifth arbiter to break the deadlock. When one party refused to name arbiters, the judge of the district court would appoint them. Judgments of the family court might be appealed only to a district court, which would pass on them as a court of last resort. In the case of a dispute between a child and a parent, an older relative, or a guardian, the family court should consist of six or, preferably, eight relatives. It might order up to a year's detention of a minor less than twenty-one years old. The court had to present its sentence to the president of the district tribunal, who might modify or dismiss it, before the judgment could be executed.[22]

The provisions of the law of August 16, 1790, were brief and ambiguous, but the intent of the draftsmen and legislators was clear. They distrusted lawyers and old-regime legal procedures, believing that disputes might be resolved without great investment of time or money. They preferred the more informal method of arbitration, which also offered greater privacy and might protect a family's reputation from scandal. By disputes within the family, the legislators meant those involving a comparatively small circle of relatives, although presumably more distant relatives might be chosen as arbiters. Most important, the authors of the family court sought to create a more democratically organized family, replacing the power of the *père de famille* with that of a council of relatives.

Once established, the jurisdiction of the court expanded rapidly. As noted in Chapter 4, the Legislative Assembly assigned it an important role in all kinds of divorce proceedings under the law of

---

21. Degrees of relationship are determined by counting up to the common ancestor and down again to the related person. For example, a nephew and an uncle are separated by three degrees of relationship. The provision did not explain whether or not it included relatives by marriage.
22. Duvergier, *Collection complète des lois*, 1:373.

September 20, 1792. The National Convention decreed that the family court should authorize the marriage of minors whose parents were dead or legally unable to give consent and should also hear disputes concerning children or property of former marriages.[23] Other decrees required that arbiters possess certificates of civic loyalty and provided procedures for chosing an additional arbiter when the parties and their arbiters could not agree on one.[24]

A frequent issue in the creation of a family court centered on the question of who should serve as arbiters. Legislators and draftsmen had clearly intended that whenever possible, the institution should permit resolution of conflicts within the family. The benefits of the institution—privacy, the useful effect of family feeling, savings in time and money, the possibility of natural and equitable justice unfettered by old legal formalities—all presupposed that the arbiters would be personally related to the parties to the dispute. Yet situations soon arose in which the parties preferred not to name their own relatives as arbiters, either because of unfriendly relationships within the family or because the relatives lacked education or sophistication. In these situations, the minister of justice concluded that there existed a "default of relatives" within the meaning of the statute and that therefore a party might name friends or neighbors as arbiters.[25]

The decision regarding the composition of the family court ultimately helped to produce an institution quite different from the one envisaged by its creators. Instead of relatives, parties to a dispute might select friends or neighbors if they wished, and these categories were broad enough to include anyone. Quite understandably, many persons wanted experienced arbiters who would promote their interests with intelligence, skill, and sophistication. Hence they began to choose business and professional men, local notables, and especially men with legal training or experience, such as judges, notaries, attorneys (*avoués*), justices of the peace, clerks (*greffiers, clercs*), bailiffs (*huissiers*), and others (*hommes de loi, juristes, jurisconsultes*).

23. The decrees may be found in AN, AD XVIII^c 453, AD II 33, and AD XVIII^c 325.
24. Ibid., AD II 30.
25. Minister of justice to Lefebvre, February 1791, AN, BB[16] 701 (Seine).

TABLE 1. Arbiters with legal expertise serving in Laon and Angoulême, 1791–95

Arbiters	1791	1792	1793	1794 [a]	1795 [b]
Laon					
Total number of arbiters	37	152	128	85	—
Number with legal expertise	22	75	83	36	—
Percent with legal expertise	60%	49%	65%	42%	—
Angoulême					
Total number of arbiters	60	174	267	436	354
Number with legal expertise	28	52	69	186	171
Percent with legal expertise	47%	30%	26%	43%	48%

[a] Figures cover all of 1794 for Angoulême but only 4½ months of that year for Laon.
[b] Nine months only.

In the judicial district of Laon during the years 1791–94, as shown in Table 1, more than half of the persons acting as arbiters were equipped with legal training or experience. In the district of Angoulême during the years 1791–95, men with legal training or expertise accounted for between one-quarter and one-half of the staff of the family court.[26] On the other hand, only 3 to 5 percent of the arbiters in both localities identified themselves as relatives of the parties to the dispute, which was usually a suit for separation or divorce. Earlier studies of the family court in Montpellier, Dijon, and Caen also indicate frequent use of legal personnel but only occasional recourse to relatives as arbiters.[27]

26. I selected the districts of Laon and Angoulême for ready availability of records and for location. Because the law of August 16, 1790, did not indicate where and how family court judgments were to be retained, in most localities they were either mixed with other court decisions or deposited in private notarial archives. In Laon and Angoulême they were classified separately. With regard to location, I had originally intended to select one district in the northern (customary-law) part of France before 1789 and one in the southern (Roman-law) area of the country. Laon met the first criterion. Angoulême, while using customary law, was influenced by adjacent Roman-law regions. In 1801, each judicial district had a population of about 100,000 persons.
27. Paul Viard, "Les tribunaux de famille dans le district de Dijon (1790–1792)," *Nouvelle revue historique de droit français et étranger* 45 (1921):424–77; Marc Ferret, *Les tribunaux de famille dans Montpellier* (Montpellier, 1926); J. Forcioli, *Une institution révolutionnaire: Le tribunal de famille d'après les archives du district de Caen* (Caen, 1932).

The figures for both Laon and Angoulême appear to indicate that the relative number of lawyers participating in family courts decreased between 1791 and 1792. The records for 1791 are probably incomplete and reflect the slowness or failure of arbiters with no legal training to deposit their judgments with the registry (*greffe*) of the district court. In Laon, the decreased percentage of arbiters with legal experience in 1794 is most likely attributable to hostility toward professional classes during the final months of the Terror. Forty-three percent of the arbiters did not list an occupation in the early months of 1794, whereas only 16 percent failed to do so in 1793.[28] In Angoulême, the family court often met at the home or place of business of a fifth party—sometimes a merchant or innkeeper, but more frequently a notary or attorney. It is not clear from the decisions whether or not the fifth party participated as an additional arbiter, but he probably often supplied advice on the meaning of the law or the way to draw up a judgment.

The distribution of arbiters within the category of legally trained or experienced persons is shown in Table 2. The category of jurists, or persons with broad theoretical training in the law, includes those arbiters identified as *juristes, jurisconsultes,* and *hommes de loi.* Attorneys (*avoués*) had been called proctors (*procureurs*) under the ancien régime They prepared and filed documents in civil and some criminal cases and paid money to clerks and process servers. Eighteenth-century critics often accused them of placing their own interests ahead of those of their clients.[29] Notaries, on the other hand, were in a position to win confidence and become trusted advisers through their involvement in major family decisions: the drafting of a marriage contract, the preparation of a will, the recording of a gift or a sale of property.[30] In both Laon and Angoulême, the relative number of notaries sitting on the family court

28. Included among the unclassified category are sobriquets that do not indicate clearly what the individual did for a living; for example, "French patriot," "mayor of the commune," "chairman of the committee of surveillance," "member of the national guard."

29. For a short time their professional status was abolished by revolutionary legislation, but those of Laon and Angoulême continued to practice, titling themselves "former attorneys" (*ci-devant avoués*).

30. Philip Dawson, "The Bourgeoisie de Robe de 1789," *French Historical Studies* 4, no. 1 (Spring 1965):2–6.

TABLE 2. Arbiters with legal expertise, by category, Laon and Angoulême, 1791–95

Arbiters	1791		1792		1793		1794[a]		1795[b]	
	Number	Percent	Number	Percent	Number	Percent	Number	Percent	Number	Percent
Laon										
Jurists	9	41%	39	52%	37	45%	15	42%	—	—
Attorneys	9	41	20	27	30	36	0	0	—	—
Notaries	3	14	10	13	9	11	16	44	—	—
Petty legal personnel	1	4	6	8	7	8	5	14	—	—
All legal personnel	22	100%	75	100%	83	100%	36	100%		
Angoulême										
Jurists	15	54	20	39	1	1	17	9	22	13
Attorneys	8	29	8	15	13	19	15	8	10	6
Notaries	4	14	8	15	38	55	111	60	96	56
Petty legal personnel	1	3	16	31	17	25	43	23	43	25
All legal personnel	28	100%	52	100%	69	100%	186	100%	171	100%

[a]Figures cover all of 1794 for Angoulême but only 4½ months of that year for Laon.
[b]Nine months only.

tended to increase with the passage of time, while the relative number of attorneys tended to decrease.

Outside the legal profession, the arbiters of Laon and Angoulême included virtually every known occupational category, from physicians, manufacturers, and merchants to carpenters, peasants, servants, and day laborers, but with the urban and rural popular classes constituting only a little more than one-tenth of the total number of arbiters in each locality.[31] Stated differently, the arbiters of the family court were often legal personnel, overwhelmingly middle class, and almost always unrelated to the parties to the dispute.

Thus the composition of the family court was significantly different from what its authors had intended, reintroducing the very legal personnel that the statute had sought to exclude. Contemporaries differed on whether or not the court was functioning well in its modified form. Some contended that lawyers ought to be excluded from the family court because their tactics delayed the resolution of disputes and cost the litigants extra money.[32] On the other hand, the evidence from Laon, Angoulême, Montpellier, Caen, and Dijon indicates that the court functioned reasonably well, although in a manner different from that intended by its founders. Complaints about the court focused on its operation under the succession laws of 5 *brumaire* and 17 *nivôse* Yr. 2, which did not permit appeal of its judgments to the district courts and which frequently overturned family arrangements for transmitting property. As explained later in this chapter, the family court suffered from its identification with these laws. In any event, when the parties desired to resolve their conflict, it could provide a prompt, economical solution. And since it was not bound by old jurisprudence and formalities, it could and often did render more flexible and equitable justice than could be obtained in the regular court system.

---

31. For a more complete discussion of the occupational and social classification of the family court's arbiters, see James F. Traer, "The French Family Court," *History* 59 (June 1974):211–28.

32. Correspondence regarding the court may be found in AN, D III 361, D XXXIX 4, and BB[16].

The family court began as a device to regulate the relationship between parents and minor children, but it seldom functioned in this area because revolutionary legislators reduced the age of majority from thirty and twenty-five for men and women, respectively, to twenty-one for both sexes. The law of September 20, 1792, establishing the rules for civil marriage, permitted young persons of twenty-one years to marry without parental consent.[33] A subsequent law of August 28, 1792, provided that parental control of a child's property, as distinct from his person, would also terminate when the child reached twenty-one.[34] Finally, in a supplementary decree of January 31, 1793, the convention declared twenty-one to be the age of majority for purposes of civil rights and all acts relating to property, such as making a will, a contract, or a gift.[35]

In practice, only a handful of cases in Laon and Angoulême family courts involved parents and minor children. One court record alone found a young woman named Bussac petitioning for release from a convent to which her parents had sent her against her will.[36] In another case, Marie Françoise Marguerite Merlieu, who had recently attained her majority, obtained a court decree instructing her parents to cease their obstruction of her forthcoming marriage.[37] On two occasions the citizen Gillebart and other minor children of a first marriage brought unsuccessful suit against their stepfather and tutor, charging him with mismanagement of their property.[38]

If the family court rarely adjudicated disputes between parents and children, it regularly heard them between husbands and wives in the form of requests for separation and, after September 20, 1792, divorce. The institution's creators had confidently assumed that the presence of relatives on the court would tend to restore marital harmony. Warring spouses did in fact often choose relatives as their arbiters, in contrast to the practice in other kinds of family court actions, but judicial records from Laon and Angoulême re-

33. Duvergier, *Collection complète des lois,* 4:562–69.
34. Ibid., pp. 375–76.
35. Ibid., 5:166.
36. Archives Départementales (hereafter cited as AD), Charente, L 2158.
37. AD, Aisne, L 2628.
38. AD, Charente, L 2158.

cord no marital reconciliations, although it is possible that suc-
cesses may have been treated informally and not recorded. Although the law of September 20, 1792, abolished separations,
spouses whose religious scruples forbade them divorce sought and
obtained separations as late as 1795. The family court also regulated the division of marital property and provided for custody and
care of the children of broken marriages.

Family court records occasionally provide intimate glimpses into
the tribulations of individual marriages. When Françoise Sardin
requested separation from her husband, Pierre Lhomme, both the
arbiters and the young husband urged her to abandon her suit.
Finally the husband, having finished his plea, stated

> that he was persuaded that the lady Sardin would not hesitate to
> receive from him the sign of marital affection. She responded that she
> would refuse it. At that moment, the gentleman Lhomme leaped up
> and sought to embrace his wife, despite her lively resistance. Im-
> mediately the gentleman Naudon [a relative] expressed much anger
> .... Taking the lady Sardin by the arm, he said to her, "Let us leave,
> let us leave. Heavens, madame! Where are we?!"

One of the arbiters attempted to intervene, whereupon

> the gentleman Naudon, still greatly agitated and not listening to
> anyone, excited the lady Sardin to cry, "Murderer!" and "Assas-
> sin!"... Many persons, who had been summoned by the cries of the
> lady Sardin, assembled in front of the house, from which the noise
> still issued.

The arbiters finally adjourned to the parlor of a Carmelite nunnery,
where they were able to reach a decision without the participation
of the parties and without disturbing the public order.[39]

In Montpellier, Anne F. requested a divorce from her husband on
the ground of his notorious moral disorder. She stated in her petition that her husband lived "*à même pot et feu*" with another
woman and that their relationship disgraced the petitioner and her
daughters. The husband replied "that it was true that he lived publicly with another woman, that it was his intention to live always
with her, that it was not a crime to have a mistress, but that it was a

39. Ibid.

rather common gallantry [*une galanterie assez en usage*], and that his wife need pay no attention to it." The husband closed by stating that he was indifferent as to whether or not his wife obtained a divorce from him.[40]

In addition to instituting divorce and reducing paternal power over minor children, revolutionary legislators modified the legal structure of the family through new rules governing adoption and illegitimacy. Prior to 1789, adoption had existed in Roman law and a few customs only as a means of altering succession. Thus a man might adopt his son-in-law, nephew, or cousin in order to make him his heir.[41] During the revolution, however, adoption also became a means of placing orphaned or homeless children in new families. This use of adoption fitted perfectly with growing eighteenth-century awareness of the child as a unique and important being.[42] It coincided with the emphasis in revolutionary legislation on ties of sentiment and affection as the constituent bonds of the family. And it offered a possible means of reducing the inequality of fortunes in instances in which well-to-do persons could be persuaded to adopt children of the popular classes.[43]

On December 2, 1792, a ten-year-old child appeared before the National Convention to contribute his savings of two gold coins to the national treasury. He explained that he was an orphan and he urged the Convention to pass a law of adoption so that a friend and protector might legally become his father. The Convention responded by instructing the Committees of Constitution and Legislation to prepare a draft law of adoption.[44] Subsequent impetus for adoption legislation came with the assassination of Deputy Louis Michael Le Peletier on January 20, 1793, just one day before the execution of Louis XVI. Le Peletier's death made him a martyr of

---

40. Ferret, *Les tribunaux de famille dans Montpellier*, p. 290.

41. Jean Carbonnier, *Droit civil* (Paris: Presses Universitaires de France, 1967), 1:582–83.

42. See Philippe Ariès, *Centuries of Childhood: A Social History of Family Life*, trans. Robert Baldick (London: Jonathan Cape, 1960), pp. 365–407.

43. Théophile Berlier, *De l'adoption: Idées offertes à la méditation de ses collègues* (Paris: Imprimerie Nationale, Yr. 2 [1794]), pp. 1–27.

44. *AP*, 54:53.

the revolution and the Convention declared his daughter, Suzanne, the "adopted daughter" of the Republic.[45]

Although it continued the practice of adopting the orphans of various prominent persons in the name of the Republic, the National Convention failed to pass a general law of adoption in 1793 or 1794. Probably it anticipated that the law would be included in the new civil code, the passage of which was viewed as imminent.[46] A decree of 16 *frimaire* Yr. 3 (December 6, 1794) confirmed the existence of adoption without defining it in detail. The Convention passed the decree in response to a petition by a justice of the peace of Beaune who had begun to settle an inheritance on a minor who had been adopted by an authenticated act. The Convention responded that he had acted correctly, stating that adoption had been sanctioned by French law and custom (*moeurs*) and that it conferred succession rights on the adopted child.[47]

While there are no statistics on the practice of adoption during the revolutionary period, some evidence of it can be found in two kinds of documents. First, the records of the festivals of youth, marriage, and old age during the Directory often include special awards to persons who had expressed their patriotism by adopting children.[48] In the festival of marriage in 1796, the commune of Caudebec recognized an aged pair of weavers who had welcomed into their home the abandoned daughter of wealthy émigrés, while in the canton of Barjols, citizens attending the festival of marriage awarded a civic crown to Joseph Antoine Cavalier, a potter who had adopted an orphan into his already large family.[49]

45. Duvergier, *Collection complète des lois*, 5:125. Mademoiselle Le Peletier was the heiress to a huge fortune. In 1797, at the age of fifteen, she decided against the opposition of her relatives to marry a Dutch youth named Jean François De Witt. The relatives appealed to the Directory, which in its inherited role as adoptive parent decided to withhold consent to the match (AN, BB¹⁶ 712 [Seine]).

46. The drafts of the civil code prepared by Cambacérès and submitted on August 9, 1793, and 23 *fructidor* Yr. 2 (September 9, 1794) included adoption (P.-Antoine Fenet, *Recueil complet des travaux préparatoires du code civil* [Paris: Ducessois, 1827–28], 1:29–30, 110–11).

47. Duvergier, *Collection complète des lois*, 7:427–28.

48. See James F. Traer, "Youth, Marriage, Patrie: The Family Festivals in the French Revolution," paper delivered at the annual meeting of the American Historical Association, Chicago, December, 1974, p. 14.

49. AD, Var, L 451; Seine-Maritime, L 359.

Second, administrative correspondence in the archives of the Ministry of the Interior includes some inquiries about the legal effects of adoption.[50] Often, however, these adoptions were undertaken by older couples to guarantee the succession rights of a young adult, sometimes a nephew or other relative. For example, in 1796 the municipal agent of the commune of Sceaux inquired on behalf of an elderly peasant couple whether they could adopt a young man of nineteen whom they had reared, but still permit him to retain his own name. The couple's goal was to ensure that he would be their sole heir.[51] Thus while it is evident that some instances of adoption did occur for reasons of childlessness, patriotism, or desire to protect an inheritance, it seems unlikely that it was a common action. Many Frenchmen had a strong prejudice against introducing a "foreign child" into the family, whether by adoption or under new legislation guaranteeing rights to illegitimates.

The question of illegitimacy gave rise to some of the most controversial family legislation of the revolution. The laws sprang from two fundamentally conflicting beliefs. On the one hand, legislators imbued with a strong sense of justice and equality wanted to treat all children alike, whether or not they were born within the bonds of marriage. On the other hand, those same men sought to reinforce and strengthen the legitimate family of husband, wife, and children founded on ties of mutual affection and respect. Under the ancien régime, both royal jurisprudence and local customary or written law governed the status of illegitimates. As a general rule, they could own property, marry, transmit property to their legitimate children, and make wills. While they usually had no claim to inherit from their parents, they might in some areas receive legacies or claim a portion of a parental estate when the parent had no legitimate children. The parental relationship might be established in legal proceedings against either mother or father. Most commonly, the unmarried mother brought suit against the putative father on behalf of herself and her child, the suit being called *la recherche de la paternité*. If the court established probable paternity by evidence of writings or cohabitation, the mother might recover not only the

50. AN, F² I 393 (Lot), 403 (Seine), 405 (Seine-et-Oise), 405 (Deux-Sevres).
51. AN, F² I 402 (Seine).

expenses of confinement but support for her child and damages for herself.[52]

Before the revolution, the question of illegitimacy often arose before a child's birth, for unmarried women and widows who became pregnant had to file a statement attesting to their pregnancy, the *déclaration de grossesse*.[53] Under the law of September 20, 1792, the question of a child's status confronted the public officer at the moment when the parent, relative, midwife, or surgeon came to make the required declaration of birth. The law of 1792 provided no instructions on how to record the three categories of illegitimate births. First, an illegitimate child might be born to two parents who were not married to each other or to anyone else. Second, an adulterine child was one born to an unwed mother but fathered by a married man. Third, a married woman might produce a child fathered by someone other than her husband.

The separations occasioned by revolution and war probably made births in the third category occur more frequently than in normal times. Public officers constantly inquired as to what action to take when the wife of a soldier gave birth one or two years after her husband had left on campaign. Often the child's actual father desired to have his name recorded in the civil records. Before the revolution, the rule "the marriage demonstrates who is the father" (*pater est quem nuptiae demonstrant*) had governed the problem, and the convention reaffirmed the principle by a decree of 19 *floréal* Yr. 2 (May 8, 1794). It stated that a child born to a married woman should be given the name of her husband, even if another

52. Crane Brinton, *French Revolutionary Legislation on Illegitimacy, 1789–1804* (Cambridge: Harvard University Press, 1936), pp. 3–9. Brinton provides a lively account of legislative attitudes toward illegitimacy. He is less clear on the substance of the law, particularly as it affected inheritance, and is inclined to label the lawmakers hypocrites, rather than recognize them as men motivated by two contradictory impulses: belief in theoretical equality and desire to protect the legitimate family. For a detailed discussion of the law of the ancien régime, see Jean-François Fournel, *Traité de la séduction* (Paris: Demonville, 1781).

53. The purpose of the declaration was to prevent induced abortion and infanticide. In practice, local officals in some areas continued to receive *déclarations de grossesse* as late as 1798 (minister of justice to president of municipal administration of canton of Annot, Basses-Alpes, 16 *fructidor* Yr. 4 [September 2, 1798], AN, BB[16] [Basses-Alpes]).

man was the father.[54] In practice, the ministers of justice and the interior enjoined observance of the law while recognizing that the husband could take legal action to disavow his paternity.[55] In instances involving an unmarried mother, the minister of the interior instructed that the birth should be recorded with the name of the mother only.[56]

The National Convention first dealt with illegitimacy in a decree of June 4, 1793, which proclaimed the right of illegitimate children to inherit from both their mothers and their fathers, leaving implementation of the general rule to subsequent legislation.[57] Its statute of 12 *brumaire* Yr. 2 (November 2, 1793) sought to establish the most far-reaching changes in the law. It provided first that an illegitimate child might inherit from both parents on the same basis as a legitimate child. When paternity had not been established before the death of the parent, it might be proved by a writing or support given under the name of paternity during the parent's lifetime. An adulterine child, however, being defined as one whose mother or father was married at the time of its birth, might inherit only one-third of what it would have received had its parents been free to marry at the time of its birth. In the case of both types of illegitimate children, the law applied retroactively to successions opened since July 14, 1789.[58]

Thus revolutionary legislators sought to reconcile their sense that all children ought to receive equal treatment in inheritance with concern for the sanctity of marriage and the legitimate family. Illegitimate children whose parents had no legitimate offspring at the time of their birth received equal treatment; adulterine children whose claims would diminish the estate of a legitimate family were limited to one-third of what they would otherwise have received. Suits by illegitimates in the family courts of Angoulême had varying

54. Duvergier, *Collection complète des lois*, 7:194.
55. Minister of justice to all departmental administrations, 5 *floréal* Yr. 4 (April 24, 1796), AN, BB¹⁶ 706 (Seine); minister of the interior to municipal agent of commune of Torigny, 17 *vendémiaire* Yr. 5 (October 8, 1796), AN, F² I 395.
56. The minister explained that if the father wished to acknowledge his child, he might do so before a notary (minister of the interior to administration of department of Aveyron, 24 *brumaire* Yr. 8 [November 15, 1799], AN, F² I 383).
57. Duvergier, *Collection complète des lois*, 5:314.
58. Ibid., 6:269–70.

success. Some were quickly dismissed. On the other hand, when Jeanne Prémont, illegitimate daughter of Pierre Prémont, brought a suit against the deceased's three legitimate children, a family court decision of 15 *fructidor* Yr. 2 (February 10, 1794) awarded her half of the estate. The evidence revealed that the father had maintained close relations with his daughter and that the daughter and her husband had cared for him in his last illness.[59]

Another suit involved the estate of Antoine Dubois, who had been a wealthy wholesale merchant, and pitted a youth who claimed to be an illegitimate son against a large band of collateral relatives. If recognized, the claimant would have been entitled to the entire estate; otherwise, it would all go to the collateral relatives. Finding themselves unable to agree, the arbiters of the family council selected a fifth member, who invited the parties to conciliate their differences by mutual sacrifices. Under his direction, the collateral heirs agreed to pay the plaintiff 1,200 livres in return for his promise to make no further claims against the estate.[60] Thus these family courts tended to apply the legislation concerning illegitimacy to achieve their sense of justice in the individual case. But in contrast to the slogan boasted by legislators—"Il n'y a plus de bâtards en France!"—administrative interpretation began to narrow the generous aims of the law of 12 *brumaire* Yr. 2, forbidding the child an action to determine his paternity despite the clear language of the statute.[61] Thus the illegitimate or adulterine child whose father refused to recognize him could not benefit from the provisions of the law, while one who had been formally recognized probably did not need its protection.

Not only did revolutionary legislation transform the relationship between parents and children, including adopted and illegitimate ones, during their lifetimes, but it modified the relationship after the death of the parents by means of new legislation governing successions. As in the case of illegitimacy, the major theme of the new succession laws was equality of treatment of all children. And the litigation that the new succession laws produced became the pri-

59. *AD*, Charente, L 2159.
60. Ibid.
61. Minister of justice to court of St-Quentin, 20 *messidor* Yr. 2 (July 8, 1794), AN, BB¹⁶ 9 (Aisne).

mary business of the family court, leading, in 1796, to its abolition. In short, application of revolutionary succession law and the fate of the family court are inextricably entangled subjects.

Revolutionary legislators dismantled the old system of succession law piece by piece, rather like workmen taking apart a badly constructed building. Their multiple statutes and decrees had a single goal: to institute rules guaranteeing absolute equality among all heirs of the same degree of relationship to the decedent, most frequently all children of a deceased parent. During the moderate phase of the revolution (1789–92) some deputies contested this goal in the name of liberty—the right of an individual to dispose of his property as he wished and in possibly unequal fashion. But absolute equality became the rule, and the major controversy during the radical phase of the revolution (1792–94) focused on the extent to which the new succession law should be retroactive, voiding prior marriage contracts, gifts, and other agreements that operated to negate the principle of equality.[62]

Legislators first attacked those special customs and statutes that created unequal rights by reason of quality of person, that is, because of nobility. Since nobility had been abolished by decrees following the night of August 4, 1789, the law of March 15, 1790, similarly abolished the right of primogeniture (*droit d'aînesse*), privileges of masculinity, and all other rules and customs tending to create unequal division of property among formerly noble families. The only exception to the rule was the instance in which the law that applied to commoners created more unequal division than did the law governing nobility, in which case the latter continued to apply.[63] On November 21, 1790, the deputy Merlin de Douai presented a report from the Constitutional Committee and the Committee on Alienation of National Lands calling for complete equality in successions, ending all customary or Roman-law provisions permitting or requiring inequality in favor of an eldest child (*aîné*), a youngest child (*puiné*), or one sex over another.[64]

62. An important monograph, despite its confusing organization, is André Dejace, *Les règles de la dévolution successorale sous la Révolution (1789–1794)* (Paris: Librairie Générale de Droit et de Jurisprudence, 1957).

63. Duvergier, *Collection complète des lois*, 1:135–36.

64. Philippe-Antoine Merlin de Douai, *Rapport sur les successions ab intestate* (Paris: Imprimerie Nationale, 1791), pp. 1–30.

Debate on the proposal took place in April 1791, with some deputies favoring a compromise bill that would have permitted a parent to dispose of a certain percentage of his property freely to one child, or to a person not a member of the family, with equal division of the rest. The compromise failed to satisfy more extreme points of view. Cazalès, a former noble from the Midi, denounced any restraint on liberty and urged that the freedom of the testator be respected, at least in those Roman-law areas where it presently existed. On the other hand, on April 2, 1791, Talleyrand read to the assembly a speech written by Mirabeau during his last illness, denouncing as despotism both primogeniture and the freedom of a testator to make unequal disposition of his property. To the words of the recently deceased Mirabeau, Robespierre added a plea for both equality of succession rights and uniformity of law throughout France.[65]

Following this debate, the assembly passed the law of April 8, 1791, which left the freedom to make a will untouched but provided that in all cases of intestate succession (the usual pattern in the north; the exceptional one in the south), division would be equal among all heirs of the same degree of relationship to the decedent. The statute further stated that representation would exist to infinity in direct line by stem (children of a deceased child taking his portion and dividing it equally) and that the new provisions would govern all successions opened from the time of its publication, but without prejudice to and not affecting rights acquired previously by marriage contract or other agreement.[66] The exception to the rule of equality for the persons of the south making a will remained until the National Convention abolished it on March 7, 1793, thereby creating a uniform rule of equality throughout France.[67]

The legislators soon discovered, however, that the equality they had decreed was in a sense illusory because of provisions maintaining the validity of prior legal acts affecting successions. In many families, succession rights of children—often highly unequal ones—had been carefully regulated by marriage contracts. When

65. *AP*, 24:506–8, 562–64, 570–77.
66. Duvergier, *Collection complète des lois*, 2:348–49.
67. Ibid., 5:232.

the parents of those families died, it was the prior stipulations and agreements, not the new law, that controlled the succession. Equality in the year 2 began to look like equality in ten or twenty years, when those young adults who were now marrying under the new law would receive the successions of their parents.

The National Convention sought to address this problem in the laws of 5 *brumaire* Yr. 2 (October 26, 1793) and 17 *nivôse* Yr. 2 (January 6, 1794).[68] The law of 5 *brumaire* stated that children might not take part in the successions of their parents unless they restored for purposes of division (*rapporter*) any gifts or advantages made to them by their parents before July 14, 1789. This was a statutory version of the Orléano-Parisian rule of "simple equality" in customary law. Furthermore, whether children took part in their parents' succession or not, they were required to restore for purposes of division any gift or advantage from their parents received after July 14, 1789. This additional provision adopted the "strict equality" provisions of the customs of western France, making them applicable to the entire country. Finally, a parent could not significantly reduce the size of his estate by disposing of his property to another person. The law permitted free disposition of only one-tenth of the property when there were heirs in direct line (descendants or ascendants) and one-sixth when there were collateral heirs.

Other provisions of the two laws limited advantages between spouses to a lifetime enjoyment (*jouissance*) or usufruct of one-half of the property of the deceased spouse, with the other half to go to the children immediately. Before the revolution, the common practice had been to guarantee to the surviving spouse by marriage contract the lifetime use and enjoyment of all of the deceased spouse's property. The law of 17 *nivôse* also tried to reduce great fortunes by limiting the amount of a gift or legacy to the sum of 10,000 livres, which could then be accepted only by a person having a fortune of less than 10,000 livres. This provision, too, was retroactive to July 14, 1789. The law regulated the devolution of

68. Ibid., 6:315-17, 372-84. Subsequent decrees of 22 *ventôse* Yr. 2 (March 12, 1794) and 9 *fructidor* Yr. 2 (August 26, 1794) confirmed the egalitarian rules of the earlier laws in response to numerous questions and objections that had been sent to the convention's Legislative Committee (ibid., 7:117-26, 315-20).

TABLE 3. Types of succession disputes, Laon and Angoulême, 1791–95

Dispute	1791	1792	1793	1794	1795[a]
Laon					
Partition requested/attacked	1	9	5	14	—
Will attacked	1	1	—	4	—
Marriage contract rights attacked/abandoned	—	1	1	11	—
Gift attacked	—	1	2	9	—
Other and illegible	2	2	4	16	—
All disputes	4	14	12	54	
Action created by laws of 5 *brumaire* and 17 *nivôse*			5	37	
Angoulême					
Partition requested/attacked	1	11	21	44	30
Will attacked	—	—	—	7	5
Marriage contract rights attacked/abandoned	2	6	4	11	15
Gift attacked	—	—	2	5	4
Other and illegible	3	8	10	23	17
All disputes	6	25	37	90	71
Action created by laws of 5 *brumaire* and 17 *nivôse*				34	38

[a]Nine months only.

successions when there were no descendants, with property moving first to ascendants and then, if there were none, to collateral relatives. Finally, the law of 17 *nivose* Yr. 2 required that any dispute concerning successions should be heard by arbiters in the family court, with no appeal from their judgment.

Even before passage of the laws of 5 *brumaire* and 17 *nivôse* Yr. 2, disputes over successions formed the largest single category of litigation in the family court. The new laws created rights on behalf of persons who had not previously enjoyed them under customary or Roman law, or who had renounced their rights in marriage contracts or other documents, and consequently the volume of litigation involving successions increased. Table 3 indicates both the growing volume of litigation and the primary (though not necessarily exclusive) issue in the various succession cases for the judicial districts of Laon and Angoulême.

Before the revolution, the succession law of the Coutume d'Angoumois placed it among the customs of "strict equality" of the west, while the provisions of the Coutume de Laon made it one of the preferential (*préciputaire*) customs permitting a parent to advantage one child.[69] In both regions, children frequently renounced their succession rights upon establishment in marriage or an office or employment. A common situation saw one or more married daughters bringing suit to reopen a succession in which their brothers had received larger shares than they had. The daughters were required, of course, to return for purposes of division (*rapporter*) their dowries or gifts at the time of marriage. For example, on 21 *pluviôse* Yr. 3 (February 9, 1795), a family court in Angoulême ordered the equal division of the estate of Jean Festis between his son and daughter. The daughter had previously renounced her succession rights in her marriage contract, but was allowed to void this transaction and to inherit equally with her brother.[70]

Parents sometimes used a variety of means to try to advantage one child. The Coutume d'Angoumois permitted a parent to transfer property to one child in return for a lifetime pension or annuity (*pension viagère*), but family courts sometimes declared these transactions invalid if they seemed designed purely to obviate the rule of equality. On 14 *nivôse* Yr. 3 (January 3, 1795), a family court voided several transfers of property that had been made to Jean Labrit by his father before the latter's death. The court decreed that the eldest Labrit had to divide this property equally with the six other children in the family.[71] Family courts also refused to permit the Roman-law device of the "universal heir," whereby a parent named one child—usually the eldest—to receive an entire estate, with the stipulation that the heir should distribute designated portions of it to his brothers and sisters. When parents sought to advantage a universal heir, family courts voided the offending will or marriage contract and required equal distribution of the deceased's property.[72] In short, family courts applied the new succession laws

---

69. Etienne Souchet, *Coutume d'Angoumois commentée et conférée avec le droit commun du Royaume de France* (Paris, 1780), 1:28–34; Jean-Baptiste de Buridan, *Les coutumes générales du bailliage de Vermandois en la cité, ville, banlieue et prévosté foraine de Laon* (Reims, 1630), pp. 141–89.
70. AD, Charente, L 2160.
71. Ibid.
72. Ibid., L 2159, 2160; Aisne, L 2628, 2629.

rigorously, thereby invalidating all prior rules, agreements, and devices that had been used to prevent equality of inheritance.

The retroactive provisions of the laws of 5 *brumaire* and 17 *nivôse* met heavy criticism. They were complicated, and their rules, requiring determination of the present or future effect of legal acts concluded both before and after July 14, 1789, created ample grounds for controversy. Successions that had been settled between July 14, 1789, and the passage of the laws were often reopened and revised, to the additional cost of the parties.[73] One result of the probably necessary complexity of the new succession laws was that persons having recourse to family courts invariably chose arbiters with legal training or expertise as being best equipped to promote their claims. Thus in a sense the law undermined an institution that was intended to yield savings in time and expense by dispensing with lawyers and formal court proceedings. The prohibition against appeals from family court judgments in succession disputes was undoubtedly intended to shorten litigation, but those who lost in the family court often bitterly protested their inability to seek a hearing in another tribunal. Finally, both the laws and the court came under attack from those who wished to return to older rules—for example, the custom of Normandy with its exclusion of daughters from inheritance, or the written law of the Midi, which permitted a testator to reward faithful children at the expense of disobedient ones.[74]

During the Thermidorian Reaction, the Convention abolished the retroactive effort of the laws of 5 *brumaire* and 17 *nivôse* Yr. 2.[75] The legislators of the Executive Directory similarly denounced what they termed "forced arbitration" and declared that all suits formerly heard in such a manner should now be brought before the

73. Complaints are collected in the records of the Legislative Committee and the Committee of Classification of Laws (AN, D III 382–391; D XXXIX 1–6).

74. See the letters and petitions in the "Collection Rondonneau," AN, AD II 48.

75. Decrees of 5 *floréal* Yr. 3 (April 24, 1795) and 9 *fructidor* Yr. 3 (August 26, 1795), in Duvergier, *Collection complète des lois*, 8:177, 304. Subsequent legislation of 3 *vendémiaire* Yr. 4 (September 25, 1795) and 18 *pluviôse* Yr. 5 (February 6, 1797) sought to resolve questions arising from the temporary period of retroactivity, to determine the rights of third-party purchasers of property, and generally to clarify the situation; it did not, however, change the basic rule of equality (ibid., pp. 289–90; 9:312–17).

nation's regular courts.[76] The ambiguity of the Constitution of the Year Three, which permitted arbitration but said nothing specific about the *tribunal de famille,* left the role of the family court in the nation's judicial system unclear. In late 1795 and in 1796, thousands of individuals wrote to the minister of justice to inquire whether or not the new constitution had suppressed the family court. A few of the letters attacked the court for its slowness or its expense, but many praised it as a useful and efficient institution. The largest number merely wanted to know whether it continued to exist and were apparently written by judges, justices of the peace, lawyers, litigants, and others who had used the family court or served on it.[77] In response, the minister of justice, Merlin de Douai, obtained the appointment of a legislative commission headed by Charles-François Oudot to study the matter. The commission recommended abolition on the ground that no citizen should be forced to submit his dispute to judges other than those sitting on an officially recognized court, and the Directory's councils so decreed on 9 *ventôse* Yr. 4 (February 28, 1796).[78]

The use of the family court in arbitration without appeal under the succession laws of 5 *brumaire* and 17 *nivôse*—"forced arbitration," as its opponents called it—was the major reason for its abolition. In addition, the court had failed to function as an assembly of relatives and friends, as its founders had intended, but rather made use of the very legal personnel it was supposed to replace. Abolition of the court was only one of a number of measures that the Directory took in an effort to centralize judicial and political authority.[79] Nonetheless, the family court continued to function until the promulgation of the civil code in divorce cases and those involving orphans and minors.[80]

76. *Moniteur universel,* 25:108–14.
77. AN, BB[16]. The series consists of more than 900 cartons of correspondence covering the period of the Directory and organized by department of origin. I examined documents from eighteen departments, ranging alphabetically from Ain to Cher, as well as those of the Seine.
78. The report of Oudot's committee is printed in *Moniteur universel,* 27:519–22. See also Duvergier, *Collection complète des lois,* 9:61.
79. Most notable among the changes to centralize the judicial system was replacement of the numerous district courts with fewer departmental tribunals.
80. Decisions of the minister of justice, AN, BB[16] 122 (Cantal); 34 (Alpes-Maritimes); 22 (Allier).

But even without the family court, the theme of equality continued to inform the law governing the organization of the family. Most important, all children were to enjoy equal rights of inheritance from their parents. And legislators hoped that equality within families would lead to greater equality of fortunes among all citizens. Adoption served to bring additional children into families and even illegitimates might inherit something from their parents, although here the principle of equal treatment yielded to concern for the legitimate family. In addition, young men and women enjoyed a greater measure of equality with their parents through a lowered age of majority and abolition of the *lettre de cachet* as a form of correction. All of these laws sought to create and sustain a new and democratically organized modern family whose members were equal to one another and united by freedom of choice and love.

6

The Civil Code

THE PRECEDING CHAPTERS have analyzed the creation and application of revolutionary legislation concerning marriage, divorce, the family court, and the relations of family members. They have also tried to explain how most legislators, publicists, administrators, and judges involved in the passage or operation of these laws were motivated at least in part by a "modern" conception of marriage and the family. Their viewpoint maintained that the parties to a marriage should choose one another freely, for affection, rather than be forced into a match dictated by parental pride or greed. The primary end of marriage, for them, was the happiness of the individual parties to the union. The laws emphasized the equality of wife with husband and children with parents and sought to reinforce the ties of sentiment that bound the family together.

Such was the conception, expressed by the legislation of 1790–94, which survived the following ten years without major change. To be sure, the belief that family sentiment could be institutionalized to provide effective means of resolving family quarrels proved misfounded. Legislators were disillusioned by the transformation of the family court into a form of private arbitration by legal personnel rather than family members. Administrators and legislators of the Directory also sometimes attempted to reduce the legal equality of illegitimate with legitimate children and to reinforce paternal authority within marriage. But beyond these exceptions, the central ideas remained intact. Divorce was an essential element of the new conception of marriage and, as such, had become a subject of intense dispute between supporters and enemies of the revolution. It had acquired symbolic value far out of proportion to its importance in society. Civil, republican marriage also generated controversy. Administrators worked hard to make it a customary and accepted act, but they often failed to endow it with a patriotic character. Many areas continued to experience substantial clerically inspired noncompliance with the law.

During the years 1800–1804, the new conception of marriage and the family met searching criticism and analysis as draftsmen prepared a civil code that would govern marriage and family relationships for generations to come. This chapter will discuss how the draftsmen combined the new conception of marriage and the family, older rules and attitudes derived from the ancien régime, and contemporary criticism to create the sections of the civil code concerned with marriage, the organization of the family, and the relationships of its members to one another.

In contrast to the early years of the revolution, public discussion of political and social issues during the Consulate was diminished and muted—the more so given the rapid application of Napoleonic censorship of the newspaper press.[1] Those few individuals writing about marriage and family law were conservative critics of the revolution and its laws. They accepted only a few aspects of the new conception of marriage and the family, principally the emphasis on the importance of children and ties of sentiment within the family.[2] They rejected measures promoting individual freedom and providing greater equality of wives and children with their husbands and fathers. Fundamentally, the critics had an understanding of human nature very different from that of the men who drafted and applied the revolutionary legislation. Instead of the optimism and environmentalist theory of the French Enlightenment, conservatives who

1. On censorship, see Robert B. Holtman, *Napoleonic Propaganda* (Baton Rouge: Louisiana State University Press, 1950), and Claude Bellanger et al., *Histoire générale de la presse française* (Paris: Presses Universitaires de France, 1969), 1:549–67.

2. In this vein, the legal scholar Nougarède declared that rearing children deepened the satisfaction of marriage and drew spouses closer to one another, while Chateaubriand celebrated the affection that united the family circle and made its members' life together happier and more civilized. See André-Jean-Simon Nougarède de Fayet, *De la législation sur le mariage et sur le divorce* (Paris: Le Normant, Yr. 10), pp. 60–64, and François Auguste René de Chateaubriand, *La génie de Christianisme*, vol. 2 of *Oeuvres* (Paris: Furne, 1865), pp. 41–43.

had lived through the revolution were skeptical about the goodness of man and the possibilities for the improvement of society. They believed that human nature included immutable and potentially dangerous elements. Laws and social institutions functioned to restrain those elements, to protect society, and to guard man against his own impulses.

Thus the critics were unwilling to leave marriage to the mercy of changing human sentiments and desires. Nougarède declared that man's heart is too inconstant to make love the basis of marriage, while other authors condemned divorce as encouraging man to indulge his passions rather than obey the dictates of reason and morality.[3] Divorce was doubly objectionable for its identification with the evils and excesses of the Republic and the Terror. Maleville spoke of "the anarchy under which we have been living," and Nougarède identified divorce with "the most disastrous of our recent civil difficulties."[4] The very existence of divorce made marriage unstable, and unstable marriages threatened society and the state. Opponents of divorce before passage of the law of 1792 had grounded their argument on the Catholic church's prohibition of divorce and had insisted that the secular state possessed no authority to change the basic principles of Christian marriage. With the exception of Chateaubriand, the conservative critics made much less use of the Catholic doctrine of indissolubility.[5] Rather than attacking the secular state's control over marriage and family law, they contended that the state must regulate such law with great care in the interest of social stability.[6]

3. Nougarède, *De la législation,* p. 62; Léonard Aléa, *Réflexions sur le divorce* (Paris: Mlle Durand, Yr. 10), pp. 29–30; Jacques de Maleville, *Du divorce et de la séparation de corps* (Paris: Goujon Fils, Yr. 10), pp. 16–17.

4. Maleville, *Du divorce,* p. 39; André-Jean-Simon Nougarède de Fayet, *Histoire des lois sur le mariage et sur le divorce* (Paris: Le Normant, Yr. 11), 2:360. This lengthy, two-volume treatise repeats the arguments of the author's earlier work.

5. The constitutional church maintained the position hostile to divorce that it had adopted during the Directory. On 25 *thermidor* Yr. 9 (August 13, 1801) the bishop Le Coz of Rennes, president of the national council of the constitutional church, sent the minister of justice a memorandum entitled *Observations sur le divorce relativement aux français,* urging complete abolition of divorce and restoration of the former action of *séparation de corps* (Archives Nationales, BB¹⁶ 738 [Seine]; hereafter cited as AN).

6. For example, Pierre-Jean Agier's *Du mariage dans ses rapports avec la religion et avec les lois nouvelles de France,* 2 vols. (Paris: Chrétienne, Yr. 9), devotes

The most determined and vocal opponent of divorce was the viscount de Bonald. Bonald was a noble from Rouergue (later Aveyron) who had fled France after the application of the Civil Constitution of the Clergy, joined émigré military forces in 1792, and lived in the Rhineland and Switzerland until 1797, when he returned to Paris under an assumed name.[7] He began publishing books attacking divorce and explaining his social and philosophical system after the coup of 18 *brumaire,* his major work being *Du divorce considéré aux XIX siècle relativement à l'Etat public de société.*[8] Like other conservative critics, Bonald emphasized man's propensity to do evil, hence the need for strong laws and institutions to control and direct him. Unlike them, however, he developed a theory of social organization with the completeness, rational order, and abstract precision characteristic of models that had been created by writers of the Enlightenment.

According to Bonald, a study of revelation and history indicated that there are three persons or elements in every society: the ruler, the minister, and the subject. In religious society, God, the priesthood, and the faithful constitute the three. The same ranking of monarch, ministers (the nobility), and subjects forms political society. Domestic society, which is the basis for both political and religious society, follows the same pattern, with the husband as the ruler, the wife and mother as the minister, and the children as the subjects. In all three cases, the ruler gives commands, the minister executes those commands, and the subjects obey them.

Bonald contended that divorce struck at the very heart of this system, for dissolution of marriage destroyed the domestic society that was the foundation of political and religious society. Furthermore, permitting a wife to divorce her husband gave her

---

most of its 1,200 pages to affirming the right of the secular state to legislate rules of marriage.

7. Despite its age, the best single work on Bonald's life and thought is Henri Moulinié, *De Bonald* (Paris: Félix Alcan, 1916).

8. Bonald's other publications concerning divorce include Citoyen Severini (pseud.), *Essai analytique sur les lois naturelles de l'ordre social* (Paris, 1800); *Législation primitive considérée dans les derniers temps par les seules lumières de la raison* (Paris: Le Clere, 1802); *Résumé sur la question du divorce* (Paris: Le Clere, n.d.); and *Lettre au citoyen Portalis, Conseiller d'Etat, sur les articles du code civil relatifs au divorce* (Paris: Le Clere, n.d.).

equality with him, whereas in her proper role she only received and executed his commands. Children in domestic society were to obey the wishes of their sovereign, just as subjects obeyed their king and the faithful obeyed God. The revolution had destroyed the proper order and balance in all three societies, with resulting irreligion, political chaos, and immorality. Therefore,

> today, in order to save the state it is necessary to close the domestic constitution to divorce, [that] cruel faculty which deprives the father of all authority, the mother of all dignity, the children of all protection, which burdens domestic society between strength and weakness, between power and duties, which makes the family a temporary agreement in which the inconstancy of the human heart stipulates its passions and its interests.[9]

Bonald's systematic opposition to divorce reached the public not only directly, through his essays, but also in the form of exerpts, letters, and reviews published in the *Journal des débats* and other newspapers.[10]

While public debate on the nature of marriage and family law was less extensive than during 1789–99, the draftsmen and legislators of the Consulate left behind a wealth of documents, projects, debates, and other materials used in the preparation of the civil code.[11] The pattern here is the very reverse of that of the early years

---

9. Bonald, *Du divorce*, vol. 5 of *Oeuvres* (Paris: Le Clere, 1818), pp. 65–66. Bonald won a personal victory over divorce in 1815–16, when he sponsored a measure to exclude it from the civil code. Despite a few objections from such men as the former *conventionnel* Lanjuinais and the literary critic Senancour, the ultraroyalist majorities of the Restoration Chamber of Deputies and the Chamber of Peers approved the proposal, which became law with Louis XVIII's signature on May 8, 1816. For a summary of the legislative history, see Jean Guillaume Locré de Roissy, *La législation civile, commerciale et criminelle de la France ou commentaire et complément des codes français*, 31 vols. (Paris: Treuttel et Würtz, 1827–32), 5:420–21. Divorce was excluded from the civil code until its restoration by the Third Republic in 1884.

10. *Journal des débats*, 4 *brumaire* Yr. 10 [1802], 16 *brumaire* Yr. 10 [1802], 11 *frimaire* Yr. 10, 17 *frimaire* Yr. 10 [1802].

11. Two major printed collections of these documents exist: P.-Antoine Fenet, *Recueil complet des travaux préparatoires du code civil*, 15 vols. (Paris: Ducessois, 1827), and Locré de Roissy, *La législation civile, commerciale et criminelle*. Locré was the secretary of the Council of State. His work contains material relating to the drafting of the codes of commerce, criminal law, civil procedure, and criminal procedure, as well as the civil code, whereas the Fenet collection is devoted exclusively

of the revolution, for which public documents are scarce and private expressions of opinion in letters, petitions, pamphlets, and essays abound. To be sure, the civil code did not emerge solely from the labors of the First Consul's four draftsmen: Tronchet, Maleville, Bigot de Préameneu, and Portalis. Codification and simplification of the law had been a goal of eighteenth-century reformers and revolutionaries.[12] The individual decrees on marriage and divorce, for example, had been intended to operate only until the passage of a complete code. Led by Cambacérès, legislators had produced four separate drafts, or *projets,* the last one by Jacqueminot having been submitted only after the coup of 18 *brumaire.* The Convention had considered Cambacérès' first draft of August 1, 1793, at length, recommending revisions and modifications, but later versions tended to gather dust owing to legislative preoccupation with foreign and civil war and governmental instability.

The four members of the commission appointed to draft the civil code were alike in many ways. They were not young; their ages in 1800 ranged from fifty-three to seventy-four, and thus they had all come to maturity well before the revolution. Although two had received their legal training in southern *pays de droit écrit* and two in northern *pays de droit coutumier,* all four were strongly influenced by Roman law and jurisprudence. All except Portalis had been supporters of the revolution in its moderate phase. Tronchet had been a member of the National Assembly and Bigot de Préameneu of the Legislative Assembly. The radical phase of the

to the civil code. For that subject, however, the Fenet work is generally more complete and easier to use.

The debates of the Council of State on the civil code were published separately in 1803: *Procès-verbaux contenant la discussion du projet du code civil,* 5 vols. (Paris: Imprimerie de la République, Yr. 12). Another compilation includes the discussions of the Tribunate and other deliberative bodies: François Frédéric Poncelet, ed., *Recueil complet des discours prononcés lors de la présentation de code civil,* 2 vols. (Paris: Firmin Didot Frères, 1850). The *Archives parlementaires,* 2d series, contain only the discussion of the Tribunate and the *Corps législatif. Le moniteur* and the *Journal des débats* also present summaries of the work of the Council of State and the legislative bodies and comments on the issues they discussed.

12. See Joseph van Kan, *Les efforts de codification en France: Étude historique et psychologique* (Paris: Rousseau, 1929); James F. Traer, "From Reform to Revolution: The Critical Century in the Development of the French Legal System," *Journal of Modern History* 49, no. 1 (March 1977):75–88.

revolution had forced all of them to go into hiding. Portalis was imprisoned in Paris and Bigot de Préameneu did not emerge into public life again until after 18 *brumaire* Yr. 8. During the Directory, Tronchet practiced law privately, while Maleville and Portalis were members of the conservative forces in the Council of Ancients. All had obtained positions under the Consulate: Portalis in the Prize Court and the others in the Court of Cassation.[13]

After about four months of deliberations, these men produced a draft law called the Project of the Year 8, which they then sent to the courts of appeal for examination and comments. In its provisions regulating marriage and the family, the Project of the Year 8 was a highly conservative document, strengthening marital and paternal authority and deemphasizing individual liberty, which the commission identified with the excesses of the Terror. Articles governing the relations of the spouses in marriage provided that the wife should have no legal personality separate from that of her husband: she could not make a gift, alienate property, accept an inheritance or a gift, or make a will without his consent. The members of the commission, particularly Maleville, were unsympathetic to divorce and thus they eliminated divorce by mutual consent or for incompatibility of temperament, retaining several specific grounds for dissolution as well as a more general standard of "habitual conduct which renders life in common insupportable."[14] Additional provisions greatly restricted the circumstances under which a wife could base a suit on her husband's adultery and denied her custody of her children during a divorce suit. Several courts of appeal suggested still more stringent safeguards against hasty or frequent divorce.

The projected code defined *puissance paternelle* in terms of the rights of both father and mother, but subsequent articles denied the mother any right to act independently of her husband, except as a

13. See the articles in Joseph François Michaud, *Biographie universelle*, 2d ed. (Paris: Desplaces, 1854–65), and *Nouvelle biographie générale* (Paris: Firmin Didot Frères, 1857).

14. Maleville publicly challenged the first consul's views on divorce at a social occasion at the Tuileries and later argued that the code would have permitted it only for adultery but for Napoleon's insistence on broader grounds. See Michaud, *Biographie universelle*, 26:237; Jacques de Maleville, *Examen du divorce* (Paris: Cerioux Jeunes, 1816), pp. 7–8.

widow. For disciplinary needs, a father might obtain detention of a minor son or daughter for a period of up to one year. While he had to pay the cost of the child's maintenance, he was not required to show good cause why the child should be detained, thus making the order another version of the *lettre de cachet*. Children might not marry without parental consent before age twenty-five, and the law denied them any legal action against their parents for establishment in marriage or in an occupation or business. Most appellate courts criticized these provisions, urging greater freedom of marriage and restraints on the exercise of paternal power. They did not object, however, to provisions in the proposed law eliminating adoption and denying illegitimate children any right to establish their paternity.[15]

After receiving the comments and suggestions of the courts of appeal, the four draftsmen made a few modifications in the Project of the Year 8 and then presented it to the Council of State. The Legislative Section of the council examined the project, but members from other sections and the consuls Cambacérès and Napoleon attended and participated in the discussions.[16] The draftsmen had wisely separated the technical provisions governing the registration of birth, marriage, and death from the requirements for the celebration of marriage, and the council spent little time with the administrative details of the way the public registers were to be kept. At one point, Napoleon strongly urged that the marriage regulations should include a requirement that the wife formally recognize her husband's position as head of the family, but the draftsmen explained that later provisions governing the celebration of marriage included a statement of the rights and duties of each spouse.[17]

Although this portion of the draft code moved rapidly through the Council of State, it failed to obtain immediate approval by the

15. Fenet, *Recueil complet*, 2:37–90. The opinions of the courts of appeal are printed in alphabetical order in vols. 2–4.
16. On the Napoleonic Council of State, see Léon Aucoc, *Le Conseil d'Etat avant et depuis 1789: Ses transformations, ses travaux et son personnel* (Paris: Imprimerie Nationale, 1879); *Le Conseil d'Etat: Son histoire à travers les documents d'époque (1799–1974)* (Paris: Editions du Centre National de la Recherche Scientifique, 1974). Charles Durand has written a number of specialized studies of aspects of the council's operation during the Empire.
17. Fenet, *Recueil complet*, 8:6–75.

Tribunate. Instead, the tribunes became involved in a lengthy dispute over Article 60, governing the registration of birth, which read: "If it is declared that the child is born outside of marriage, and if the mother designates its father, the name of the father will be inserted in the birth certificate only with formal mention that it was designated by the mother."[18] Benjamin Constant and another tribune argued that the provision was unfair to illegitimate children, suggesting their parentage without giving them any legal basis for proving it. Other legislators objected that the law would permit women of low repute to slander the reputations of innocent men by falsely attributing paternity to them, even though the designation could have no legal effect.[19]

The Tribunate finally voted to recommend passage of the section of the code to the *Corps législatif*, but meanwhile the government decided to suspend discussion of the code for about six months. During that time, Napoleon purged the Tribunate of members who had criticized his actions as arbitrary or had otherwise shown too much independence. After the discussion of the code resumed on 7 *messidor* Yr. 10 (June 26, 1802), the Tribunate abandoned any real effort to analyze or change the proposals submitted to it. It obediently approved each new title and section with a minimum of debate.

The Council of State made a few changes in the provisions of the Project of the Year 8 governing marriage. In response to the suggestions of numerous courts of appeal, the commission of draftsmen had already decided to permit young women to marry without permission of their parents at age twenty-one, while young men still had to wait until age twenty-five to obtain the same right. Maleville, who invariably favored application of rules of Roman law, argued at length for restoration of a woman's right of action against her father for a dowry in marriage, but the council rejected his proposal. To objections that the provisions governing the relations of the spouses made the wife's legal personality excessively dependent on that of her husband, Tronchet replied that the code

18. Ibid., pp. 130–31.
19. Ibid., pp. 121–56.

left married couples free to use the marriage contract to organize their property as they wished.[20]

While the members of the council could agree on the provisions governing marriage, the issue of divorce proved far more controversial. Napoleon initially demanded a vote on the question of whether or not divorce should be retained in some form. The minutes of the session show only that the motion was approved, without indicating who voted for or against it.[21] Then the discussion progressed to the controversial grounds of incompatibility of temperament and divorce by mutual consent, both of which were strongly opposed by the four draftsmen and several members of the legislative section of the council. Napoleon argued for retention of both grounds, supported in the case of incompatibility by Berlier and Crétet and in the case of mutual consent by Berlier, Emmery, and Réal.[22] The first consul finally abandoned his insistence upon retention of the ground of incompatibility, but he continued to maintain that mutual consent was necessary for cases in which disclosure of spe-

20. Ibid., 9:6–75. Tronchet's statement was only partly accurate. According to Articles 1387–1581 of the civil code, married couples might select a regime of community property (embracing all movable property either brought to marriage or acquired subsequently and all immovable property acquired subsequent to marriage) or one including a dowry, or variations of either. The law assigned couples who failed to conclude a marriage contract the standard community property system. In any case, the husband alone controlled and administered property held in community or by dower right.

21. Fenet, Recueil complet, 9:252.

22. Berlier, Crétet, Emmery, and Réal were all former Jacobins. Berlier had been a member of the Convention and had voted for the death of Louis XVI; Réal became the public prosecutor of an extraordinary criminal court created after the Revolution of August 10, 1792. Crétet belonged to a prosperous family involved in commerce and had profited from the revolution by large purchases of nationalized church properties. All four men were involved in public life during the Directory: Berlier, Crétet, and Emmery as members of the Council of Five Hundred, Réal as commissioner of the Directory at the general administration of the department of the Seine. They all owed their positions on the Council of State solely to Napoleon. All four men could support divorce out of loyalty both to the goals of the revolution and to the interests of the first consul. See Michaud, Biographie universelle, 2d ed., and Nouvelle biographie générale; Pierre-Louis Roederer, Journal: Notes intimes et politiques d'un familier des Tuileries (Paris: H. Daragon, 1909), pp. 57–58; Jean Bourdon, Napoléon au Conseil d'Etat: Notes et procès-verbaux inédits de Jean-Guillaume Locré, secrétaire général du Conseil d'Etat (Paris: Berger-Levrault, 1963), p. 324.

cific and substantial grounds for divorce would bring shame to the parties and their families.

While Napoleon participated in most of the legislative section's deliberations on portions of the code relating to marriage and family matters, only in the area of divorce did he organize and take charge of the discussion. He seemed proccupied with the question of adultery, particularly that of an unfaithful wife:

> Many members of the council maintain that divorce on account of incompatibility is immoral, but this is not strictly true. A man knows his wife is an adulteress. If he is himself a man of good morals her conduct is abhorrent to him, and he can no longer live with her. Yet he is unwilling to claim a divorce on this ground, partly because he has no desire to be a mark for those witticisms which society showers on a deceived husband, and partly to save their children from being dishonored by the misconduct of their mother.
>
> Laws are made in support of morals. It is not right to leave a husband no option but to plead before the courts of law for divorce on account of adultery. It should be made possible for the parties to obtain a divorce by mutual consent, which although not in itself a reason for divorce is a sufficient indication that divorce is necessary. The family council would examine into the facts and decide.[23]

Cambacérès suggested that the code might permit divorce by mutual consent, while surrounding it with limitations and formal procedures in such a way as to ensure that it did not become an easy or popular method of dissolving marriage. Ultimately, the council adopted this solution.[24] In addition to approving mutual consent,

---

23. Antoine Claire Thibaudeau, *Bonaparte and the Consulate,* trans. G. K. Fortescue (New York: Macmillan, 1908), pp. 188–89. The statements of the first consul in the sessions of the Council of State were carefully edited before publication by Fenet and Locré. Thibaudeau's volume first appeared anonymously in Brussels in 1827 under the title *Mémoires sur le Consulate.* It purports to quote Napoleon's statements before the council, but the author gives no indication whether he was writing from notes taken twenty-five years earlier or simply from memory. Even so, the book is the most useful and apparently complete item of memoir literature produced by anyone who served on the Council of State and participated in the debates on the code.

After two years of marriage to Josephine Beauharnais, Bonaparte learned of her infidelity while he was on campaign in Egypt in 1798. The couple was reunited upon his return to France in 1799, but the shock of betrayal seems to have destroyed Napoleon's earlier passionate attachment to his wife. See Felix Markham, *Napoleon* (London: Weidenfeld & Nicolson, 1963), pp. 72–73.

24. Fenet, *Recueil complet,* 9: 387.

the Council of State reduced the large number of grounds for divorce in the Project of the Year 8 to adultery, infamous punishment of one spouse, and outrageous conduct, ill usage, or grievous injuries *(excès, sévices ou injures graves)*. The involvement of parents and family in a divorce proved to be another area where the First Consul's opinions contradicted those of the draftsmen and most members of the council. Napoleon argued that the law should require family approval when a couple sought divorce by mutual consent. Tronchet replied that the use of family councils or family courts had not served to discourage divorce during the revolution. Bigot de Préameneu insisted that only foolish relatives intervene in a quarrel between spouses. Napoleon finally won his point, but with the understanding that the intervention of families in this form of divorce did not supplant the function of the court.[25] Many of the courts of appeal had proposed reviving the action of *séparation de corps* for those persons who could not in good conscience seek a divorce. The council agreed to the change without any difficulty, but spent a good deal of time debating how soon one of the spouses might convert a separation into a divorce. Conservatives such as Boulay de la Meurthe suggested a delay of five years or longer; Napoleon proposed that it be limited to one year only. Ultimately, the codifiers compromised on a three-year delay.[26]

The discussion of adultery as a ground for divorce offers excellent evidence of how far the drafters of the code had departed from the revolutionary ideal of equality of husband and wife. Tronchet explained that the Project of the Year 8 had adopted the distinction between adultery of a wife and that of a husband found in Roman law. The adultery of the wife was considered far more serious than that of the husband because it might introduce a "foreign child" into the family. When Emmery suggested that adultery as a ground for divorce should be defined equally for husband and wife, other members of the council objected that such a step would be unjust and offensive to public morals and decency. The council retained the provision from the Project of the Year 8 permitting a husband

25. Ibid., pp. 270–90.
26. Ibid., pp. 281–329.

to obtain a divorce for any act of adultery by his wife, but limiting a wife to the situation in which her husband introduced his concubine into the parties' common home. While neither spouse might marry an accomplice in adultery, the definition of adultery permitting an action of divorce made it more likely that the prohibition would be applied to the wife than to the husband. Furthermore, the council stipulated that a wife divorced by reason of her adultery should thereafter be confined to a house of correction for a period of three months to two years.[27]

The hostility of the authors of the Project of the Year 8 to children born outside of marriage was also evident in their failure to include in the draft any provisions for adoption. Tronchet and Maleville argued that adoption was used mainly to circumvent the rules governing successions, and that few persons wished to introduce "foreign children" into their families anyway. The majority of the council, led by Napoleon, decided to include sections permitting adoption and friendly guardianship, reasoning that adoption to modify a succession or to care for a minor orphaned child had existed for ten years without inconvenience.[28] In the area of enforcement of paternal power, the draftsmen had yielded only slightly to the criticism of the courts of appeal, limiting to six months instead of one year the time a father might initially have his son or daughter confined for disciplinary purposes. The law provided no real means for examining the father's motives and determining whether or not the confinement was justified by any objective standard. Only Berlier called the action by its true name: it was a modified version of the ancien régime's *lettre de cachet*.[29]

While the code's framers excluded illegitimate children from the family circle and viewed adopted ones with suspicion, they guaranteed legitimate children at least a share in their parents' estate. When a person died intestate, the code followed the provisions of the laws of 5 *brumaire* and 17 *nivôse,* maintaining absolute equality among heirs of the same category of relationship to the deceased person. Legislators contended, quite reasonably, that in the absence of other stated intentions, equal division was likely to

27. Ibid., pp. 299–429.
28. Ibid., 10: 1–58.
29. Ibid., pp. 246–48, 479–543.

have been the desire of the decedent. Yet these same men were anxious to reintroduce an element of freedom, whereby an individual might dispose of part of his property outside of the family or might favor some family members over others.

Thus in the law of 4 *germinal* Yr. 8 (March 25, 1800), before consideration of the code had begun, the legislative bodies of the Consulate declared a certain portion of an individual's property freely disposable by him, with the amount dependent on the number and kinds of heirs he left at his death. An individual might freely dispose of one-fourth of his estate by gift or will if he left at death three or fewer children, or their descendants. The amount freely disposable was one-fifth if he left four children, one-sixth if he left five children, and so on. Furthermore, the same individual might convey or will one-half of his estate if he left at death only ascendants or brothers and sisters or their descendants, and three-fourths of the estate if there survived only uncles, aunts, cousins, or their ascendants or descendants.[30]

The provisions of the civil code modified this law somewhat, permitting a person to transfer between one-fourth and one-half of his property, but no more. According to Article 913, a parent with one child might convey or will half of his property to someone else; with two children the freely disposable part shrank to one-third, and with three or more children it became one-fourth. The freely disposable portion might be used to favor one child over others. That portion of the property guaranteed by law to heirs went to descendants, and failing them, in equal portions to paternal and maternal ascendants or collateral relatives. At the end of the line of heirs established by law stood illegitimate children, who inherited only in the absence of blood relatives, and finally the wife. The code clearly expected a husband and wife to provide for the survivor of the marriage by means of a marriage contract.[31]

As to the succession rights of children in a family, the civil code represented a compromise between the revolutionary dogma of ab-

30. Jean-Baptiste Duvergier, *Collection complète des lois, décrets, ordonnances, règlements, et avis du Conseil d'état* (Paris: A. Guyot, 1825–), 12:186.

31. Late-nineteenth-century legislation remedied this much-criticized provision of the code. See Esther Sue Kanipe, "The Family, Private Property, and the State in France, 1870–1914," Ph.D. dissertation, University of Wisconsin, Madison, 1976.

solute equality and the wide range of exclusions, advantages, and testamentary freedom found in many regions during the ancien régime. It reintroduced the notion of advantaging one child, using the old term *préciput*. But it guaranteed to each child a fixed share that was more substantial than had been the *légitime* in Roman law and the *réserve coutumière* in most customs.[32] It made no distinction between the rights of daughters and those of sons. Renunciation of succession rights was possible only after the death of the person who had formerly possessed the property. Article 791 forbade renunciation, even by marriage contract, to the succession of a living person. In other words, the code sought to prohibit family arrangements designed to exclude some children from a succession. Thus the code's framers required a measure of equality among all sons and daughters of a deceased person and, when that person failed to indicate another intention, established a regime of absolute equality.

Critics of equal division of inheritance, both during the revolution and afterward, charged that it inevitably meant subdivision of land and hence unprofitable agricultural practices. And they blamed it for a dropping birthrate, which they contended was caused by the desire of peasants to limit their families in order to conserve their lands intact. Thus the opponent of equality in the National. Assembly, Lambert de Frondeville, charged that if the ancien régime favored the eldest son, the new regime favored the only son![33] And later polemicists frequently quoted Alexis de Tocqueville's remark that the civil code was a device to cut up the land (*"une machine à hacher le sol"*).[34] Not surprisingly, both men came from the part of Normandy where customary law under the ancien

32. The code's provisions governing property rights in marriage permitted the spouses to stipulate community property, separation of property, a regime protecting the wife's dowry (which had previously been widely used in the Midi), or other types of property relationships. If the spouses failed to elect a regime by marriage contract, the law established the system of community property. See Jacqueline Brisset, *L'adoption de la communauté comme régime légal dans le code civil* (Paris: Presses Universitaires de France, 1967).

33. Jérôme Mavidal and Emile Laurent, eds., *Archives parlementaires de 1787 à 1860: Recueil complet des débats législatifs et politiques des chambres françaises*, 1st ser. (1787–99), 2d ed. (Paris: Paul Dupont, 1879–), 24:47. Hereafter cited as *AP*.

34. Quoted in Ambroise Colin, "Le droit de succession dans le code civil," in *Le code civil: Livre du centenaire* (Paris: Arthur Rousseau, 1904), 1:309.

régime had strongly favored the eldest male child. Nineteenth-century criticism reached its peak in the writings of Frédéric Le Play, who sought unsuccessfully to promote reform of the civil code to protect family holdings.[35] But the causal link is far from proven. Areas of sizable farms, such as La Beauce, south of Paris, were governed in the eighteenth century and afterward by rules of equality, just as were regions of very small farms in Brittany and the Angoumois. The subject awaits study in depth.

After the Council of State had debated and revised the various sections of the civil code dealing with marriage, divorce, and relationships within the family, they were quickly approved by the Tribunate and the *Corps législatif* in 1802 and 1803. Only a few persons outside of the government commented on them. The jurist Dufour de Saint-Pathus restated all of the old goals of revolutionary legislation: broad freedom of marriage and divorce, minimal restriction on the family by the state, a low age of majority, and equality of family members. Rather than paternal power to control the marriage of children, he argued, "let fathers rear their children better; let them make the children feel at an early age how they should behave; the children will choose well. So few fathers know how to be friends with their children; so many fathers believe always that they must hold themselves at a great distance, that it is little surprising that their ideas coincide so little."[36] Another pamphlet proclaimed that the principal goal of marriage was happiness.[37] Other writings more specifically urged retention of divorce by mutual consent or for incompatibility of temperament.[38]

Despite occasional expressions of revolutionary goals or ideals, more typical criticism directed at the work of the Council of State attacked the provisions in the code governing marriage, divorce,

35. Frédéric Le Play, *La réforme sociale en France* (Paris: Henri Plon, 1864), 1:102–44. For a discussion of Le Play's work and ideas, see Michael Z. Brooke, *Le Play: Engineer and Social Scientist* (London: Harlow, Longmans, 1970).

36. Julien-Michel Dufour de Saint-Pathus, *Observations sur le nouveau projet de code civil* (Paris: Courcier, n.d.), p. 43.

37. A. Clesse, *Je cherche le bonheur, ou le célibat, le mariage et le divorce* (Paris: Moutardier, Yr. 10).

38. Chevallier, *Objections aux articles du projet de code civil relatifs au divorce* (Paris: Lemarchand, 1081 [*sic*]), pp. 13–16; Félix-Marie Faulcon, *Aux membres de Conseil d'Etat: Précis historique de l'établissement du divorce* (Paris: Baudouin, n.d.), p. 14.

and the family as being too liberal. In the Tribunate, Carrion-Nisas argued violently that divorce should have no place in a Catholic state recovering from the evils of revolution and among a people governed by their passions. Instead of encouraging worship of innovation and pleasure, society's laws should maintain order and call men to obedience to their duties.[39] Carrion-Nisas cited Bonald's works favorably, as did other authors who urged rules that would restore equilibrium in families as in the state.[40] In the press, the influential *Journal des débats* presented prominent favorable reviews of Bonald's writings, published his letters and articles, and campaigned in other ways for abolition of divorce and strict measures upholding paternal authority.[41]

While liberal and conservative critics debated, the Council of State worked steadily to complete the task of codification. Marriage and family law had been only a beginning, but in another year the draftsmen finished their efforts and formally promulgated the civil code on March 1, 1804. In 1807 its name was changed officially to the Code Napoleon. Unlike much of the revolutionary legislation, the civil code endured, establishing in the law a basic pattern of marriage and family relationships that endured for more than a century. The wars of the Napoleonic era led to application of the code throughout Europe, and it remained influential in other countries as a model for emulation long after it was no longer imposed by French military power.

Scholars analyzing the provisions of the civil code dealing with marriage, divorce, and organization of the family have stressed the significance of a variety of themes and interpretations. Some authors have emphasized that the code maintained civil control of marriage and family law, which had been begun by the monarchy

39. After the purge of Benjamin Constant and other tribunes who had criticized articles controlling the registration of vital statistics, Carrion-Nisas was the only tribune to attack any provision submitted by the Council of State (Fenet, *Recueil complet*, 9: 510–41).

40. François-Dominique de Reynaud de Montlosier, *Observations sur le projet de code civil* (Paris: Giguet, 1801); Edmé-Hilaire Garnier-Deschennes, *Observations sur le projet de code civil* (Paris: Huzard, Yr. 9).

41. Henri Hayem, *Polémiques de presse sur l'institution du divorce (an IX à an XI)* (Paris: Arthur Rousseau, 1908), pp. 14–136.

and which was completed during the moderate phase of the revolution.[42] For these historians, civil control went hand in hand with toleration of minority religious beliefs, including the practice of divorce by Protestants and Jews.[43] Another line of interpretation has stressed the contributions of the code to extreme individualism or even atomization of French society.[44] René Savatier, a distinguished legal scholar, has argued that the draftsmen were so hostile to the interposition of corporate or intermediate bodies between the individual and the state that they did not even include the word *family* in the code, save in a few minor provisions.[45] The hostility of legislators to these intermediate or corporate bodies is clear, for example, in the hasty abolition of the family court in 1796, but Savatier's textual analysis leads him to overlook the concern for the stability of the family so evident in the discussions of the Council of State.

The personal role of Napoleon in the preparation of the code has fascinated other historians.[46] The first consul presided over about half of the sessions held by the Council of State, and he did not hesitate to offer his comments and criticisms. As has been noted, he was particularly interested in divorce, adoption, and the legal subordination of a wife to her husband, and these concerns acquire greater significance against the background of his disappointment

42. Ernest Glasson, *Le mariage civil et le divorce dans l'antiquité et dans les principales législations modernes de l'Europe*, 2d ed. (Paris: Durand et Pedone, 1880), pp. 270–71; Jules Basdevant, *Des rapports de l'église et de l'état dans la législation du mariage du Concile de Trente au code civil* (Paris: Sirey, 1900), pp. 199–200.

43. During the Consulate, legislators frequently justified their support of divorce by arguing that tolerance required the law to allow actions permitted by minority religious beliefs. Treilhard relied heavily on this line of reasoning when he presented the Council of State's final version of the divorce provisions to the Tribunate and the *Corps législatif*. See Fenet, *Recueil complet*, 9: 468–70.

44. Julien Bonnecase, *La philosophie du code Napoléon appliqué au droit de famille*, 2d ed. (Paris: E. de Boccard, 1928), pp. 83–167.

45. René Savatier, *Le droit, l'amour et la liberté*, 2d ed. (Paris: Librairie Générale de Droit et de Jurisprudence, 1963), pp. 13–26.

46. For example, see Adolphe Thiers, *Histoire du Consulat et de l'Empire* (Paris: Paulin, 1845), 3:299–302; Amédée Madelin, *Le Premier Consul législateur: Étude sur la part que prit Napoléon aux travaux préparatoires du code civil* (Paris: Auguste Durand, 1865); Jean-Joseph-Marie-Honoré Perouse, *Napoléon Ier et les lois civiles du Consulat et de l'Empire* (Paris: Auguste Durand, 1866). All of these books glorify and exaggerate Napoleon's contribution.

at Josephine's infidelity and his growing fear that their marriage might not produce an heir. In one sense, Bonaparte's personal role was of utmost significance, for it was he who selected the draftsmen of the code and members of the Council of State, who brooked no interference from the Tribunate, and who saw the project through to speedy completion. Also, his comments during the discussions, even assuming they have been edited by Locré and Fenet, indicate an acute mind that could grasp problems readily and weigh the competing policy considerations of several possible solutions. On the other hand, it is inaccurate to credit him with legal genius, which he did not possess, or with great involvement in the solution of technical problems found in the areas of contracts, successions, and marital property.

Another common method of evaluating marriage and family law in the code has been to label it "bourgeois." The argument may be stated in a syllogism. The revolution resulted in a victory of the bourgeoisie. The code is a product of the revolution. Therefore the code is bourgeois. While both premises and hence the conclusion may be true, they add little in the way of explanation or illumination of the provisions governing marriage, divorce, and family law. This kind of reasoning mars Georges Lefebvre's otherwise excellent summary of the content of the civil code. Lefebvre initially states that the code was "conceived in the interest of the bourgeoisie" and later that it was "the product of the evolution of French society insofar as it [the evolution] created the bourgeoisie and carried it to power."[47]

As an example of the way the code favored bourgeois interests, Lefebvre cites the detailed regulation of the marriage contract, which he states made the agreement a "moneyed transaction." It is true that the law governing the marriage contract provided for detailed regulation of property arrangements between spouses and their families, but this was nothing new. Marriage contracts from the sixteenth through the eighteenth centuries illustrate the same preoccupation. If marriage or the marriage contract had become a moneyed transaction, the change had taken place long before 1804

47. Georges Lefebvre, *Napoleon: From 18 brumaire to Tilsit*, trans. Henry F. Stockhold (London: Routledge & Kegan Paul, 1969; first published 1935), pp. 151–54.

or 1789.[48] The point is, simply, that while some features of the civil code may fit the Marxian pattern of class analysis, many do not. The conclusion that the code was bourgeois because the revolution was bourgeois invites cloudy generalization and error.

Other types of interpretation relate to the origin of rules or provisions in the code. One scholar has separated them according to their antecedents in Roman or customary law, while another has classified them as revolutionary or as belonging to the ancien régime.[49] Finally, national pride has encouraged many commentators to adopt the "perfect balance" approach. They assert that the civil code achieved a perfect balance between the revolution and the ancien régime, between Roman and customary law, between abstract reason and concrete tradition, between social control and individual liberty, between general legal principle and detail, between formal structure and flexibility.[50]

In some ways, the provisions of the civil code maintained the revolutionary conception of marriage and the family that had been written into the laws of 1790 and 1792. First, they preserved the exclusively secular nature of the institution of marriage for purposes of public law. The only explicit concession to the older Christian pattern of celebration of marriage appeared in Article 63, which provided that formal publication of intent to marry should be made on a Sunday. Thus the public notice required by the state

---

48. See Elinor G. Barber, *The Bourgeoisie in Eighteenth-Century France* (Princeton: Princeton University Press, 1955), pp. 99–102, and Adeline Daumard and François Furet, *Structures et relations sociales à Paris au milieu du XVIIIᵉ siècle* (Paris: Armand Colin, 1961).

49. Most contemporary secondary works adopt the latter technique. For example, see Herbert Albert Laurens Fisher, "The Codes," in *Cambridge Modern History of Europe* (New York: Macmillan, 1918), 9:148–79; Geoffrey Bruun, *Europe and the French Imperium, 1799–1814* (New York: Harper & Row, 1938), pp. 25–29; and Jacques Godechot, *Les institutions de la France sous la Révolution et l'Empire,* 2d ed. (Paris: Presses Universitaires de France, 1968), pp. 691–96. Fisher's discussion is very useful, despite its age. Philippe Sagnac emphasized the revival of Roman legal tradition and the return to what he called the "juridical" spirit, as opposed to the "philosophic" spirit of the revolution (*La législation civile de la Révolution française* [Paris: Hachette, 1898], pp. 388–95).

50. Marcel Planiol's famous work, *Treatise on the Civil Law,* with the collaboration of Georges Ripert, trans. Louisiana State Law Institute (St. Paul, Minn.: West Publishing Co., 1959), vol. 1, presents this argument, which also appears in a volume of essays celebrating the first century of the civil code: *Le code civil, 1804–1904: Livre du centenaire,* 2 vols. (Paris: Arthur Rousseau, 1904).

would appear at the same time as the religious banns published by the church. In contrast to the laws of the ancien régime, the code paid no attention to the religious beliefs of the parties to a marriage. Persons of differing religions or of no religion at all might marry one another without any restriction or special formality. Thus, in one sense, strictly civil marriage furthered the principle of freedom of marriage.[51]

Negotiation of the Concordat of 1804 with the Catholic church made it less difficult to enforce the secularization of marriage decreed by the civil code. Before the agreement, local officials had frequently suggested passage of effective legislation requiring curés to refrain from celebrating religious rites of marriage unless a couple could prove they had already been married civilly.[52] On behalf of the Council of State, Portalis advised the minister of the interior that such a requirement would achieve the state's goal without infringing on freedom of religion, and the rule became part of the agreement with the church. Title 3, Article 54 of the "organic articles" that supplemented the general provisions of the Concordat of 1804 provided that curés "shall give the nuptial benediction only to those who shall justify, in good and due form, that they have contracted marriage before the civil officer."[53] After the conclusion of the Concordat, the complaints coming to the ministries of Justice and the Interior about religious opposition to civil marriage virtually ceased. Thus, agreement with the church achieved what administrative efforts and patriotic festivals had never fully realized: the establishment of civil celebration of marriage for all French men and women.

The articles relating to the formation of the marital tie sought to balance the competing considerations of freedom of marriage and

51. Civil code, art. 63.
52. Extract from the registers of the prefecture of the department of Morbihan, 23 *brumaire* Yr. 10 (November 14, 1801), sent to the minister of the interior, AN, F² I 397; prefect of Beauvais to minister of the interior, 5 *germinal* Yr. 9 (March 26, 1801), AN, F² I 398.
53. Duvergier, *Collection complète des lois*, 13:323. Later provisions in the organic articles extended this regulation to include Protestant pastors. The law of 1 *prairial* Yr. 10 (May 21, 1802) applied the same prohibition to marital benedictions pronounced by rabbis (ibid., pp. 450–51). The opinion of Portalis is dated 16 *frimaire* Yr. 10 (December 7, 1801), AN, F² I 401.

family solidarity, both of which were revolutionary ideals.[54] Article 148 established the age at which a young person could marry without obtaining parental consent as twenty-one for women and twenty-five for men, striking a compromise between the rules of the ancien régime and those of the legislation of 1792. The law required that young persons beyond age twenty-one or twenty-five notify their parents of their intended marriage by respectful acts (Articles 152–57), but this formality was a type of courtesy rather than a significant barrier to marriage. The provisions governing formal oppositions to marriage (Articles 173 and 174) sought to limit them to parents and grandparents, or in very restricted circumstances to brothers, sisters, aunts, uncles, and cousins. A person who wished to prevent a marriage had to prove his relationship to one of the parties and establish in court that his objection was well founded.

The authors of the code limited the scope of actions seeking to nullify a marriage, even when it had been celebrated without having satisfied all legal requirements. Even if a marriage lacked parental consent, for example, the parent had to attack it promptly or the flaw would be cured by passage of time. In this indirect way, the framers furthered the principle of freedom of marriage. According to Article 183, parents or other relatives might not attack a marriage for failure to obtain family approval when they had expressly or tacitly given consent, or had allowed one year to elapse without taking any action. If the wife became pregnant within the first six months after celebration of the marriage, they also might not attempt to have it nullified (Article 185). The only truly rigorous nullity provision in this area applied to the circumstance in which

54. Administrators generally supported the principle of freedom of marriage in their interpretation of the civil code. For example, in an order of 5 *thermidor* Yr. 8 (July 21, 1800), the minister of war, Carnot, affirmed the right of soldiers to marry like any other citizens, with the stipulation that they obtain the consent of the administrative council of their unit before the ceremony (AN, F^2 I 401). Questions from public officers concerning projected marriages between blacks and whites met a similar response. Both the minister of the interior in 1802 and the minister of justice in 1803 rejected complaints based on the ancien régime's ordinance of 1778 forbidding marriages of blacks and whites and ordered public officials to celebrate them like any others (mayor of Château-Gontier to minister of the interior, 2 *messidor* Yr. 10 [June 21, 1802], AN, F^2 I 395; minister of justice to Citizen Télémaque, 22 *messidor* Yr. 11 [July 11, 1803], AN, BB^{16} 745 [Seine]).

the marriage was not celebrated publicly and before a competent public officer. Article 191 provided that in this case, the parties, parents, relatives, and public official were all qualified to have the marriage declared null. The prohibition was clearly an effort to support the requirement of civil marriage and to deter individuals from celebrating only a religious ceremony before a priest.

Retention of divorce in the civil code indicated at least some acceptance of the belief that individuals should have the liberty to dissolve unsatisfactory marriages and to seek happiness with new spouses.[55] Without Napoleon's support of divorce, however, the draftsmen probably would have limited its scope and lengthened the delays required to obtain it. The Council of State's refusal to re-create the family court, except in a modified form for divorce by mutual consent, expressed its wariness of excessive personal liberty. The main argument against the family court in this area was that it had failed to dissuade parties who had decided on a divorce. The provisions regulating divorce by mutual consent (Articles 275–305) were so elaborate and complicated that it is hard to escape the conclusion that they were drafted solely to meet the possible need of the first consul.[56]

55. Divorces were much less frequent under the Empire than during the preceding years. According to Gérard Thibault-Laurent, the average yearly number of divorces during 1803–16 was less than one-tenth of the average yearly number during 1792–1803. He estimated that 30,000 divorces occurred during the earlier period, but only 2,500 during the latter (*La première introduction du divorce en France* [Clermont-Ferrand: Moderne, 1938], pp. 189–91). Detailed studies of the vital statistics of the cities of Metz and Nancy corroborate this conclusion. See Jean l'Hote, "Le divorce à Metz sous la Révolution et l'Empire," *Annales de l'Est*, 1952, pp. 175–83; P. Clemendot, "Evolution de la population de Nancy de 1788 à 1815," in *Contributions à l'histoire démographique de la Révolution française*, ed. Marcel Reinhard, vol. 18 of Commission d'histoire économique et sociale de la Révolution française, Mémoires et documents (Paris: Bibliothèque Nationale, 1965), pp. 199–202. For recent work on demographic change during the revolutionary and Napoleonic periods, see *Hommage à Marcel Reinhard: Sur la population française au XVIIIᵉ et au XIXᵉ siècles* (Paris: Société de Démographie Historique, 1973).

56. Napoleon and Josephine agreed to a divorce by mutual consent in 1809 and explained their reasons on December 15 to a gathering of the imperial family, which constituted the family council required by the code. The Senate approved the divorce and a committee of French ecclesiastics declared their religious celebration null on the ground that Napoleon's consent to it had been "defective." Accounts of the divorce may be found in Henri Welschinger, *Le divorce de Napoléon* (Paris: E. Plon, Nourrit, 1889); Frédéric Masson, *Joséphine répudiée (1809–1814)*. (Paris: Albin Michel, 1901); Michel l'Hospice, *Divorce et dynastie* (Paris: Bibliothèque d'Histoire

The articles of the code governing procedure in cases of divorce for a specified ground were designed to guard the privacy of spouses and family whenever possible. Thus according to Article 241, the judge was to examine the complaint in a divorce suit in a private hearing and determine whether or not it appeared to have a reasonable foundation. Article 253 instructed that evidence and depositions of witnesses should be heard by the court behind closed doors. Only the final judgment in the case was to be pronounced in open court (Article 258).

Finally, in its provisions on filiation, adoption, and friendly guardianship, the code emphasized the cohesion of the legitimate family and the barriers that separated it from other persons in society. Illegitimate children might be legitimated by subsequent marriage of their parents, and indeed the law encouraged such an action (Articles 331–33). The adulterine child had no right to establish his paternity, however, and the law expressly prohibited a married man from recognizing the paternity of a child he had conceived outside of marriage. The goal of protecting the legitimate family was so important that the code's draftsmen denied the adulterine child any claims against his father (Articles 335, 342).

The sections dealing with friendly guardianship regulated the situation in which an individual might wish to assume parental responsibilities toward a minor, but they carefully stipulated that a friendly guardian had to be at least fifty years of age and without children or legitimate descendants (Article 361). The code permitted adoption as a means of making a person one's potential heir, but not if the adopting party had children or other legitimate descendants. In this area, the code's concern for the nuclear family was quite in harmony with earlier revolutionary legislation, but in its refusal to permit outsiders to enter that family, it differed from earlier revolutionary enthusiasm for equality of illegitimate children and adoption of those who were orphaned or homeless.

The revolutionary conception of marriage and the family survived in some aspects of the civil code relating to secularization of marriage, formation of the marital tie, nullity, divorce, privacy in

---

du Droit et de Droit Romain, 1958). On April 1, 1810, Napoleon married Marie Louise, the daughter of the Austrian emperor, and the passage of another year brought the birth of a son and heir to the imperial crown.

legal cases involving the family, and protection of the cohesion of the nuclear family. In contrast, most provisions of the code governing internal organization of the family abandoned the principle of equality or relative equality of family members for one of authority. Almost every article concerned with family relationships reinforced the authority of the husband and father. Even in the section dealing with registration of vital statistics, Article 37 foreshadowed the attitude of the rest of the code, stipulating that witnesses to acts of civil status (birth, marriage, divorce, death, adoption) had to be adult males. According to the law of 1792, adults of either sex might be witnesses.

A wife was instructed to obey her husband and to follow him wherever he might judge it convenient to reside (Articles 213, 214). A husband owed protection to his wife and was responsible for providing those things necessary for the wants of life, according to his means and station. The law did not permit the wife to plead in court in her own name, even if she were a businesswoman or separated from her husband (Article 215). She might not give, mortgage, or receive property or make a will without the consent of her husband. As discussed earlier, the provisions governing divorce discriminated against the wife in a number of ways.

In the area of relations between parents and children, the code provided that married persons contracted with one another to nourish, support, and rear their children. That is, by their marriage agreement they undertook obligations toward the children to be born of their marriage (Article 203). Adult children were held responsible for providing their parents with maintenance when the latter needed it, but they were denied any right of action against their parents for an establishment in marriage or a career (Articles 204–11). The law required a minor child who wished to marry to obtain the consent of both parents, but if the parents disagreed, the consent or refusal of the father controlled the issue (Article 148).

The provisions governing the relations of parents and children assumed, of course, a valid and legitimate marriage. As previously noted, an illegitimate child might hope to obtain recognition of his paternity, but he could not establish it by a legal action. The law forbade the father of an adulterine child to recognize it. Article 373 provided that the father alone exercised the paternal power during marriage, and Articles 376–82 permitted confinement of minor children according to his will. Children under age sixteen might be confined only a month, while those sixteen or over could be held as long as six months. In either case, confinement was a privilege of the father; the law did not require any writing or judicial examination of the father's motives for requesting punishment of the child.

Scholars who have analyzed these provisions of the civil code often claim that the rules governing the organization of the family revert to the Roman law of the *pays de droit écrit* before 1789, but the contention is not completely correct. While the ancien régime's version of Roman law did permit a wide exercise of marital and paternal power, it also guaranteed a wife a measure of separate legal personality and permitted a daughter to bring an action against her father for establishment in marriage—rules that the civil code eliminated. The provisions of the civil code establishing the authority of the husband and father can be better understood in terms of both the wishes of Napoleon and the theories of Bonald. Whether because of Corsican background or personal experience or both, Napoleon favored subordination of wife and children to the authority of the head of the family. He sought and obtained this goal in the deliberations of the Council of State. For Bonald and many lesser thinkers, the family was the fundamental unit in society and hence the key to social stability. Therefore the law had to discard revolutionary notions of equality in order to guarantee the authority of the husband and father in the family just as it did that of the ruler or monarch in political society.

7

Conclusion

THE THOUGHT of the French Enlightenment, the legislation of the French Revolution which sought to apply the ideals of liberty and equality to the relationships of husband with wife and children with parents, and the actual experience of millions of men and women shattered permanently the structure of traditional marriage and family in France. The rule of equality in succession law, introduced during the revolution and largely maintained in the civil code, affected every adult who possessed property or received it by inheritance. Similarly, while relatively few marriages terminated in divorce, most persons in cities and towns knew someone who had ended one marriage and initiated another. Everyone who married did so in a civil ceremony. Most men soon had the experience of informing the civil authorities of the birth of a child or the death of a child, parent, or other relative. Educated persons became increasingly aware of literature that advanced the claims of sentiment in human relations. Everyone who had lived through the revolution knew at least some meanings of the words *liberty* and *equality*.

To be sure, modern marriage and family relationships did not automatically replace their traditional antecedents on some particular date or within a short period of time. Marriage and family in the nineteenth century frequently retained traditional patterns, particularly in rural areas and among the less educated and less prosperous everywhere. There was no dearth of submissive wives and obedient children. Even wives and children who wished greater independence and equality must often have yielded to the age, physical strength, and economic power of the *père de famille*. But just as the attempt to restore absolute monarchy during the Bourbon Restoration became increasingly attenuated with succeeding decades, so the authority of traditional rules, attitudes, and social patterns diminished with the passage of time. Although the subject is beyond the treatment of this work, the coming of agrarian and industrial revolutions to France in the nineteenth century, with corresponding increases in prosperity, geographical and social mobility, and urbanism, undoubtedly aided the development of the modern marriage and family. Finally, certain new rules, particularly those of divorce, became intimately identified with republicanism and reappeared in the law at the end of the century, when republicanism became the nation's accepted political system.

The law and social custom governing traditional marriage and family were the products of a long conflict between the Roman Catholic church and the French monarchy. For centuries after the Roman era the church had sought to define clearly the nature of Christian marriage and to apply its precepts to the disorderly habits of medieval men and women. Definition of marriage culminated in the decrees of the Council of Trent, which responded to the criticism of Protestant reformers with a reaffirmation of the sacramental nature of marriage and its indissolubility.

Meanwhile, the French monarchy and its secular courts had long exercised authority over feudal obligations and property matters connected with marriage and family relationships. From the end of the sixteenth century, French kings began to issue ordinances governing marriage directly, thus initiating two centuries of direct conflict between royal and clerical law. Royal lawyers never challenged the authority of the church over the sacrament, but they developed a contractual theory whereby the secular power would regulate all civil aspects of marriage. They then defined the contract to include almost everything.

Thus royal ordinances, applied in royal courts, came to control impediments and restrictions on marriage, especially the requirement of parental consent for minors, and governed separations of persons and property in instances of marital discord. Royal courts similarly supervised relationships between parents and children, including the right of a father to discipline his child through detention under a *lettre de cachet,* and inheritance rights established by gift, will, marriage contract, or intestate succession. The church's involvement in marriage was most visible at the moment of celebration, for only a priest, and not a notary or judge, could create the marital tie. And it was the priest alone who kept the records of marriages, births, and deaths among his flock—the documents that would later be called records of vital statistics, or *état civil.*

The writers of the French Enlightenment challenged the prevailing assumptions of both church and state regarding the traditional marriage and family. In response to the insistence that there was a unique Christian doctrine of marriage governed by a single royal law, *philosophes* and travelers, both real and imaginary, described varying marriage practices in classical times, in Protestant states, and in the exotic lands of the East. In so doing they questioned the Catholic rule of marital indissolubility and sometimes monogamy as well. Other social theorists developed the theme of utility, arguing that such practices as paternal control, which delayed marriage, and separation of the spouses as a remedy for marital unhappiness were harmful to the state because they tended to reduce the number of legitimate children. These writers contended that freedom of marriage, plus the possibility of divorce and remarriage in instances of marital discord, would contribute to population growth.

Proponents of tolerance of religious minorities also raised the standard of utility on behalf of the marriage practices of Jews and Protestants, who they urged were useful and productive members of society. Thus prominent lawyers in two celebrated suits contended that Jews residing in France should be permitted divorce under their own customs. Similarly, many enlightened men urged the legal validity of the marriages of French Protestants, whose unions were concluded outside the Roman Catholic church. Otherwise conservative magistrates found ways of upholding these privately contracted marriages, and the issue generated a reform movement that led in 1787 to a special statute creating for Protestants a form of civil marriage.

Finally, a variety of reformers, authors, and pamphleteers promoted the cause of affection and freedom of choice in marriage. They denounced marriages dictated by parental despotism in search of social and economic gains. Instead, they insisted on sentiment and liberty as the constituent bonds of marriage. And they urged the availability of divorce and remarriage as a means to human happiness when parental influence had prevailed over inexperience, or when love had fled from marriage. Thus the key elements in the traditional conception of marriage and the family advanced by the church and the monarchy can be summarized in the words *sacrament, contract, authority,* and *indissolubility.* In contrast, the *philosophes* offered the notions of liberty, equality, diversity, utility, and affection.

The clash of ideals might have remained largely theoretical but for the bankruptcy of the French monarchy and the ensuing Revolution of 1789. The men of the National Assembly and subsequent legislatures shared a common viewpoint of environmentalism drawn from John Locke. They believed in their capacity to reform men and society by means of better laws and institutions. Thus they sought to re-create the "little commonwealth" of marriage and the family, as well as the larger commonwealth of France.

Civil control of marriage and of the records of marriage, birth, and death offers the best example of continuity with the ancien régime: here was the final triumph of contract over sacrament. The assumption of civil control over marriage might not have occurred, however, but for the widening conflict resulting from nationalization of church lands and the application of the Civil Constitution of the Clergy. The dispute led to a breakdown in the maintenance of civil records which, together with pressure from some anticlerical deputies and the assent of others who viewed marriage as the responsibility of the *patrie,* ultimately yielded the law of September 20, 1792, creating civil marriage and a system for the registration of the records of civil status. The other decree of the same date, establishing divorce, was more a product of Enlightenment theory about the proper nature of the modern marriage and family and of an articulate campaign of pamphlets and petitions. It, too, might not have been achieved without the conflict between church and state.

The proponents of secular marriage and divorce constantly justified them in terms of liberty—freedom of choice as to whom one married and liberty to terminate an unhappy marriage by divorce. Additional laws reorganizing the internal structure of the family echoed the second of the revolution's ideals: equality. The best example of the insistence on equality is the legislation on successions, which ended special privileges based on former nobility, on sex (almost always masculinity), and on parental favoritism. All children were to inherit equally from their parents, including within the inheritance any prior benefits or advantages granted under gift or marriage contract. Equality meant a common age of majority fixed at twenty-one, so that adult daughters and sons no longer remained under the legal tutelage of their fathers until age twenty-five or thirty. Equality of rights included enlarging the family circle to welcome adopted as well as natural children and even guaranteeing some inheritance to illegitimate children. Finally, equality meant the same requirements in marriage and divorce for both men and women.

To enforce these laws, revolutionary legislators created a new kind of tribunal, a family court, which would function as a form of private arbitration. They confidently believed that sentiment and family solidarity would quickly resolve disputes, but their expectations proved unfounded. The family court functioned as a form of private arbitration, but with ever increasing numbers of men of law serving as its judges. It ended as a scapegoat for the unpopular provisions of the successions laws—retroactivity and a ban against appeals—and disappeared in a reorganization of the judicial system in 1796.

A decade of application and experience led to the final revision of marriage and family law with the creation of the civil code under the supervision of Napoleon. The first consul served as a kind of chemist, or alchemist, bringing together the substance of earlier laws and drafts with the more volatile elements of doctrine and jurisprudence contributed by the code's draftsmen. If Napoleon served as chemist, a returned noble *émigré*, Bonald, provided the formula for the new law. Bonald's influential writings urged that the code should create and protect the small, indissoluble family governed by the authority of the husband and father. Only such a family could guarantee the security of the larger institutions of church and state.

Yet while both Napoleon and Bonald rejected the revolutionary ideals of liberty, equality, and affection, the code retained some elements of the revolutionary legislation that preceded it. It maintained the civil control of marriage and of the records of marriage, birth, and death. It authorized divorce, including all but one of the grounds established by the law of 1792. The most persuasive arguments for dissolution of marriage had become not the ideals of liberty and happiness but the toleration of the practices of non-Catholics and the blunt opinions of the first consul. As to the age of majority, the code compromised between revolutionary and ancien régime rules. Similarly, it maintained a substantial measure of equality of inheritance rights among all legitimate children, while permitting a parent to dispose freely of a portion of his property to one child or to someone outside of the family.

Within the family, the code consistently reestablished the authority of husband and father. Thus it revived a form of the *lettre de cachet,* permitting a father to obtain a judicial order for the detention of a minor child. It transformed adoption into a means of creating succession rights, rather than a legal device for introducing orphaned children into families, and it denied inheritance rights to illegitimate children who had been recognized by their parents, unless there were no legitimate heirs. Finally, the code stressed inequality of husband and wife, denying the latter any separate legal personality and often creating more exacting rules for women than for men, as in the case of a suit for divorce on grounds of adultery.

By combining elements of both traditional and modern conceptions of marriage and family, the civil code appropriately reflected a transition in French society. The new principles of modern marriage were already the property of the educated and prosperous; gradually they began to influence everyone else. To be sure, romantic love, freedom of choice, equality, and domestic happiness did not always carry the day against economic realities, family ambitions, and the inevitable disappointments of marital and family life. But in the law, in literature, and in everyday affairs the direction of social change was clear. The ideals of liberty and equality, together with romantic love and domesticity, had created a modern conception of marriage and family that would become the norm for France and, indeed, for much of the Western world.

Bibliographical Essay

MOST PRIMARY AND SECONDARY SOURCES used in this work are cited in the footnotes; consequently they are not listed here. After briefly discussing valuable bibliographic tools and published collections of laws and documents, I shall list the classifications of sources I have used in national and departmental archives in France.

Research for this study began in the United States, in the General Library of the University of Michigan and the Law Library of the University of Michigan Law School. The latter has a particularly complete collection of primary and secondary French legal materials. I also consulted the collections of the Newberry Library in Chicago, the Harper Library of the University of Chicago, the Cornell University Libraries, and the Hamilton College Library.

In France, the Section Moderne of the Archives Nationales at Paris holds the national archival sources cited in the bibliography. The departmental archival sources are located in the prefecture of each department. The Bibliothèque Nationale in Paris provided a wealth of secondary sources. In addition, I consulted the collections of the Bibliothèque de l'Arsenal, the Bibliothèque Mazarine, and the Bibliothèque de la Faculté de Droit at the Sorbonne.

Bibliographies of late-eighteenth-century France, the revolution, and the Napoleonic era are legion. One useful set, readily available to American readers, may be found in George Lefebvre's *The French Revolution,* vol. 1 trans. Elizabeth Moss Evanson, vol. 2 trans. John Hall Stewart and James Friguglietti (New York: Columbia University Press, 1964; first published 1957), and in his *Napoleon,* vol. 1 trans. Henry F. Stockhold, vol. 2 trans. J. E.

Anderson (New York: Columbia University Press, 1969; first published 1935); Jaques Godechot, *Les révolutions (1770–1799)* (Paris: Presses Universitaires de France, 1965), is a valuable part of the Nouvelle Clio series, and may be supplemented by works cited in the second edition of his *Les institutions de la France sous la Révolution et l'Empire* (Paris: Presses Universitaires de France, 1968). Despite its age, Pierre Caron, *Manuel pratique pour l'étude de la Révolution française*, new ed. (Paris: A. et J. Picard, 1947), remains an important primary guide. The subject of French law may be approached through the works cited in René David, *Bibliographie du droit français, 1945–1960* (The Hague: Mouton, 1964), and in James F. Traer, "From Reform to Revolution: The Critical Century in the Development of the French Legal System," *Journal of Modern History* 49, no. 1 (March 1977): 73–88.

Two older standard bibliographies are Gaston Brière and Pierre Caron, *Répertoire méthodique de l'histoire moderne et contemporaine de la France, 1898–1906, 1910–1913* (Paris, 1899–1914), and A. Grandin, *Bibliographie générale des sciences juridiques, politiques, économiques et sociales de 1800 à 1925–1926* (Paris: Sirey, 1926), with irregular supplements until 1950. More recent compilations include Gabriel Lepointe and André Vandenbossche, *Eléments de bibliographie sur l'histoire des institutions et des faits sociaux, 989–1875* (Paris: Montchrestien, 1958), and Comité français des sciences historiques, *La recherche historique en France de 1940 à 1965* (Paris: Centre National de la Recherche Scientifique, 1965).

Publications from the revolutionary and Napoleonic periods may be located by means of André Martin and Gérard Walter, *Catalogue de l'histoire de la Révolution française*, 5 vols. (Paris: Bibliothèques Nationales, 1936), and André Monglond, *La France révolutionnaire et impériale: Annales de bibliographie méthodique et description des livres illustres* (Grenoble: B. Arthaud, 1930–). Jules Gay, *Bibliographie des ouvrages relatifs à l'amour, aux femmes et au mariage* (Paris, 1861), is a nineteenth-century guide to popular literature.

For the ancien régime, the best collection of royal laws is François André Isambert, ed., *Recueil général des anciennes lois françaises, depuis l'an 420 jusqu'à la révolution de 1789*, 29 vols. (Paris: Belin-le-Prieur, 1822–33). Court decisions, opinions of commentators, and other elements of jurisprudence may be found in Jean-Baptiste Denisart, ed., *Collections de décisions nouvelles et de notions relatives à la jurisprudence* . . ., 9 vols. (Paris: Desaint, 1783), and Nicolas-Toussaint Le Moyne Desessarts, ed., *Causes célèbres, curieuses et intéressantes, de toutes les cours souveraines du royaume* . . ., 165 vols. (Paris, 1775–87).

With regard to the revolution, John Hall Stewart, ed., *A Documentary Survey of the French Revolution* (New York: Macmillan, 1951), includes constitutions, important laws, and a bibliography. The laws and decrees of the revolution are published by Jean-Baptiste Duvergier, *Collection complète des lois, décrets, ordonnances, règlements, et avis du Conseil d'état* (Paris: A. Guyot, 1825–), while legislative history can be reconstructed from *Moniteur universel*, reprint, 32 vols. (Paris: H. Plon, 1858–70), and Jérôme Mavidal and Emile Laurent, eds., *Archives parlementaires de 1787 à 1860: Recueil complet des débats législatifs et politiques des chambres françaises*, 1 ser. (1789–99), 2d ed. (Paris: Paul Dupont, 1879–). Both of the latter are now available in microfilm or microfiche.

The drafting of the civil code may be followed in the collections of P.-Antoine Fenet, *Recueil complet des travaux préparatoires du code civil*, 15 vols. (Paris: Ducessois, 1827–28), and Jean Guillaume Locré de Roissy, *La législation civile, commerciale et criminelle de la France ou commentaire et complement des codes français*, 31 vols. (Paris: Treuttel et Würtz, 1827–32).

The archival sources used in this book fall into four basic categories, two located in the national archives in Paris and two situated in departmental archives. The first category consists of sources of legislative history, primarily documents produced or collected by the committees of the various revolutionary legislatures. A second category comprises administrative records and correspondence between Paris bureaucrats and local officials. Most of the materials in this classification are found among the archives of the ministries of Justice and the Interior.

In writing this book, I used the records of the family court for the departments of Aisne and Charente. I also sampled notarial records from the ancien régime in these two departments. In addition to these major categories, I consulted a variety of local records, including those of city and departmental administrations, reports of public festivals, parish registers, and declarations of pregnancy.

The archival sources are listed below as they are cited in the various guides and inventories.

NATIONAL ARCHIVAL SOURCES

Series D (Mission des représentants du peuple. Comité des assemblées)

D III (Comité de législation [Legislative Assembly, National Convention]), 336, 361, 363–67, 379, 380, 382.

D IV (Comité de constitution [National Assembly]), 13.

D XVII (Comité de judicature [National Assembly]), 5.

D XXXIX (Commission de la classification des lois [Directory]), 3–8.

Series F (Administration générale de la France)

F^2 I (Administration départementale: Objets généraux), 379–409.

Series AA (Collection de lettres et pièces diverses), 18, 45, 49, 62.

Series AF III (Archives du pouvoir exécutif de 1789 à 1815: Directoire), 32–36.

Series BB (Versements du Ministère de la justice)

BB^{16} (Correspondance générale de la Division civile), 1, 2, 8–10, 21, 22, 27, 31, 35, 41, 45–47, 68, 84, 85, 87, 107, 122, 128, 129, 136, 137, 148, 701–20.

BB^{30} (Versements de 1904, 1905, 1908, 1929, 1936, 1939, 1941, 1943, 1944), 80, 88, 266.

Series AD (Archives imprimées)

AD II (Justice et droit civils), 30, 33, 34, 35, 38, 44, 45, 48, 50–56.

AD XVIII^C (Impressions des assemblées), 160–64, 192, 324, 325, 365, 393, 453, 454, 456.

DEPARTMENTAL ARCHIVAL SOURCES

Series EE and E (Ancien régime)

Archives notariales: Angoulême, EE 6464 (Lescalier); 6492 (Lhoumeau); 6504 (Mathé-Dumaine, *père*); 6635 (Pineau); 6697 (Texier); 9175, 9176 (Aubin).

Archives notariales: Laon, E 22, 23 (Delacampagne); 34, 35 (Belin).

Series L (Période révolutionnaire)

Tribunal de famille et tribunal de l'arbitrage
Charente, judicial district of Angouleme, L 2158–60.
Aisne, judicial district of Laon, L 2628–30.

Fêtes publiques
Maine-et-Loire, L 417–18.
Nord, L 1259–61.
Puy-de-Dôme, L 660, 662, 665.
Rhône, L 446–48.
Seine-Maritime, L 359–60.
Var, L 447, 451, 456.

Déclarations de grossesse
Eure, 238 L 70–72.

Index

Library of Congress Cataloging in Publication Data

TRAER, JAMES F.   1938–
Marriage and the family in eighteenth-century France

    Bibliography: p.
    Includes index.
    1. Marriage law—France—History. 2. Domestic
relations—France—History. 3. Marriage—France
—History. 4. Family—France—History. I. Title.
LAW   346.4401′5   80-11121
ISBN 0-8014-1298-6